Surplus to Subsistence

A Critique of British Land Revenue Policy in Rajasthan 1870-1910

Surplus to Subsistence

A Critique of British Land Revenue Policy in Rajasthan
1870-1910

M. S. Jain
M.A., Ph. D.
Professor of History (Retired)
University of Rajasthan, Jaipur

AGAM KALA PRAKASHAN
DELHI

First Pub. 1994

Published by
Dr. Agam Prasad, M.A., Ph.D., Diploma in Museology
for AGAM KALA PRAKASHAN
34 Central Market, Ashok Vihar
DELHI 110052 Phone: 7113395

Typetset at
SanPark Press Pvt. Ltd.
29, Central Market, Ashok Vihar I, Delhi-110052
Ph.: 7241869

Printed at
Garg Offset Works,
B-76, Naraina Ind. Area, Phase II, New Delhi

Preface

The prosperous trade and commerce of Rajasthan, at the beginning of the 19th century, had been conceded by Tod. Different political agents and officers had, till 1870, written about the prosperous and contented peasantry in various states, particularly Bharatpur and Mewar. The special censuses conducted at Bharatpur and Alwar, in 1867 and 1872 respectively, had revealed that less than 50% population was dependent on agriculture. By the second decade of this century, the dependence on agriculture had increased to about 70% population, and the prosperity was nowhere to be seen. Agriculture had become overwhelmingly dependent on rainfall; famines stared in the face every few years. How did this come about? Any inquiry into the impoverishment of a peasantry which had been prosperous half a century earlier, would naturally be directed to the operational aspects of the new land revenue policy which transformed the traditional system of assessment and realisation of land revenue in the khalsa.

The present work is primarily a micro level study of the British land revenue policy in such states of Rajasthan as came under regency administration in the last quarter of the 19th century and in Ajmer Merwara. It is an attempt to analyse the impact of land revenue settlements in a region which had remained, till 1870, largely unaffected by British legal notions of ownership. The land revenue settlements were part of the positive process of integrating the states' economy with colonial Indian economy. The first chapter describes the growth of British land revenue policy in Ajmer district in the pre 1870 period and the introduction, during regency administrations, of land revenue settlements in the states of Rajasthan. The second chapter discusses the transformation of the hereditary and secure land ownership right of the peasant in to an occupancy right subject to the payment of land revenue. In some states, the joint ownership of land was broken up leading to fragmentation of land holdings. The functions of hereditary local officials who used to determine the state revenue demand, after an evaluation of the gross yield, were overhauled completely since the revenue demand had been fixed for the term of the settlement and was not affected by the vagaries of weather or decline in the gross produce of the field. The changes in service conditions, dismissal and termination of a sizeable percentage of the local officials were enough to convey the change in the priorities of the new masters. It resulted in a complete alienation between the revenue collecting agency and the peasantry.

The next chapter highlights the resource crunch which the states in the region began to experience by the middle of the 19th century. It had been created by the diversion of transit trade from Rajasthan to different areas. The British acquisition of monopolistic control over the opium trade and salt manufacturing sources deprived the states of traditional sources of income. The famine of 1868 was utilised to persuade the states to abolish or reduce customs duties on trade. The establishment of railways further reduced the states' income from customs duties. The civilising phase of British imperialism had introduced newer items of expenditure on state durbars, reception and visits by the Viceroys and other dignitaries from England. Faced with resource crunch, enhancement of land revenue became the easy way out. Changes in natural and artificial classifications of soil helped the process. This was also accompanied by a new approach to the whole question of revenue payment by the peasantry. The revenue demand was raised at every revision of the settlement. Irrigated land was given relief which unirrigated land was subjected to a heavier rate of revenue.

The fourth chapter highlights the settlement officers' attempt to find an equitable justification for the enhancement of revenue demand. The principle of finding out the cash rents paid by the tenant to the proprietor cultivator was advocated, but it was not found helpful in justifying enhancement. The principle of one fourth gross produce as state revenue demand was then put forward. But the gross produce was not the actual produce; it was an assumed produce calculated on an arbitrary assumption of yield per acre/bigha for an area which was much more than the actual cultivated area. The revenue demand became still heavier when the conversion price of the crop into money was much higher than the price obtained by the cultivator for his crop. The result was that one-fourth gross produce was often about 2/3rd or more of the gross produce. The peasantry had been compelled to cultivate even for subsistence.

The next chapter discusses the investment of capital in land, emphasized by almost all land settlement officers. They had different notions about the way to encourage the investment of money in land. Wingate wanted investment of capital in the digging of wells in dry areas so that the new cultivator, who had no resources, could take to agriculture. Pears and Abbott understood the encouragement to manotidars and discouragement to ijaredars as equivalent investment of capital; Raw restored the ex-zamindars hoping that they would invest capital in land. Dwyer provided 50% land revenue as profit rent to the new intermediary class and hoped that it would lead to investment of capital in land. At Ajmer and Mewar, the bankers were provided facilities in realising their loans from the agriculturists. The end result everywhere was the same:

increase in the sale and mortgage of lands by the cultivators. In the post 1895 period, the mortgage and sale was restricted only to agricultural classes but it did not check the process of alienation of land to the richer classes. The peasantry was getting impoverished. With a view to cover up the reality, the settlement officers began to highlight the growth of cattlewealth and to hold it as an indication of the prosperity of the agricultural community. The attempt could not carry conviction because the growth of cattlewealth was accompanied by decreasing availability of pastures and culturable land; the increased cattle-wealth wealth was far in excess of requirement for agricultural purposes. Statistical data has been given from some states to show that the increase of cattle-wealth meant increased dependence on animal husbandry as a means of providing sustenance since agriculture had ceased to provide it. Land, meant for cultivation of food and other crops, had to be diverted to growing fodder.

In retrospect, the land revenue settlements helped to build up a 'leviathan' of state power; considerable social engineering was brought about through a 'record of rights'. The process of increasing dependence on agriculture took place during the years when the total population of the states concerned and the region as a whole was declining. The land settlements had helped in the mopping up of accumulated reserves of the peasantry. The result was an increasing incidence of famines in the region and greater mortality when severe famines did occur. This mortality was heavier in states where the new land revenue settlements had been introduced under British settlement officers. In years of normal rainfall, only the barest subsistence had been left with the peasantry; even a slight variation in normal rainfall caused scarcity conditions and forced them to migrate in search of food for themselves and fodder for their cattle. Famines which had been infrequent earlier, became frequent in the post 1890 era.

The work has kept me fruitfully engaged for three years after my retirement from the University of Rajasthan. I have been tremendously benefitted by discuss the subject with two of my young friends. Dr. G.S.L. Devra, Professor of Culture and Tradition, Kota Open University has helped me, with his special knowledge of 18th century Rajasthan economy, to understand the background of the peasantry much better. Dr. U.C. Chaturvedi, Reader in History, University of Rajasthan, has been helpful, on account of his special interest in economic history, in ways more than one. Both the scholars have shaped the finer nuances of some of the approaches in this book.

I am thankful to the authorities of the National Archives of India, New Delhi and of the Rajasthan State Archives, Bikaner who have provided all necessary research facilities. My thanks are specially due to Dr. G.S. Sharma, Dy. Director, Rajasthan State Archives, Bikaner, who made my access to records easier. I am thankful to Dr. Agam Prasad and his son Rahul for bringing out the book in a very short time. My gratefulness to my wife, Urmila, is unbounded; she has made it possible for me to devote my time and energies to research.

B-144, Vijaypath
Tilaknagar, Jaipur-302004

M.S. Jain
Professor of History (Retd.)
University of Rajasthan,
JAIPUR

Contents

List of Tables

Chapter 3

Appendices

1

Historical Background

I

A major transformation in the economic condition of the peasantry in Rajasthan was brought about by the land revenue settlements made after 1870. The treaties of subordinate alliance signed by the states of Rajasthan during 1817-18 had specifically excluded the introduction of British jurisdiction (civil and criminal) in thirteen out of eighteen states. Half a century later the civilising phase of British imperialism had emerged and by 1870 British attitude and policy towards the internal administration of the states had undergone a complete change. New responsibilities and a fresh definition of imperial duty towards the states, dependent on its alliance, had come to be advocated. The changed policy perspective after 1870 led to revenue settlements in the different states of Rajasthan under British settlement officers. Land settlements made during 1818-70 by British administrators in Alwar and Bharatpur were thoroughly revised during 1896-1900 to implement new goals.

The district of Ajmer-Merwara had been retained under direct British administration. It comprised of revenue circles which reflected the climatic variations of different parts of the region. The types of land tenures, prevalent in the bordering states, were also reflected in different circles of the district. Lord Hastings gave an insight into the motivating factors behind change in land revenue settlements. He noted on February 1, 1814 that the Government was in 'a state of great pecuniary embarrassment'. The Directors were asking him to "send home treasure" urgently.[1] Prinsep argued that one of the great achievements of Hastings had been the addition of not less than a crore of revenue, realised from the districts acquired in 1817-18 and the tribute from the Indian states brought under British protection during those years.[2] Hastings was opposed to the policy of permanently settling land revenue demand which accounted for nearly 2/3rd of the Company's total receipts.[3] He believed that an upward revision of the land revenue was an easy way of enhancing the government income.

Wilder, the first Superintendent of Ajmer, was keenly anxious, to 'increase the government revenue'. The district had been valued at Rs. 505484 in the treaty with the Sindhia. Without looking into the past history of revenue collections by the Marathas, he presumed that the traditional demand had been 'one half of the estimated value of crops'; he accordingly realised a sum of Rs. 159746 in the first year. It was Rs. 44686 or 38% more than what the Marathas had realised. In 1820 he forwarded a proposal for a 3 year progressive revenue settlement beginning at Rs. 179457 and rising to Rs. 249306 (217% higher than the Maratha collections) at the end of 3 years. Wilder justified his heavy enhancement of land revenue on the basis of his impressions abut the richness of the district at the time of taking over possession in 1818. He did not furnish information about the reasons which led him to recommend the progressive assessment. The settlement was approved despite the disadvantages of an assessment framed on anticipated improvement which might not come about. Such an arrangement was likely to prevent the accumulation of capital as also the growth of an industrious peasantry. The settlement broke down in the very first year. Wilder consequently revised his revenue demand and proposed a fresh settlement at an annual amount of Rs. 164700 (8.22% lower than his previous demand) for a 5-year period.[4] This was also approved by the Government. Wilder claimed that the basis for his settlement was the ancient custom of estimating the crops and realising ½ produce. His innovation consisted in asking the cultivators to continue to pay the money equivalent of 50% produce at the 1818 prices for a few years to come regardless of the fall in produce or prices.

Middleton, his successor, was loud in condemning the severity of land assessment. He reported that many cultivators who had been attracted to Ajmer in 1818 had been driven away by high assessments and bad harvests. The wells and tanks were falling into disrepair because the people were left with no money to repair them. He talked of the oppression unleashed by the British administration and suggested in November 1826 a 5 years' settlement at an annual *jama* of Rs. 144072 (12.5% less than the reduced demand of Wilder) which was approved. In October 1827 he was replaced by Cavendish who had been associated with the Saharanpur Settlement in the N.W. Provinces. He considered the annual land revenue demand to be excessive, and recommended the reduction of revenue demand to Rs. 87645 only. He, for the first time, pointed out the original mistake which had led to heavy assessment. The year 1818-19 was a year of very high prices in Ajmer district on account of demand of foodgrains from Jodhpur and Mewar. The realisation of 50% revenue at 1818-19 prices was extremely unfair; it resulted in the impoverishment of the peasantry. He argued that the peasants had never paid half produce and could not pay such a high revenue demand calculated at a stipulated price. He was transferred in 1831 before he could revise the settlement due for renewal in November 1831. His plea that the peasantry had been "highly nay oppressively over-assessed" fell on flat ears.

TABLE: 1.1

Incidence of land revenue demand in Ajmer Merwara 1818-32

Year	Seers Per Rupee				Total For 4 Rs. P1+ P2+P3+P4 = T	Average Rate Per Rupee T/4	Qty. of Grain (Seers) Required to Pay Rs. 100.00	% of Total Produce to Pay Land Revenue	Incidence Higher By % (1818 = 100)
	Wheat P-1	Barley P-2	Maize P-3	Moth P-4					
1818	14	22	22	13	71	17.75	1775	50	100.00
1819	15	26	27	24	92	23.00	2300	65	129.58
1820	13	21	24	21	79	19.75	1975	56	111.27
1821	16	22	28	23	89	22.25	2225	63	125.35
1822	21	30	36	26	113	28.25	2825	80	159.15
1823	21	38	46	36	141	35.25	3525	99	198.59
1824	20	35	36	30	121	30.25	3025	85	170.42
1825	17	21	21	21	80	20.00	2000	56	112.67
1826	21	29	29	29	108	27.00	2700	76	152.11
1827	25	42	49	35	151	37.75	3775	106	212.67
1828	27	52	69	37	185	46.25	4625	130	260.56
1829	25	45	51	42	163	40.75	4075	115	229.58
1830	26	39	44	39	148	37.00	3700	104	208.45
1831	26	38	39	40	143	35.75	3575	101	201.4
1832	32	55	68	47	202	50.5	5050	143	284.5

Based on La Touche's Settlement Report, p.68

The impact of excessive land revenue realisation on the condition of the peasantry need not be left to the opinion of Middletone or Cavendish. It can be easily seen in the context of the prevalent prices of foodgrains in Ajmer from 1818 to 1832. (Table No. 1.1)

The fall in prices from year to year increased the incidence of a fixed land revenue demand; it became oppressive when the produce of fields was adversely affected. Even if we accept, for the sake of argument, that Wilder had only demanded 50% produce as land revenue and that the land produce had remained stationary, the same revenue demand operated to take away 56% in 2, 60 to 80% in 3, 80 to 85% of the total produce in 2, nearly the total produce in 1 and more than the total produce (101 to 143%) in 6 out of the 14 years. The resulting impoverishment of the peasantry during the period can well be visualised.

The peasantry had not been rack rented by paying 50% of the produce; it was impoverished by transforming the two variables into two constants—the quantity of produce and the rate of conversion into money. The peasantry had been made to pay a fixed amount of money when the prices were falling and the crop yield remained uncertain on account of the vagaries of weather. The table given above shows convincingly that during the 14 years, the peasantry was living on and paying revenue out of the surplus which it had accumulated over the years. The fact that the Ajmer peasantry had been able to sustain itself after paying such an exhorbitant revenue demand for years was proof, if any were needed, of the surplus reserves it had built up during the pre-1818 period which had been called by British administrators and writers as one of anarchy and plunder. A famished, poverty stricken peasantry, living on subsistence production, if the British administrators were to be believed, could not have borne this burden. The impoverishment of the peasantry which commenced in 1818 was unparalleled in its severity. The district had receded from prosperity because a fair assessment on land had not been fixed even for a single year during 1818-1832.

The settlement which was due for renewal in 1831 continued till May 1836 when Edmonstone was able to recommend one. He was candid enough to confess that the Ajmer district, during the last 18 years, had receded in prosperity because "in no one year had a fair assessment been fixed on land". The peasantry had become poverty stricken and indebted. He recommended a revenue demand of Rs. 127525 (29% less than Wilder's original demand) on the basis of 50% produce. He was aware that even the reduced settlement demand was twice as heavy as the settlement made in N.W. Provinces. The settlement was sanctioned for 10 years. Thought the revenue demand had been reduced, but a new principle of 'distributing the village assessment over the entire holdings and of making all the *khewatdars* jointly responsible for paying the village revenue demand' was introduced. This novelty made the settlement very unjust. It was enough for an industrious cultivator to pay his revenue demand, but it was inequitous to subject him to pay for other cultivators also who had either migrated out or turned to manual labour for livelihood or had abandoned or carelessly cultivated their lands.[5]

Face to face with the naked truth of peasant impoverishment, the British administrators began the exercise of finding scape-goats and alibi for the poverty of the peasantry caused by their policies. By 1836, two arguments had been put forward to cover the evil effects of their land revenue administration. The recklessness and improvidence of the peasantry and the role of the bohras and mahajans were held responsible for peasant poverty. Of the two arguments advanced, the first was apparently wrong because the life style of a conservative peasantry could not have been acquired suddenly. The second argument was also wrong because it did not pay attention to the fact that the bohras and mahajans were now called upon to play a role which was different from what they had played earlier. They had been concerned with converting the land revenue, collected in kind, into cash on behalf of the state; now the peasant was asked to himself convert the food grains into cash. A great leverage was now made available to the mahajans and bohras in dealing with individual cultivators who had to come to the former for help in paying the land revenue. The terms of trade had been transformed with harmful consequences for the peasantry. The British had themselves invited leading bankers and businessmen from the various states of Rajasthan to come and settle in Ajmer by offering them various privileges and concessions. The mahajans had been assured full help by the government in the realisation of their money and loans.

Sutherland, Commissioner of Ajmer-Merwara, reported in 1841 that the results of British land revenue policy had been very bad; he confessed that the prosperity of the khalsa lands had tremendously declined during the last 23 years; he also informed that about 500 families of cultivators had left the district because they could not pay the high revenue demand. About half the number of water-tanks which had been in existence for ages had become delapidated because the peasants had not been left with enough funds for their repair. After about two decades of British rule in Ajmer-Merwara, the irrigated lands under cultivation had gone down considerably. The government was forced to think of repairs of tanks—a major source of irrigation in Merwara tehsil. Dixon, Superintendent, Merwara (1836-47), undertook repair and construction of tanks with local help; materials were obtained gratis and labour was also not always paid for.

Dixon considered Edmonstone's assessment as standard and added a moderate profit (about 8%) on the money invested in repairs of tanks and reservoirs. He pitched his assessment at the highest amount which he believed should be collected in good years. He sought for remission of what could not be collected. He confessed that his labours to convince the people that their welfare had been kept in view in the new settlement did not carry conviction. Everyone - the Lt. Governor, N.W.P., the Government of India, and the Court of Directors - was apprehensive that Dixon's assessment was heavier than the villages could bear, yet it was sanctioned because of Dixon's insistence and involvement. He had been able to project his heavy revenue realisations as 350% return on capital invested in the construction of tanks; the authorities believed that probably the tax paying capacity of the peasantry had really been enhanced. The Court of Directors, for this reason, asked the Government to publish the work done in Mairwara, as a publicity drive 'to let others know what had been achieved by Dixon'. It took more than a decade to realise the harmful consequences of Dixon's excessive realisations. La Touche, the Settlement Officer in 1874, cited the case of village Akhri as not an uncommon example of Dixon's settlement. Edmonstone had assessed it at Rs. 650/-; the average collection had been Rs. 608/-; Dixon added Rs. 864/- (8% of the cost of repair of a tank) to the earlier demand. The assessment was not realised even once; by 1873-74, the villagers had abandoned the below subsistence level agriculture, and became labourers on earthwork on the railway line.[6] Dixon's Merwara Settlement was propagated a success because the reality had been kept hidden from the government and the public. He took advantage of his position as Commandant, Merwara Battalion, and used to deduct the amount of unpaid revenue out of the monthly salary of the soldiers of the Battalion who were also cultivators. The system broke down after he departed. In his eagerness to ensure realisation of land revenue, he had also introduced the 'saad' system whereby a merchant banker stood guarantee for the revenue demand, paid it himself and realised his money later on from the cultivators, if necessary through the legal process. he had popularised the cultivation of opium in Todgarh tehsil of Merwara, hence many defects of his settlement were overlooked. The oppressive character of his settlement began to be talked about only after his death in 1857.

The available data for sale and mortgage of land in the district portrayed the consequences of realisation of heavy revenue from the cultivators. The phenomenon of sale and mortgage of land had not been talked over by Dixon in his 'Sketch of Mairwara'. The manifold increase in the occurrence of mortgages and sales in the post 1849 period was the result of Dixonian heavy assessment. It became visible to everyone after 1871.

TABLE: 1.2[6a]

Mortgage and Sale of Land in Ajmer-Merwara (1849-1874)

Circle	Mortgaged land (acres)	Amt. of Debt Rs.	Area sold (acres)	Sale money Rs.
Beawar	5541	168624	2325	47798
Todgarh	8430	641401	459	73587
Ajmer	12561	344412	2878	80762
Total	26532	1155432	5662	202147

Considerable importance had been given to the cultivation of commercial/cash crops. Todgarh tehsil had devoted its best irrigated lands to opium cultivation. The evaluation of the return to the cultivator from difference kinds of crops was calculated by La Touche in 1874 (Appendix A).

Some derivations from this return are significant. The area under fully irrigated commercial crops (1st class) was 1%, 1.5% and 8.4% in Ajmer, Beawar and Todgarh tehsils respectively. The staple foodgrain crops (IInd class) grown either in irrigated lands or in land submerged in the bed of tanks, covered 38, 60 and 60% area, and the coarse grain crops (IIIrd class) grown in unirrigated lands covered 61, 38 and 31.6% area in the above three tehsils respectively. On the basis of the quality of crops cultivated and facilities of irrigation, Todgarh tehsil should have been very well off.

TABLE: 1.3

Crop Valuation in Ajmer - Merwara

Tehsil	Value of agricul-tural pro-duceRs.	Land Rev. Demand Rs.	Cost of produc-tion Rs.	Interest paid to Money lender	Total of cols. 3 to 5	Net Income 2-6	Number of owners	Per Capita Income Rs.
1	2	3	4	5	6	7	8	9
Ajmer	865454	166362	336182	82896	585440	280014	23403	11.96
Beawar	531412	75142	212564	40470	328176	203236	13826	14.70
Todgarh	368506	63089	14742	153962	364453	4053	20401	00.20

Source : La Touche's Settlement Report, pp. 99-100

But such was the impact of land revenue demand and the cumulative burden of borrowing money to pay land revenue in lean years that the Todgarh peasant was the poorest. The result of one year's crop valuation is given in Table No. 1.3.

Todgarh tehsil had the highest percentage of land under first class crop, particularly opium. Out of 2849 acres devoted to opium cultivation, 80% was in Todgarh and 93% of the tehsil's best lands were devoted to opium and yet the tehsil peasant was the poorest. Thus with the availability of all conditions for prosperous agriculture - secured irrigation, cash crop cultivation, hard working peasantry - the Todgarh peasantry was left with below subsistence income and was overburdened with debt to meet the incidence of land revenue.

The Dixonian settlement continued for over 20 years with harmful consequences for the peasantry. The British administrators covered up the evil consequences of the settlement by depicting them to have been the result of a decade (1860-70) of excessive, deficient or untimely rains in the district. And yet the land revenue continued to be collected in full. This was a high watermark of administrative indifference to public suffering. Even in the famine of 1868, 60% of the total land revenue was collected from people who were dependent on famine relief works. After remitting a paltry sum of Rs. 42000/-, the rest was added to next year's revenue demand. Next year the locusts ate away the kharif crop, even then the government succeeded in collecting more than the annual revenue demand. The people had borrowed heavily to pay off the government. Col. Brooke, in his report on the famine of 1868, conceded that much of the indebtedness of the cultivators was caused by the necessity of borrowing to pay the government demand.[7] Similar views were expressed by the official report on famine relief operations in Merwara in 1891-92. It wrote: 'there is no doubt that the indebtedness of the rural population of the district was very largely increased by indiscriminate recovery of Government revenue immediately after the famine

TABLE: 1.4

Incidence of Dixonian Settlement During a Decade of Normal Rainfall (1849-1859)

Year	Seers per Rupee				Total=T (P1+2+3+4)	Average rate per rupee= T÷4	Revenue incidencehigher by % with 1849 as Base-year	Amt. of grain required to pay a revenue of Rs. 100.00	Percentage of total produce required to pay fixed land rev. of say Rs. 100/-
	Wheat P-1	Barley P-2	Maize P-3	Moth P-4					
1849	14	19	23	16	72	18		1800 Seers	50
1850	18	22	28	22	90	22.5	25	2250 "	62.5
1851	21	29	29	22	101	25.25	40.28	2525 "	70
1852	22	33	34	27	116	29	61.1	2900 "	80.5
1853	24	33	33	26	116	29	61.1	2900 "	80.5
1854	27	30	31	24	112	28	55.5	2800 "	77.7
1855	24	35	35	30	124	31	72.2	3100 "	86.1
1856	24	38	38	36	144	36	100	3600 "	100
1857	26	39	26	37	128	32	77.7	3200 "	88.8
1858	27	43	38	36	144	36	100	3600 "	100
1859	24	34	33	26	117	29.25	62.5	2925 "	81.25

of 1868-70'. La Touche cited the example of village Rassolpura in Ajmer tehsil where there were no mortgages prior to 1868; the policy of realising land revenue, even during a famine year, resulted in mortgages and sale of land; by 1874 half the *chahi* and *abi* lands (there was no *talabi* land) had been mortgaged. Even after a reduction of 22% demand from the villages in 1874 settlement, the mortgages and sales continued to increase.

The British administrators found an easy way out of increasing peasant indebtedness and passed on the responsibility to the vagaries of weather. The approach may have been justified if it could be shown that the years of normal rainfall (1850-59) had led to peasant prosperity.

The incidence of land revenue demand during years of normal rainfall may be analysed in order to see whether the cultivators could save in normal years. The administrative unconcern with the impact of falling prices of principal crops on the peasantry for a decade after the settlement and the consequent below subsistence level agriculture bears ample witness to the results of the land settlement. (Table No. 1.4)[9]

Thus in both types of decades - normal and subnormal - the impact on the condition of the peasantry was uniform. The phases of high prices were attributable to scarcity and low productivity; the cultivator was not benefitted because he had very little to sell. La Touche had found that high prices and low revenue were generally coexistent since deficiency of produce had been the cause of high prices which did not help the cultivator because he produced for the maintenance of his family. In case of lower production he had to borrow to pay the land revenue; in case of abundant production and low prices, the land revenue demand consumed the bulk of production. In both the cases his purchasing power was cut down by the land revenue demand which compelled him to borrow in years of scarcity and did not leave enough with him in years of abundance. After 1884, there was a long spell of 15 years of agricultural prosperity; this was also a period of increasing land mortgages and sales in Ajmer district where 54% more land was mortgaged during 1884-1910. The incidence of land revenue was 231% higher than what the settlement officers claimed it to be. (Table No. 4.4)

Face to face with widespread calamitous effects of the famine of 1868-69, the British Government ordered a fresh land revenue settlement at Ajmer to find out 'what the several village *could* pay for a series of years with some degree of certainty and ease'. The attempt was to ascertain those villages 'in which an appropriate demand had been collected' and, taking them as standard, to assess the rest accordingly.[10] This had practically foreclosed an enquiry into the causes of impoverishment of the peasantry.

TABLE: 1.5[11]

Percentage of Irrigated Land Sold and Mortgaged During the Dixonian Settlement (1849-1874)

Tehsil	Total Irrigated land (acres)	Land sold or mortgaged (acres)	Percentage of land mortgaged & sold
Ajmer	34664	15439	44.8
Beawar	21926	7866	35.0
Todgarh	11797	8889	75.3
Total	68387	32194	47.1

Looking back at half a century of British land revenue administration in Ajmer Merwara, one is struck by the phenomenon of transformation of 'surplus' agriculture to 'below subsistence' level. Every administrator, from Wilder onwards, was aware of the inequitious nature of land settlements and yet the same were renewed with marginal changes. Cavendish who had located the real cause of this unjust revenue demand, was transferred before he could initiate policy to lower the assessment. Dixon alone had been allowed to stay for long because he not only maximised the revenue demand but also aimed at collecting an amount of revenue which would be the maximum in a good year. If it was not realised, he used to get orders for remissions. This practice had a very demoralising effect on the peasantry. He had also popularised the practice of asking a bohra (moneylender) to pay for the peasant and thus delivered the cultivator into the clutches of the moneylender. The impact may be seen by some data on land mortgaged or sold during the continuation of Dixonian settlement.

II

The most important feature of the land tenure in Rajasthan in the pre-settlement period was that the cultivator's proprietorship of land was not dependent on the fulfilment of any condition. In other words, his ownership was secure and he could not be dispossessed of his land except in case of rebellion against the state. This right was based on the theory that the inhabitants of a village were the lineal descendants of the original settlers. This secure ownership was called by different names in different states but its content lay in absolute security. On the same analogy, the village community had control over the surplus lands, common pasture lands, woodland and tanks etc. in the village. If some cultivator felt that his patrimony fell short of his requirements, he could clear some extra land and make it usable for agriculture. The two features - security of tenure for the individual cultivator and community ownership of surplus land - were fundamental to the maintenance of the rural structure. The peasant did not pay a rent in cash or kind for his ownership of land. He was not under any compulsion to cultivate his land or any minimum portion of it. If he cultivated, he paid portion of the produce to the state. This ensured a healthy independence of the average cultivator who was a far more independent person than his counterpart in British India. He was not a rent paying tenant; he was free from any liability of land tax if the land could not be cultivated either on account of war, internal disturbance or famine or for personal or family reasons. The ownership of land was unaffected by non-cultivation of land even for long periods. If the peasant migrated out and returned after a couple of years, his ownership of land was intact; if his land had been given by the state to someone else, he could claim it back.

The land revenue was collected in cash and kind. Though the general practice was collection in kind, the practice of cash collection in case of some crops was equally old. The state demand had been based on realising a customary part of the produce, termed as '*banta*' (a portion). Even where cash rents were applicable per *bigha*, the rents in essence conformed to the concept of the '*banta*'. The peasant had the option of disagreeing with the estimated '*banta*' by the local officials and he could insist on an actual division of the crop yield. The peasant was cushioned against the bad effects of the harsh weather since the revenue demand (*bhog*) was generally dependent on the produce. There were no large arrears of land revenue; the cultivator could mortgage or sell his land; there was no foreclosure of mortgage.

The land revenue, collected in kind, was partly preserved in kind and partly converted in cash. It was the responsibility of the state to convert the produce into cash. This saved the peasant from the clutches of the trader who could manipulate the market rates. Thus the independence of the peasant was protected from being trampled on either by the state or the trader or the local official.

The pre-British system of land revenue collection and fixation of state demand had been shaped in accordance with forces of nature - climate and availability of irrigation. The land revenue demand depended on the produce. In case of agricultural output being adversely affected by excess, scarce or untimely rain, the state shared the difficulty of the cultivator. The land revenue was not rent; it was a tax on the gross produce; in other words, if the gross produce was less, the state demand was also less. Secondly the state demand was basically governed by the consideration that the cultivator should be left enough for the maintenance of his family and for the preservation of the social system. Wingate made special mention of this feature of the pre-settlement period as a defect of the land revenue system prevalent in Mewar.[12] Prior to 1818, the rulers as also the nobles had depended on the willing support of the people (cultivators included) in their political struggles. The maintenance of the village social order - the artisans and craftsmen and the service sector - was the responsibility of the producing classes. The political order in the states was considerably decentralised; the officials at the village level had considerable autonomy; the antagonistic relationship between the tax collectors and tax payers did not grow. The harmonious relationship between them led the British administrator to often postulate an unholy alliance between them to defraud the state of its legitimate dues.[12a]

During the decade after the great upheavel of 1857-58, some British Political Officers had started advocating a 'positive policy to fulfil the paramount power's duty of ensuring the proper functioning of the feudal order'. Some new entrants to the Political branch of the covenanted civil service were imbued with a crusading zeal to establish their racial superiority and to implement their ideas of social and economic progress. They felt that they had a 'duty' to give 'advice' to the ruling princes. Since the Indian states had been assured continuation due to considerations of state policy, indirect rule was relied upon to achieve British goals. The British, so their argument ran, would be held responsible for the decline of the Indian feudal order which 'had been guaranteed protection but not properly trained and educated'. The policy of exposing the rulers to western liberal education and of re-structuring the judicial and land revenue administration on new rational principles were considered two aspects of this 'great duty'.[13] The emphasis on the introduction of judicial reforms to check the waywardness of the feudal nobles and the establishment of land revenue settlements to ensure to the cultivator, as the called it, 'the rewards of his labour' were complementary expressions of the new definition of the paramount power's duty. This was the essence of the 'white man's burden' which aimed at social and economic restructuring in Indian states. It was, they felt, the duty of the government to make the ruling princes worthy feudatories of the Crown.

Simultaneously, self righteousness began to be loudly proclaimed by these Political Officers. A state, managed by a Political Agent during the minority of its ruler, was held up as having improved considerably in its administration. In 1869 when Bharatpur was handed over to its ruler, the AGG proudly wrote: 'There is no state in Rajputana which has anything approaching to so strong a Government or such efficient establishment as we now make over to the young Maharajah'. In 1871 another AGG wrote: 'In those capitals which have had the advantage of British management during a minority, much good has been effected, which has not died out with the withdrawal of our interference.[14] If states like Alwar fell back into anarchy and disorder after being handed over, they felt strengthened in their sense of superiority about their management. The most emphatic assertion of this new concept was made by Keatinge, the AGG, in his annual report when 'self-reliance, a high toned morality and a judicial mind' were declared to be the good qualities of a Political Agent who was expected 'to act impartially like a judge and not be involved in the partisan disputes'. Gone were the days when linguistic or departmental accomplishments of a Tod or a Metcalfe were considered as assets. The confident tone of imperialism around 1870 had been accompanied by a high moralising superiority. It was reflected in their estimate of two states' chief executives both of whom had been docile and obedient to the British. Kothari Kesri Singh (Mewar) was called 'hardworking, conscientious, able financier and qualified in every respect' for the post he held but he was not 'inclined to a liberal policy' because he clung to an antiquated revenue system' which, as the British put it, was tending to impoverish the people. On the other hand Sheodeen (Jaipur) was considered as a capable and far-sighted administrator because he had enhanced the state revenues from Hindaun tehsil from 3 to 6 lakhs by persuading the cultivators to grow opium and tobacco.[15]

In pursuance of the same objective, Mayo decided in 1870, to move out to Ajmer to tell the ruling princes 'what they should do' and 'what they shall not be allowed to do'. The foundation stone laying ceremony of the Mayo College for the sons of the ruling aristocracy in October 1870 was utilised as an occasion to spell out the new attitude. He sought heavy and cordial assistance from the princes in fulfilling the goal set by the British Government. He said: 'if we respect your rights and privileges, you should also respect the rights and privileges of those who are placed beneath your care. If we support you in your power, ... we demand that everywhere throughout the length and breadth of Rajputana ... the cultivator should enjoy the fruits of his labour ... you should undertake the construction of those works of irrigation which will improve the condition of the people and swell the revenues of your states ... '.[16] Mayo's emphasis on land revenue administration was an indication of future lines of state policy. Lytton, on December 5, 1879, exhorted the Mayo College audience: 'the leading Rajput families are mostly landowners; many of them (are) the lords of very large estates ... you (the students) are also the future landowners ... the future administrators ... (You should be able) to discharge the high duties of your inherited station with credit to yourselves'. Bradford, AGG, said on March 8, 1883: "There can be no higher ambition than that of desiring to manage your estates in such a manner as to create esteem amongst your tenants and dependants ... ".[17] The emphasis on improvement of land revenue system was indicative of the 'a priori' need to change it. The class of introspective British administrators who had considered government land revenue policy in Ajmer during 1818-36 as oppressive, had become a thing of the past by 1870. This sermonising about the need to improve the management of their landed estates was being done when the British knew that there was no peasant discontent in the khalsa areas of the various states.

The fact that British officers had introduced land revenue settlements in some states in the pre-1870 period, did not prevent them from emphasising the need to have fresh settlements; only the justification was now different. Where the settlement had not been introduced, the argument was that the interest of the state demanded it; vast fields of uncultivated rich soil were waiting to be cultivated (Mewar). In states where the land settlements had been introduced, it needed to be revised because either, the sources of irrigation have increased and the revenue demand could be easily raised (Bharatpur) or, the local officials had not implemented the settlement rules and there was need to restructure the whole system (Alwar) or, the record of rights was not properly maintained or a different type of survey was needed (Ajmer, Alwar and Bharatpur).

Imbued with a sense of their superiority, the British Political Officers changed their pre-1871 evaluation of the prevalent land revenue system in the states of Rajasthan. Mewar is an apt illustration of this process and is doubly significant because the British made a determined effort to change the land settlement in the state against passive resistance offered by the peasantry.

Political Agents at Mewar, during 1868-71, had considered the land revenue system to be 'simple, primitive and patriarchal'. The land revenue demand, varying from ½ to ¼ of produce was collected in a manner which was very popular because remissions in bad seasons were nearly automatic whilst full dues were paid in good ones. There were very few arrears. The agricultural population of Mewar was, as a rule, held to be very well off; the village communities had the administration of their own petty affairs, both civil and municipal, in their own hands; the elders of the village were held responsible for all the crimes committed within the limits of their villages. The system of government was more acceptable and coincided more with their views than the mode of government adopted in British provinces. The absence of litigation and complaints, about the rights to their lands between the landlords and the tenants, was particularly remarkable since the British Indian courts were flooded with such suits and complaints. Such matters were disposed of by the heads of village communities who decided them according to local customs; cases of injustice were rare.[18]

After 1871 the British Officers began to project a picture of docile and submissive cultivators who, being uneducated, were not mindful of their rights and interests. They argued that a new land revenue settlement would ensure their safety against exploitation by subordinate civil officials. When the peasants expressed resentment and opposition to a new land revenue settlement, the British, without caring to inquire into the genuineness of the grievances, found a ready scapegoat in the role of state officials who were considered corrupts and inefficient and were held to be working for the preservation of their ill-gotten gains which were likely to be reduced by the new land settlements. The British officials did not substantiate their charges. Mewar and Jhalawar offered instances of this type.

In Mewar a summary land settlement was introduced in 1870-71 which provided for a fixed annual revenue payment by the peasantry irrespective of crop yield. The revenue had been fixed on the basis of the average of 10 years (1860-69) which were years of scarcity and high prices. Originally the settlement was introduced for 3 years but was continued thereafter. In 1875 heavy rains and floods caused extensive damage to the crops and compelled the peasants to organise a resistance movement against the oppressive fixed revenue demand. The British retreated temporarily, and allowed payment according to past practice.

Here was an instance of a state where the peasants did not consider the settlement introduced by the British to be in their interests, and the British were keen to change the prevalent old system. Lyall appointed W.H. Smith to prepare a report justifying the need for a regular (as contrasted with a summary) land revenue settlement. Smith had the experience of N.W. Provinces settlement work and had recently introduced a settlement at Dholpur. He stayed for less than four months at Udaipur; this was enough for preparing a report finding fault with the prevalent state of affairs. He held the local officials - Hakims and Patels - to be responsible for the failure of the last settlement. His general low opinion about an average Indian led him not only to deny 'spotless integrity' to the Mewar officials but also to condemn the whole system which was pronounced to be 'vicious in every way, full of openings for every kind of fraud and embezzlement'. He presumed that the cultivator was 'continually harassed' by the officials who had to be conciliated by bribes. His conclusion was that the whole system was '*ba-ittbar-i-Hakim*' i.e. dependent on the integrity of the pargana officials. His general prejudice against the system and local officials led him to pronounce the judgment that if the 1871 settlement had succeeded, it would have resulted 'in the certain loss of much of their influence and nearly all their illegitimate profit'.[19] He thus held the officials culpable for the failure of the settlement, and prepared a case for change of the prevalent land revenue system.

Wingate, the succeeding Settlement Officer in Mewar, was, on the other hand, very critical of the settlement of 1871 which had imposed 'a full revenue'. He exonerated the local officials from blame for the failure of the settlement.. He conceded that the fall in prices of foodgrains, sugar and cotton in the post-1871 period made the burden of a fixed revenue more and more intolerable with every passing year.[20] The only result was to increase the indebtedness of the peasantry as the following table reveals.

TABLE: 1.6

Price in Rupees per Mani = (12 maunds of a seer of 44 tolas) in Rashmi Pargana (Mewar)

Year	Makki P-1	Jowar P-2	Jau P-3	Wheat P-4	Total of P-1 to P-4=T	Average Price of 1 Mani=T/4	Qty. in Mani to pay Rs. 100/- land revenue	Percentage of increase in burden of payment
1871	15	14.5	16	24	69.5	17.4	5.75	base year
1872	10.25	10	13	20	53.25	13.30	7.52	30.78
1873	14.75	14.75	15	18	62	15.5	7.1	23.47
1874	14.25	14	14.25	17	59.2	14.88	6.7	16.5
1875	12.75	12.33	10	14	49	12.25	8.16	41.9
1876	12	11.5	12	15	50.5	12.62	7.93	37.9

Source : Wintage : Settlement of the Jat Pergannahs of Mewar, p. 12

The burden of land revenue had increased on an average of 30% annually as a consequence of fall in prices of agricultural commodities; the revenue demand equivalent to 50% gross produce had thus become 65% of the gross produce. Wingate thus conceded that the main cause of failure of the revenue settlement of 1871 was the fall in prices. The heavy rains and floods of 1875 only provided the occasion for the passive resistance movement by the peasants against the oppressive land revenue settlement. This phenomenon should have been apparent to Smith in 1878 but he chose to throw a blanket over it. He did not even hint at it. This suppression of the significant factor for the failure of the land settlement makes one suspect British motives in enforcing a land settlement in the state.

Jhalawar came under regency administration in 1875 when Prithvi Singh died without any direct or adopted heir. The British overruled Kota's claim for reversion of the state even though it had been granted to Zalim Singh's heirs only; and allowed one of the widowed queens to adopt a 9 year old Bakhat Singh. For the next 9 years the state was run by the Political Agent. This provided the much awaited opportunity for a land revenue settlement - summary settlement in the year 1878 for 5 years to be followed by a regular settlement, announced before the expiry of the summary settlement. Preparations for the regular settlement began in April 1880 itself. When Zalim Singh II was entrusted with the administrative control of the state in February 1884, he was not allowed to change the land revenue administration.[21]

Land Revenue Settlement During Regency Council Administration

All land revenue settlements in the different states of Rajasthan were introduced during the minority of the rulers in the post-1870 period when the state administration was run by a regency council under the presidentship of the Political Agent or other British Officers. This was the highest common factor (H.C.F.) of all land revenue settlements in the states of Rajasthan and lends one to ask the significant question: Why did the British do so? The question acquires added significance in the light of AGG Lyall's observation that "it would be a difficult undertaking in a state like Mewar" to attempt the introduction of a 10 year settlement "during a short minority".[22] Sajjan Singh had sat on the gaddi in 1874 and was of about 16 years of age. Lyall had also observed that introducing a settlement at Alwar when there was a longer minority and there was time enough for `more systematic reform', was more correct. It appears that the type of changes which the British aimed at, might not have been possible if they did not have the final administrative authority of the state in their hands. The generally docile rulers alongwith their advisers might not have agreed to the far reaching socio-economic engineering which was brought about by the land revenue settlements. The political events in the various states which preceded the introduction of land revenue settlements may be briefly reviewed.

Bharatpur came under regency council administration in 1853 when Jaswant Singh, aged 2½ years, ascended the *gaddi.* The regency council administration lasted till 1869. A summary 3 year land revenue settlement was introduce in 1855 by Henry Lawrence, the AGG, in three northern tehsils of the state and by Nixon, his assistant, in the remaining tehsils. In order to ensure its acceptance by the zamindars, a new class sought to be created at the time, the revenue demand had been reduced by 10 to 15%. The settlement was extended for another 3 years. Since the zamindars could not be created, the 6 year settlement made in 1862-63 enhanced the revenue demand by Rs. 80000/-. Jaswant Singh, even after attaining majority was restrained from changing the land settlement. He was succeeded in 1893 by his son who was deprived of all powers in 1895 and a regency council under the Political Agent was established. Since the British perspective towards land settlements had changed after 1870, a fresh land settlement was undertaken after 1895 which took more than 4 years for completion.

At Alwar the British got an opportunity to establish a regency council in October 1858 on account of a rebellion of Rajput nobles against the ruler. Impey, the Political Agent, introduced a 3 year summary settlement in February 1859; a 10 year settlement was established in 1862 enhancing the revenue demand by 25%. In 1874 Mangal Singh, aged 16, ascended the gaddi; regency council administration was re-established. Powlett had been appointed Settlement Officer in the state in 1872; but a 16 year settlement was established only in 1876. Mangal Singh died in 1892 and was succeeded by Jai Singh aged 10 years. The regency council decided upon a thorough revision of the land revenue settlement. It was done during 1896-1900 with considerable socio-economic restructuring.

Mewar came under regency council administration in 1861. Here priority was given to reorganisation of judicial and police apparatus. A summary land settlement was thrust on an unwilling peasantry in 1871. The peasantry led a passive resistance movement in 1875 resulting in the cancellation of the settlement. The peasant resistance was misrepresented as a plot by local officials to preserve their illegal gains. The accession of Sajjan Singh, aged 16, in 1874 and his subsequent conduct in being guided totally by British advice, gave the British the desired opportunity to introduce a land revenue settlement. Wingate, the Settlement Officer, with the help of Mehta Pannalal and leading members of the business community, took 8 years to introduce the land settlement in stages.

In Jhalawar it was only after the accession in 1876 of Zalim Singh II, aged 10 years, that the British thought of changing the prevalent land revenue system. Abbott, Political Superintendent of the state, first established a summary settlement for 5 years in 1878. After 3 years, steps were taken to commence a regular survey. Zalim Singh II, though educated at Mayo

College (1876-83), was entrusted with state powers with some restrictions in 1884. Land revenue settlement had been completed by 1884.

In Bikaner the accession of 7 years old Ganga Singh in 1887 led to the establishment of a regency council. Full advantage was taken of the opportunity to establish a regular land revenue settlement under Fagan. He took more than four years to propose a land settlement which was implemented after 1896.

Even in small states like Dungarpur, the British took advantage of minority administration in the post 1870 period, to introduce land revenue settlements. With the accession of Bijay Singh, a minor, in 1898, Dungarpur came under regency council administration for a period of 11 years. A 10 year land revenue settlement was introduced during 1904-05. On its expiry in 1915, the state was advised, for reasons of economy, to continue the settlement with necessary minor revisions. The real reason was that the state was not under regency administration. When the state came under regency administration after the accession of Laxman Singh, aged 10, in 1918, the settlement was thoroughly revised in 1924-25 with major changes affecting Bhil villages.

At Dholpur, it was only after the accession of 9 year old Nihal Singh in 1873 that the British appointed La Touche as officer on special duty to report on the revenue system. W.H. Smith was deputed in 1875 to undertake a regular settlement and he established a summary settlement for 12 years in 1878. On its expiry in 1891, Nihal Singh was continuing on the *gaddi*. Hence the settlement was revised by his confidant, Uma Charan Mukhopadhya in 1894. Nihal singh died in 1901 and was succeeded by his son Ram Singh, aged 8 years. A new settlement was undertaken by the British in 1909 which was completed by 1912.

The land revenue settlement of Tonk is a theoretical exception to the general observation made above. But the exception itself proved the rule. It is true that Tonk was not under a minority administration when the land revenue settlement was established in 1891 after 5 years of labour. But the events which preceded the land revenue settlement and the conditions under which it was introduced had reduced the state virtually to the status of a state under regency administration. The British had deposed the nawab in 1867; the new nawab Muhammad Ibrahim had landed the state in a state of insolvency. On account of his financial difficulties, the nawab first bound himself in writing in February 1885 to abide by all arrangements which may be made to make the state financially solvent. He agreed to remove some of his advisers, to limit his expenditure, and promised not to grant landed property or cash allowance to anyone.[23] On March 28, 1886, he expressed his inability to extricate the state out of debt and solicited a loan of 12.5 lakhs at a low rate of interest.[24] It was not enough. He was asked to give 'more definite guarantees for the improvement of the administration' before any assistance could be given. On August 30, 1886, the nawab surrendered to be guided by the advice of the Political Agent in the conduct of administration.[25] In Novemeber 1886 T.C. Pears was deputed to carry out a land revenue settlement. The state administration was entrusted to a council of administration in May 1887; accounts and finances were controlled by an Accounts Officer loaned by the British Government.[26] Pears was given instructions by the Political Agent about the manner in which the settlement was to be introduced. these arrangements reveal the extent to which Tonk administration had come under the control of the Political Agent.

Even in the case of a small state like Karauli under a ruler with full authority, W. Raw carried out a settlement which was discussed with Pinhey, Offg. AGG, and finally approved by the Government of India.[27] Pinhey visited Karauli in January 1909 and agreed that the land revenue work of the small state (population 1.46 lakhs) might take 2½ years. At the end of

March 1909, the principles of the settlement were submitted to the Government for approval. Later on the same were discussed with Harcourt Butler, foreign secretary to the Government, in July 1910 at Agra. Thus the changes that were brought about were decided not by the ruler but by the British government.

The land revenue settlement in all states were thus carried out at a time when the British Government had full administrative control in its hands. Mostly the state was under a regency administration; in other cases the ruler had agreed in advance to accept the policy guidelines and their implementation. Despite the regency administration, specific sanction of the Government of India was sought for all major changes brought about through the settlement, e.g. the status of the zamindars in relation to the state, the writing off of old arrears and the enhancement of revenue demand at Bharatpur.[28] When there was a possibility that a settlement officer might be appointed for Mewar at the request of the ruler who was not a minor, the offg. AGG had specifically brought it to the notice of the Government of India that the Settlement Officer 'should be in constant communication with, and under the guidance of, the Political Agent, in all matters not strictly technical: that, even in these, the latter should be kept fully informed, from time to time, of the progress of the work and should be the channel of communication' with the AGG and the Government.[29]

Appendix-A

Evaluation of Crop yield in Ajmer Merwara Circa 1874 A.D.
(La Touche's Report p. 95)

Crop.	Ajmere Tehsil										
	Area in acres	Average produce per acre		Amount of produce		Average price current			Value in Rupees		
		FIRST CLASS									
		M.	S.	M.	S.	Per Rupee. M.	S.	C.	Rs.	a.	p.
Sugarcane	292	8	0	2,336	0	0	8	0	11,680	0	0
Poppy	69	3	30	258	30	0	10	0	1,035	0	0
Vegetables	354	per acre.		Rupees		30	0	0	10,620	0	0
Melons	287	"		"		25	0	0	7,175	0	0
Lucerne grass	9	"		"		100	0	0	900	0	0
						M.	S.	C.			
Pepper	39	3	0	117	0	0	3	0	1,560	0	0
Tobacco	57	10	0	570	0	0	10	0	2,280	0	0
						Per Rupee M.	S.	C.			
Onions	20	18	0	360	0	2	0	0	180	0	0
Roses	14	20	0	280	0	0	10	0	1,120	0	0
Total	1,141	...		...		...			36,550	0	0
		SECOND CLASS									
						M.	S.	C.			
Cotton Irrigated	5,215	4	10	22,163	30	0	8	0	1,10,818	12	0
Dry	592	1	10	740	0	0	8	0	3,700	0	0
Maize Irrigated	6,177	10	0	61,770	0	0	22	0	1,12,309	1	5
Dry	895	1	20	1,312	20	0	22	0	2,440	14	7
Wheat Irrigated	2,517	7	20	18,877	20	0	16	0	47,193	12	0
Dry	87	1	0	87	0	0	16	0	217	8	0
Barley Irrigated	16,075	10	0	1,60,750	0	0	24	0	2,67,916	10	8
Dry	609	2	0	1,218	0	0	24	0	2,030	0	0

Crop.	Ajmere Tehsil										
	Area in acres	Average produce per acre		Amount of produce			Average price current		Value in Rupees		
Bejar	1,496	6	0	8,976	0	0	24	0	14,960	0	0
Gojee	502	7	10	3,639	20	0	21	0	6,932	6	5
Gram	8,150	2	20	20,375	0	0	23	0	35,434	12	6
Rice	69	4	0	276	0	0	8	12	1,261	11	5
Hemp	...	...					...		...		
Sarsoon	7	1	10	8	30	0	12	0	29	2	8
Unsown	126	...		...			...		...		
Total	42,517	...		...			...		6,05,244	11	8
				THIRD CLASS							
							Per Rupee				
Jowar	26,161	2	20	65,402	20	0	23	8	1,11,323	6	5
Bajra	12,168	2	20	30,420	0	0	19	12	61,610	2	0
Moong	2,218	2	30	6,099	20	0	16	12	14,565	15	6
Moth	16,696	2	30	29,414	20	0	20	0	58,828	0	0
Mosh	155	1	20	232	20	0	16	0	581	4	0
Kangni	33	3	0	99	0	0	13	4	298	14	0
Til	13,736	1	10	17,170	0	0	11	0	62,436	5	10
Linseed	30	1	10	37	20	0	11	0	136	5	10
Gwar	623	4	0	2,492	2	1	0	0	2,492	0	0
					S.						
Indigo	4	0	3		12	0	0	8	24	0	0
Chaula	404	4	0	1,616	0	0	20	0	3,232	0	0
Maddoon	14	1	3	15	0	0	20	0	30	1	7
Kuluth	1,385	2	0	2,770	2	[illegible]	26	0	4,261	8	7
Unsow	427	...		...			...		...		
Total	68,054	...		...			...		3,19,819	15	9
Grand Total	1,11,712	...		...			...		9,61,614	11	5

(Contd.)

(Contd.)

Crop	Beawur Tshsil				
	Area in acres	Average produce per acre	Amount of produce	Average price current	Value in Rupees
FIRST CLASS					
		M. S.		Rs. a. p.	Rs. a. p.
Sugarcane	5	Per acre	Rupees	35 0 0	175 0 0
		M. S. C.	M. S. C.	Per seer.	
Poppy	551	0 6 8	89 21 8	8 15 10	32,196 3 3
Vegetables	53	Per acre.	Rupees	30 0 0	1,590 0 0
Melons	43	"	"	25 0 0	1,075 0 0
Lucerne grass	13	"	"	50 0 0	650 0 0
				M. S. C.	
Pepper	5	4 0 0	20 0 0	0 6 6	125 7 11
				Per Maund.	
Tobacco	62	10 0 0	620 0 0	10 3 7	6,336 5 8
Onions	...	...	...	...	...
Roses	...	...	...	...	...
Total	732	...	...	...	42,148 0 10
SECOND CLASS					
				M. S. C.	
Cotton Irrigated	1,677	4 0 0	6,708 0 0	0 8 0	33,540 0 0
Dry	356	1 10 0	445 0 0	0 8 0	2,225 0 0
Maize Irrigated	8,182	10 0 0	81,820 0 0	0 28 7	1,15,087 7 6
Dry	1,502	2 0 0	3,004 0 0	0 28 7	4,225 6 6
Wheat Irrigated	1,269	7 0 0	8,883 0 0	0 18 6	19,336 12 9
Dry	16	1 0 0	16 0 0	0 18 6	34 13 3
Barley Irrigated	13,887	10 0 0	1,38,870 0 0	0 28 5	1,96,196 0 5
Dry	955	3 0 0	2,865 0 0	0 28 5	4,047 11 0
Bejar	470	6 0 0	2,820 0 0	0 28 5	3,994 1 8
Gojee	881	7 0 0	2,685 0 0	0 18 6	5,851 7 10
Gram	1,288	2 20 0	1,230 0 0	0 25 9	5,038 10 1
Rice	123	10 0 0	1,230 0 0	0 7 6	8,671 3 0
Hemp	269	2 0 0	538 0 0	0 28 5	760 1 5
Sarsoon	124	1 10 0	155 0 0	0 20 13	297 14 6
Unsown	...	...	...	...	...
Total	30,502	...	...	...	3,97,306 9 11

THIRD CLASS

				Per Rupee	
Jowar	5,267	3 3 0	16,196 0 0	0 24 7	26,510 1 6
Bajra	4,215	2 39 0	12,539 25 0	0 23 8	21,342 15 8
Moong	1,486	5 22 8	8,265 35 0	0 17 9	18,826 3 1
Moth	1,185	5 0 0	5,925 0 0	0 23 4	10,193 15 0
Mosh	190	5 6 0	978 20 0	0 18 14	2,073 10 3
Kangni	47	5 0 0	235 0 0	0 28 5	332 0 1
Til	3,267	5 6 8	16,865 35 8	0 12 14	52,398 14 0
Linseed	...	...	...	...	...
Gwar	42	6 10 0	262 20 0	0 23 5	370 11 4
Indigo	...	...	...	...	...
Chaula	697	7 20 0	5,227 20 0	0 21 10	9,669 5 6
Maddooa	3	5 0 0	15 0 0	0 28 5	21 3 2
Kuluth	1,132	5 0 0	5,660 0 0	0 24 7	9,264 7 3
Unsown	1,306	...	...	...	...
Total	18,837	...	...	...	1,51,003 6 10
Grand Total	50,071	...	...	...	5,90,458 1 7

Crop.	Todghur Tehsil				
	Area in acres	Average produce per acre	Amount of produce	Average price current	Value in Rupees
		FIRST CLASS			
		M. S.		Rs. a. p.	Rs. a. p.
Sugarcane	58	Per acre	Rupees	50 0 0	2,900 0 0
				Per seer.	
Poppy	2,229	0 7 4	404 0 4	6 9 0	1,06,051 10 0
Vegetables	55	Per acre	Rupees	30 0 0	1,650 0 0
Melons	4	"	"	25 0 0	100 0 0
Lucerne grass	...	...	...	....	...
Pepper	36	4 0 0	144 0 0	0 7 0	822 13 9
				S. C.	
Tabacco	9	7 20 0	67 20 0	10 0	270 0 0
Onions	...	...	...	...	...
Roses	...	...	...	...	...
Total	2,391	...	...	...	1,11,794 7 9

(Contd.)

Crop.	Todghur Tehsil											
	Area in acres	Average produce per acre			Amount of produce			Average price current		Value in Rupees		
SECOND CLASS												
Cotton Irrigated	262	5	10	0	1,375	20	0	13	8	4,571	6	2
Dry	117	2	0	0	234	0	0	13	8	693	15	4
Maize Irrigated	6,617	12	20	0	32,712	20	0	31	10	1,04,616	9	7
Dry	1,287	3	20	0	4,504	20	0	31	10	5,045	13	3
Wheat Irrigated	1,081	10	0	0	10,810	0	0	20	5	21,287	6	2
Dry	13	1	20	0	19	20	0	20	5	38	6	5
Barley Irrigated	6,459	12	20	0	80,737	20	0	30	8	1,05,845	4	0
Dry	686	3	0	0	2,058	0	0	30	8	2,884	14	8
Bejar	...	...						...		...		
Gojee	75	7	0	0	525	0	0	26	0	807	10	8
Gram	105	3	0	0	315	0	0	26	0	484	10	8
Rice	295	10	0	0	2,950	0	0	20	5	5,809	3	8
Hemb	1	2	20	0	2	20	0	32	0	3	2	0
Sarsow	23	2	0	0	46	0	0	28	8	64	9	0
Unsowu	...	...			...			...		...		
Total	17,021	...			...			...		2,52,152	15	7
THIRD CLASS												
								Per Rupee				
Jowar	2,420	4	0	0	9,680	0	0	26	8	14,611	5	2
Bajra	431	2	0	0	862	0	0	24	4	1,421	13	10
Moong	848	3	0	0	2,554	0	0	20	5	5,009	11	8
Moth	76	3	0	0	228	0	0	26	0	350	12	4
Mosh	327	2	0	0	654	0	0	23	4	1,125	2	7
Kanjni	32	4	0	0	128	0	0	25	0	204	12	9
Til	1,254	2	20	0	3,135	0	0	17	10	7,114	14	5
Linseed	...	...			...			...		...		
Gwar	...	...			...			...		...		
Indigo	...	...			...			...		...		
Chaula	590	2	0	0	1,180	0	0	22	2	2,133	9	11
Maddoon	67	4	0	0	268	0	0	26	5	407	6	7
Kuluth	2,589	4	0	0	10,356	0	0	31	9	13,124	7	0
Unsown	331							...		...		
Total	8,965	...			...			...		45,504	0	3
Grand Total	28,377	...			...			...		4,89,451	7	7

Crop	Ajmer-Mhairwara	
	Area in acres	Value in Rupees
FIRST CLASS		
Sugarcane	355	14,755
Poppy	2,849	1,39,283
Vegetables	462	13,860
Melons	324	8,350
Lucerne grass	22	1,550
Pepper	80	2,508
Tobacco	128	8,887
Onions	20	180
Roses	14	1,120
Total	4,264	1,90,493
SECOND CLASS		
Cotton Irrigated	7,154	1,48,430
Dry	1,065	6,619
Maize Irrigated	20,976	1,32,013
Dry	3,684	12,362
Wheat Irrigated	4,867	87,818
Dry	116	291
Barley Irrigated	36,421	5,69,998
Dry	2,250	8,773
Bejar	1,966	18,954
Gojee	961	13,591
Gram	9,543	40,958
Rice	487	13,742
Hemp	270	763
Sarsoon	154	392
Unsown	126	...
Total	90,040	12,54,704
THIRD CLASS		
Jowar	33,848	1,52,445
Bajra	16,864	84,375
Moong	4,552	38,402
Moth	11,957	69,373
Mosh	672	3,780

(Contd.)

(Contd.)

Crop	Ajmer-Mhairwara	
	Area in acres	Value in Rupees
Kangni	112	836
Til	13,257	1,21,950
Linseed	30	136
Gwar	665	2,863
Indigo	4	24
Chaula	1,691	15,035
Maddoon	84	458
Kuluth	5,106	26,650
Unsown	2,064	...
Total	95,856	5,16,327
Grand Total	1,90,160	19,61,524

M = Maund
S = Seer (1/40 of a maund)
C = Chatank (1/16 of a rupee)
a = anna (1/16 of a rupee)
p = pie (1/12 of anna)

Notes & References

1. The Private Journal of the Marquess of Hastings, vol. 1, p. 40
2. H.T. Prinsep: History of the Political and Military Transactions in India, vol. II, p. 431
3. The Private Journal, vol. II, pp. 62-63
4. La Touche: Report on the Settlement of the Ajmer and Mhairwarra Districts, 1875 (published 1900), p. 70. This report has given a good historical section and has been the basis for the pre 1874 account of British land revenue policy in the district.
5. Ibid., p. 75
6. Ibid., p. 83

6a. La Touche : op. cit., p. 90; Whiteway : Report, p. 30

7. Brooke's Report on the Famine of 1868, para 52. Foreign, General A, March 1871, nos. 3-4.

8. A similar view was expressed in 1892-93 when the Government was warned against recovering the arrears of suspended revenue during the famine of 1891-92 in Ajmer. Report of Famine Relief in Ajmer Merwara, 1891-92, p. 111
9. The rates have been given by La Touche. op. cit., p. 68.
10. La Touche: op. cit., 110
11. Data compiled from La Touche's Report (p. 90) and Whiteway: Report on the Settlement of Ajmer Merwara Districts, p. 30
12. A. Wingate: Proposals for the Settlement of the Jat Pergannahs of Meywar (1885), p. 19
13. Report on the Political Administration of the Rajpootana States (later cited as R.A.R.), 1868-69, p. 141
14. R.A.R., 1868-69, p. 14; R.A.R., 1871-72, p. 5 The reference in both the Report is to AGG's remarks.
15. R.A.R. 1868-69, p. 34. The observations have been made to the Political Agent, Mewar; also R.A.R., 1870-71, p. 11
16. Sherring: History of Mayo College, Vol. I, p. 11
17. Ibid., Vol. 1. p. 194
18. R.A.R., 1868-69, p. 35; 1869-70, p. 29; 1870-71, p. 44
19. Foreign Revenue A, October 1879, no. 1-17. Smith's Settlement Report of Mewar, paras 82 and 87
20. Wingate: op. cit, paras 8 and 31
21. Foreign Political, Internal A, February 1888, no. 53
22. R.A.R., 1874-75, p. 5
23. R.A.R., 1884-85, p. 156
24. R.A.R., 1885-86, pp. 46 and 186
25. R.A.R., 1886-87, p. 175
26. R.A.R., 1887-88, p. 94
27. W. Raw: Rinal Report of the First Settlement of the Karauli state. 1909-12, pp. 14-15
28. AGG, Rajputana to Secretary, Government of India, letter no. 124-C dated 1/7th January 1899; the Government approved the recommendations vide letter no. 677-1A, dated 11 March 1899. Both the letters have been printed along with the Report of the Northern Tehsils of Bharatpur.
29. Foreign Revenue A, October 1879, Nos. 1-17. Letter of AGG to Secretary, Government of India, dated 30.7.1878.

2

Socio-Economic Engineering Through Land Revenue Settlements

I

J.C. Brooke had been impressed during the famine of 1868, by the healthy independence of the peasantry of the region, which was not willing to come to relief works and accept doles.[1] Alfred Lyall, AGG, one of the advocates of the imperial civilising mission, expressed his bewilderment in 1875, at the successful revolt of the peasantry led by the cultivators of five Jat pargannahs of Mewar against the land revenue settlement of 1871 in the state. He wrote[2]:

> The experiment of fixing the revenue demand at a money rate ... has not succeeded ... When the revenue was demanded (after the failure of autumn crop on account of excessive rain) the cultivators of 100 villages set off in a body for Malwa with all their property, followed by the revenue collectors and the money lenders, both entreating them to stay. The curious thing was that there seemed to be no disposition to stop the cultivators forcibly by seizure of person or property. The cultivators appeared to be masters of the situation and eventually dictated their terms.

This healthy independence of the peasantry of Rajasthan was in sharp contrast to the submissiveness of the peasantry in British India around that time. It had been the result of generations of security of land tenure and absence of oppressive revenue collection in the region. Half a century later, this independence would become a thing of the past. The report of famine relief operations in 1905-6 in Ajmer Merwara said that "the people of Merwara have no shame about coming to famine relief".[3]

The security of land tenure of the cultivators in the different states of the region, prior to the enforcement of the land revenue settlements under British officers, has been conceded by writers on 18th century land system. Tod had written that "the *ryot* (cultivator) was the proprietor of the soil in Mewar.[4] The peasant compared his right therein to *akshay doob* which no vicissitudes could destroy. Land was considered by him as his *bapota* (patrimonial inheritance). The popular adage in the whole region was: *`bhog ra dhani raj ho; bhum ra dhani ma cho"*. (The government is the owner of revenue, but I am the owner of land). His right to alienate by sale or a temporary mortgage indicated his proprietorship. In many cases of mortgages, the proprietor cultivator continued to cultivate the lands his ancestors may have mortgaged 4 or 5 generations ago; even such an old mortgage did not impair his proprietary rights. Any length of time of mortgage or his absence from his village did not affect his *bapota*.

A similar adage was common for the Jat states in eastern Rajasthan. O'Dwyer had noted the popular saying at Bharatpur. It was: *"bhej tumhara, dharti hamara"* (the revenue is yours, the land is ours).[5]

The peasant paid nothing for his ownership of land; he paid a portion of the produce of his land and was under no compulsion to cultivate his land. The revenues of the state on every description of corn were realised by either *kankut* or *batai*; other crops like sugarcane, opium, hemp, tabacco and cotton were subjected to money payment. The cultivators usually had large holdings but cultivated only a portion of it, leaving the rest fallow to regain fertility. The inviolable right of ownership of land was the secret of their healthy independence and profound attachment to their lands. The village community zealously guarded its right over the village land which was its preserve to be used as pasture for its cattle or for future needs of increased population of the village. Every cultivator had a right, as a member of the village community, to partake in the communal property of the village - the pastures, the village tank. Absolute security of the peasant's title of ownership to his land was fundamental to an understanding of his relationship with the state. His liability to pay land revenue was determined by his produce. He was cushioned against the vagaries of weather and harshness of climate in as much as his liability to pay was proportionately reduced.

It is legitimate to ask: Why were the British settlement officers interested in curtailing the secure and inheritable ownership of land? Smith and Wingate knew that Mewar was sparsely populated and that the best lands in the state were already being cultivated. Why did they want the cultivation to be extended to inferior *barani* lands? There had been no mechanisation of agriculture requiring larger fields for cultivation; there had been no substantial enhancement in state irrigation works in any state during the later half of the 19th century, and there had been no increase in population to justify the settlement officers' attempt to extend cultivation to inferior lands. In fact the population had declined substantially by 1901. There was no migration of people to the states of the region from British Indian provinces; if at all, there was some migration out of the states into various provinces of British India. Some population statistics are given below[6]:

States' Population during 1872-1901

State		1881	1891	1901
Alwar	(1872) 778596	682926	767786	828487
Bharatpur	(1867) 743710	645540	640303	626665
Mewar		1443144	1710579	1018805
Karauli		148670	156587	156786
Kota		707402	718771	544879
Pratapgarh		79298	87975	52025
Tonk		338029	380969	273267
Dungarpur		86429	98448	100103
Rajasthan as a whole (Excluding Ajmer Merwara)		10283121	12153631	9842482

The total population even in 1931 was 11225712.

And still Wingate was insistent that the *assamis* should be discouraged to keep lands they could not cultivate. He argued that some one else will take up the cultivation of the vacant land. The settlement process was thus an attempt to encourage a cultivator to give up lands he could not cultivate. The fixation of land revenue per bigha was a subtle device to press the *assami* hard to give up extra land. The apparently innocuous but potentially significant principle was announced from house tops. 'No right of ownership is recognised in any land for which assessment is not paid'. He made a specific mention that the people 'stubbornly resist any effort of the *hakim* to introduce new settlers'.[7] But the important question was: From where was the new cultivator to come?

The new cultivators came from a large scale closure of various crafts and cottage industries in the last quarter of the 19th century under the impact of import of consumer goods from industrial England. Every state under regency council administration experienced financial changes leading to a great displacement of people from handicrafts and cottage industries or from state employment. Some idea of the nature of changes may be formed by what happened at Alwar during 1871-72. The manufacture of iron was a great industry in the state but it fell off greatly on account of large quantities being imported from Europe. This single change affected a large number of people employed in cutting wood and bringing it to the iron furnaces; or the expenditure on stables was reduced by 41%, on courtiers by 66% and on the charitable and religious endowments by another 66%. The number of saddle and carriage horses was reduced from 690 and 164 to 272 and 101 in 1870-71. Such sundry details have been given to indicate the process of displacement of people from traditional sources of income in state service. Large numbers of people so displaced had to be provided alternative sources of living; they were diverted to agriculture necessitating a change in the ownership rights of individuals and the system of land tenure. The land revenue settlements weakened the ownership right of the peasants so as to enable the state to provide land to the persons displaced from state service and handicrafts. The *barani* land, made available for cultivation after the assertion of state authority over all lands, was the only means of earning their livelihood. The central point which was put forth as the main advantage of curtailment of *bapota* and assertion of state ownership of land was that the state would be free to allot those lands to any one who was desirous of cultivating them.

The British used the land revenue settlement to bring about socio-economic engineering. It was a two-fold process. The negative part of this process consisted in weakening the secure land ownership of the peasant proprietor and in changing the process of fixation and realisation of land revenue demand. The positive part of the process lay in either creating a new class of intermediaries between the cultivating peasantry and the state or in changing the attitude of local officials towards the peasantry. The secure land ownership of the peasant was projected as a hindrance in the adoption of measures of public welfare by the state. The local machinery's responsiveness to the peasant interests was projected as its corruption and inefficiency. The conditions of service of the local officials - *patels, patwaris, lambardars* and *kanungos* - were changed; they were freed from their dependence on the village community and were fully subordinated to state control. These local officials who had been spokesmen of the peasantry in the past, soon became state officials who conveyed and implemented state decisions. The peasant proprietor's healthy independence, as a result of the above changes, became a thing of the past; in the course of a quarter century he found himself suddenly isolated in his own rural setting. The process of weakening the peasant's secure ownership and of creating a class of intermediaries was accompanied by a transformation in the character of the local officials.

The time taken in bringing about the land revenue settlement was, in a large number of cases, disproportionate to the area and population of the state concerned.

TABLE: 2.2

State	Cultivated Area (Bighas)	Population Pre-1881	1901	Time taken for land revenue Settlement
Alwar	1392765	778596	828487	1896-1900 = 4 yrs
Bharatpur	1598989	743710	626665	" "
		1881		
Dholpur	436257	249657	271496	1909-1912 = 3½ yrs
Jhalawar	1385682 Acres.	150361	90175	1883-1885 = 2½ yrs
Kota	1763244	707402	544879	1904-1909 = 5 yrs
Karauli	154137	148670	156786	Jan. 1909- Aug. 1912 = 3½ yrs
Mewar	388067	1443144	1018805	1879-1893 = 15 yrs
Pratapgarh	29172 acres.	79298	52025	1903-1906 = 3 yrs

Alwar and Bharatpur had already had five land revenue settlements each; at Alwar all of them were done by British officers. The earlier settlements had been completed generally in less than a year.

The 'operation' of this process of weakening the peasant's secure ownership began from Mewar where the peasantry had openly revolted in 1875 against the summary settlement of 1871. The passive resistance movement of the peasantry was looked upon as a challenge to the policy of subordinating the state economy to imperial and colonial interests. A.C. Lyall, after joining the Executive Council at Calcutta, took keen interest in preparing a case for changes in prevalent land system. Smith had been sent to Mewar to justify the need of the settlement. His report of 30 foolscap printed pages, written during his stay of less than four months, is a document full of 'a priori' assumptions based on "could be" or "might be".[9] He conceded that the prevalent classification of soil was simple and reasonable; that the boundaries of every field were not only well known and clearly marked but 'strongly defined'; that it would be 'most unwise' to abolish the privileged holdings of the Brahmins, Rajputs and the mahajans. He wanted to fix rates for soils in accordance with custom and declared capabilities of each particular village; he accepted that immediate enhancement of revenue was 'not the object of the proposed settlement'. The question that needs to be asked is: Why was he sent? He confessed that his real object was to change the cultivator's indestructible proprietorship of soil called *bapota*.[11] By a process of defining, he limited, restricted, and ultimately weakened this secure and heritable ownership right in land. He first divided the *bapota* into *pucca* and *kutcha*, limited the former to consist in the right to sell land, restricted the operative *pucca bapota* only to some parganas in the state and then weakened it, by making it conditional on the payment of the '*bhog*' (mistranslating it as rental) to the state.[12]

The tenor of Smith's report was highly conjectural and biased mainly against the peasant proprietors in the state. His batteries were directed against their '*bapi*' rights in Mewar. He refused to accept Tod's description of "patrimonial inheritance" of peasant's right to land 'without grave reservations'. His opinion, unsubstantiated by any instances or documents, was that the land under *pucca bapota* was secure to the peasant as long as he paid '*bhog*' i.e. the rent of his land. He contradicted himself in the next para when he declared that the claims of *bapota* holders and state's rights in *bapota* villages were 'still unsettled'. He could not cite instances of the dispute being in existence. He misrepresented the payment of *nazrana* by a peasant for reclaiming waste land for addition to his *bapota* as an admission of state's right of ownership though he confessed that this was not a universal practice in the state. On the basis of his experience, he hesitatingly dèclared the prevalent method unreasonable. He accepted that the '*ryot* only pays for as much land as he cultivates' but he wanted the state to assert its right over 'the vast areas of magnificent soil' which the cultivator either refused or was unable to bring under the plough himself.[13]

The modification of the *bapota* by Smith, apparently marginal, was in reality substantial and fundamental. The patrimonially inheritable and indestructible *bapota* was replaced by an ordinary right of ownership dependent on compliance with state revenue demand. This was a complete transformation of the nature of land tenure. It was for reasons of this nature that the land revenue settlements were always carried out at a time when the Political Agent had full administrative authority in the state concerned. Once the cultivator's land tenure was made dependent on the fulfilment of some condition (e.g. payment of land revenue), his dependence and subservience to the state increased, affecting his prosperity in the long run. He did not pay rent either in cash or in kind for his possession of land; he paid a portion of the gross produce.

Smith deliberately misrepresented by saying: 'the ryot pays for as much land as he cultivates'. If there was no produce, he did not pay. Having misrepresented the prevalent land tenure and the rationale behind state demand of land revenue, Smith went on to restructure land relations when he projected the state trying to bring large tracts of land under cultivation and put forth the cultivator as obstructing the growth of state prosperity since he himself was not able to cultivate vacant land and was not allowing the state to do so because of his *bapota.* The theoretical right of the state to enhance its revenue by increased cultivation was put forward as a justification to acquire ownership of vacant lands in the villages.

Wingate preferred to ignore a discussion of the nature of *bapi* tenure in Mewar. He did not mention the tenure in his report of Five Jat *parganahs* and devoted only 2 out of 80 pages report for Sadri *parganah.* He re-echoed Smith when he said that the *pucka bapi* tenure gave the cultivator rights of mortgage and sale and an indestructible title to the land.[14] Without giving any instance, he represented that a cultivator could be ejected for nonpayment of land revenue but he modified himself soon by conceding that he could claim the inheritance of his ancestors. He did not repeat the rider 'after payment of state dues' because such a conditionality was non-existent. Like Smith, he was interested in weakening the right of ownership. He misinformed that *pucca bapi* tenure prevailed only in two villages of Choti Sadri *parganah* and the *kutcha bapi* tenure was held equivalent to tenancy-at-will. He corrected himself immediately that actual facts were different and went a step ahead of Smith by saying that there was practically no difference between *pucca* and *kutcha bapi* tenure.

Smith had put forward a theoretical justification for change of land revenue settlement. It was left for his successor, Wingate, to implement the changes suggested. He argued that the summary settlement of 1871 had offered to the ryot nothing 'in exchange for punctual payment' of land revenue. He put forward the ownership right as being given in exchange for punctual payment. By declaring that there was no right of ownership over land for which land revenue was not paid, Wingate introduced a fundamental change without announcing it in so many words. By one stroke, the peasantry had been deprived of its secure *bapota* and was given an ordinary right of ownership dependant on payment of state revenue demand.[15] The nature of land revenue had also been changed from a tax on produce to a rent for land. The cultivator did not understand the difference for long; when he came to know its implication, he felt an increasing sense of insecurity at the loss of his traditional right. The difference was that in years to come, he would have to cultivate land even if it meant cultivating at a loss. He could not afford to lose his means of livelihood; he borrowed money to pay land revenue in a year of low productivity. He hoped that next year he might be able to repay the loan plus interest plus the government revenue and save enough to make his both ends meet. The burden of payment increased with every passing year and the peasant became permanently indebted not for meeting his social or traditional obligations but for protecting, as he thought, his '*bapi*' right which had now been reduced simply to an occupancy right. He was now under an obligation to pay fixed government revenue demand even if the field produced an insufficient crop. This was a new situation which he had not faced earlier. The cultivators did borrow money earlier but that had been either for meeting his special social and personal obligations (like marriage or other similar occasions) or for professional requirements to increase the productivity of the soil by digging a well or by reclaiming new lands. It had never been for protection of his right to cultivate. More importantly, the payment of land revenue became the first charge which had to be made under all situations.

The transformation and termination of '*bapota*' was really of fundamental significance in reducing the independence and prosperity of the peasantry in the state. The new doctrine of state ownership of all land snapped the roots of basic harmony between the political power and the peasantry. The possibility that the peasantry could stop cultivation and starve the state financially, had kept the political authority responsive to its needs and problems. Once the peasantry was deprived of this leverage, it was reduced to a community of cultivators tied down to the soil. The British land revenue settlements not only succeeded in smothering the healthy independence of the peasantry, visible in 1875 and later on in 1880, but also in generating a feeling of alienation between the peasantry and the political power in the state. The modification of the '*bapota*' tilted the 'terms of trade' very much against the peasantry (as explained later) which came to be subjected to a life of exploitation and misery.

This transformation and termination of the indestructible *bapota* was brought about through the instrumentality of the land revenue settlement in Mewar, primarily because the British had failed to create a class of zamindars or intermediaries. Land ownership rights elsewhere were transferred from the cultivating peasantry to an intermediary class either within the agricultural or the trading and money lending communities depending on the conditions prevalent in the individual state. The two intermediaries - zamindars and mahajans - were not created to compete at one and the same place; they were alternative choices. There was a third class of intermediaries - the *ijaredars* - which existed mainly at Dholpur and Tonk; this was deliberately wiped out in favour of either of the above two classes. The novelty of the new intermediaries - the zamindars and the mahajans - created by the land revenue settlements lay in the rights conferred and the privileges allowed to them. The similarity of nomenclature - zamindar - has been primarily responsible for this feat of socio-economic engineering remaining largely unnoticed.

The creation of an intermediate class of landed proprietors at Bharatpur had been attempted soon after the establishment of regency administration in 1852. Henry Lawrence, the AGG, himself came down to the state to establish a land revenue settlement in 1855. This was the only instance when the AGG had himself done so. He had also taken his assistant, Nixon, with him to implement the principles in the state. Though the stage was well set for bringing about the desired change, but the whole scheme misfired. Morrison, the Political Agent incharge of regency administration in the state, dissented and wrote such a discordant note that even Lawrence found it difficult to overrule him. Morrison wrote to Nixon[16]:

> In all Native States the Raj retains the proprietary right to all the land. In our Regulation Provinces this right has been vested in the *lambardar*; and, as you have been required to proceed in your settlement in the spirit of these regulations, the result will be that the proprietary rights of the Raj will be transferred to the *biswadar* of villages who have never yet been recognised as having any.
>
> A revenue arrangement which tends to alienate the rights of the Raj in so summary a manner appears to me to be liable to strong objections; and, as it does not fall in with my own ideas of right or duty or necessity in our management of a Native State, I think it proper ... to record my dissent against the principle on which the settlement is being made.

Lawrence disowned himself and took a defensive posture. He wrote to Nixon[17]: 'I never proposed *to give* proprietary rights, but to *record* existing ones ... if *biswadars* are now only farmers, they will remain for the present only farmers, and it will rest with the Maharaja hereafter to raise them to the status of proprietors; the settlement will be a lease, not a proprietary settlement'. While writing to the Government of India, he repudiated the idea that he was infringing the rights of the Raj and that he was declaring a proprietary right in opposition to the custom of the native states.[18] He alleged that the Political Agent had been influenced by the complaints of some native officials.

The reality was that Lawrence's plan had been exposed. Nixon had confessed, in a routine manner, in his report of March 1858[19]:

> Hitherto in Bharatpur the Rajas have exercised the functions of proprietors or Zamindars ... and in every way exercised signorial and proprietary rights. But henceforth by the introduction of a regular settlement these rights will be nullified, in as much as it is our system in making such a settlement to confer proprietary rights on the *Biswadar*. ... I solicit your explicit instructions as to whether you desire to confer proprietary rights on these people, for if not, it would be as well ... to cease from prosecuting the settlement any further, and thus leave the position between Raja and *Biswadar* and *Biswadars* and cultivators for the present undefined ... ***should you desire to confer proprietary rights*** on the *Biswadars*, the definition of these rights can be proceeded with as in our provinces.

A better explanation could not have been given of the reason why the settlement remained a summary settlement when the British had full control for more than a decade in the future. The settlement demand had been lowered in 1855 by about 15% in order to leave a greater margin of profit to the zamindars, who had earlier been allowed a *hakk-i-mokaddami* ranging from 2 to 5% of the revenue realised. When this class could not be created, the revenue demand was enhanced by the British Political Officers in 1858, 1862 and afterwards. This was the reality behind revenue enhancements during 1858-70. This example was utilised to propagate that the rulers wanted higher revenue realisation and the British settlement officers had fixed lower demands.

The next opportunity to introduce such a fundamental change in the socio-economic structure came only with another regency administration in the state which happened in 1895. O'Dwyer, Revenue Settlement Commissioner, attached great significance to the nature of land tenure and wanted this question to be decided even before the survey had begun. He was firmly of the opinion that the stumbling block of the earlier settlement officers had been that they did not lay emphasis on ascertaining the tenure. He, however, proceeded fairly cautiously. Instead of saying that there should be a class of intermediaries, with proprietary rights in land, he posed the problem in the form of two questions: Did such a proprietary class, separate from the cultivators, exist? What was the relationship between that proprietary body and the state? Having posed the two questions, he considered the determination of the status of the zamindars as a fundamental issue. He browsed through the correspondence between past British officers to find evidence for his view point, conveniently ignoring what did not suit him. He found the report for the year 1873-74 using the word zamindar. It said[20]:

> The land tenures of the State may be divided into two classes - zamindari or crown (Khalsa is the more usual term) land, and mafi or rent free holdings. Zamindari tenures are those in which the land is cultivated for the zamindar by lessees who pay him a certain rent for the same ... A deduction of one-third is made in favour of the zamindars, the net balance being fixed as the regular amount of assessment.

O'Dwyer conceded that the term 'zamindar' had been loosely used. He did not quote more from the report which could have revealed the understanding of the Political Officer who had also written in the same place.

> The percentage per rupee paid to the Raj is one-sixth, the zamindar received one-twelfth, while the share of the tillers is three-fourths of a rupee.

Of the extensive records available on the land revenue demand, this was perhaps the only report which said that the state demand was so low and the savings margin of the peasant so high. Even the most optimistic advocate of the prosperous condition of the peasantry would find if difficult to accept this account. The Administrative Report of 1870-71 had specifically denied the existence of an intermediary class in land.

Dwyer did not have a smooth sailing even during the second regency administration. But he was more assertive. He met with the opposition of Rai Sohan Lal, the chief revenue officer of the state, who relied on the fact that

> all cultivators, both the so-called proprietors and others, usually contribute equally to the state demand, (and) contended that the distinction between proprietors and other cultivators, if it had ever existed, had now ceased to exist ... all actual cultivators should now be regarded as tenants holding on the same level, direct from the state, and that a ryotwari settlement should now be made direct with them all.

Dwyer had to concede the fact that all contributed equally to the state demand; but his argument was that 'to infer from a temporary equality to revenue liability, a permanent equality of status is a deduction illogical and unreasonable'. His reasons in favour of a proprietary body distinct from and superior to the ordinary cultivators were: (i) 'To refuse the Meos of Bharatpur a right which ... has long been conceded to their brethren in Gurgaon, Alwar and Mathura, would at once create a blaze of discontent'. (ii) The Jat landholders held on a species of feudal tenure from the crown. Some earlier rulers, it was argued, had remitted all or three-fourths of state demand from them. "To treat them now as having the same status as their *Chamar* and *Mali* tenants would be a grievous injustice and would set the state in a blaze". Dwyer then talked about the social privileges enjoyed by some landowning families, and sought to justify the existence of a superior landowning class. Finally he said: "For the above and *other reasons, which need not be adduced,* it has been decided that in each estate there is a proprietary body having a position distinct from and superior to that of the ordinary cultivators.[21] His plan was on the point of proving a non-starter because the zamindars were not willing to come forward unless some concessions regarding arrears were announced. Hence O'Dwyer conferred some extra privileges on them, and recommended the remission of all arrears prior to the years 1890-91 (i.e. Rs. 43.58 lakhs) out of a total arrear of Rs. 51.49 lakhs. He presented these arrears to have accumulated from sheer inability to pay in years of famine or scarcity. The famine of 1877-78 did not affect revenue realisation for such a long period in other states. Here the arrears had accumulated on account of a large scale migration of population from Bharatpur after the Salt Agreement of 1879. The remission of arrears was a gift to them and was expected to 'put new heart into the zamindars'. Secondly the future liability of the zamindars was limited at the figures of the Settlement. What ever cultivation they could extend hereafter, the demand was not to be revised during the next two decades. Moreover these concessions to the zamindars were accompanied by a specific and complete record of their rights, a long term of assessment, guarantee against imposition of any cess or tax. It was thus hoped that the settlement will be accepted willingly and adhered to loyally by the zamindars.[22]

Even more brazen than the attempt at Bharatpur was the attempt to introduce at Dholpur a new class of intermediary proprietors - the zamindars - replacing a class of *mustajjirs*. The British had succeeded at Bharatpur and hence they did not care much for the susceptibilities of a small state like Dholpur. The first summary settlement of Dholpur had been introduced during 1875-78, but social engineering was not then attempted as it had misfired at Bharatpur. Both W.H. Smith, the Settlement Officer and La Touche, Officer on Special Duty, had found a land revenue system which was in essence *ryotwari*. There was a class of persons engaged in collecting revenue for the government which was entitled to receive 5% of the revenue collected as '*hakk mokaddami*' (and not *malikana*) plus the cost of revenue collection. The terms 'rent' (i.e. money paid by the tenants) and revenue (i.e. money paid by the revenue collectors) were used synonymously at that time. The revenue was usually fixed each year by the diwan on the basis of estimates prepared by the *tehsildars* and *kanoongos*. Tenants' rates were the same as those paid by the revenue collectors. The state considered its zamindars to be nothing more than cultivators with the right of general management. During the famine of 1877-78, many zamindars had abandoned their duties because they could not collect the revenue. A large number of villages were made over to either outsiders or *mustajjirs*.

This settlement was revised during 1891-92 by Umacharan Mukhopadhyaya, the private secretary to the ruler. He considered the prevalent system as modified zamindari. The state did not deal directly with the *ryot*. The zamindar had no real proprietary rights whatsoever. He was a mere collector of revenue and entitled to a remuneration of 5%. He was a middleman between the state and the actual tillers of the soil. The rights of the zamindars were held to be similar to those of the tenants with 'occupancy rights' in the British provinces. The concept of joint responsibility of the co-sharers in villages was introduced in 1894. Another new condition was added that a defaulting zamindar who failed to pay the village revenue in time, would lose all his proprietary rights in the estate, and the village would either be taken over by the state or else made over to a new farmer of revenue (*mustajjir*).[23]

In 1901 as soon as the state came under British regency administration, a revision of the 1892 settlement was contemplated thought there were still two years left of the term fixed by the 1892 settlement. Col. Thornton was deputed to suggest the lines for the next settlement. His recommendation was not in favour of the zamindari system since he felt that the situation was basically for a ryotwari settlement. His recommendation was based on the central fact that rent and revenue were synonymous terms and that the zamindars got nothing but a small percentage for the cost and trouble of management. He had also observed that the state considered its zamindars as mere cultivators with a right of general management. Therefore, in 1903 another settlement officer, E.H. Blakeslay, was put on special duty to suggest revision of the settlement along a 'modified' zamindari system. Raw knew that there was no difference between rent and revenue, and the tenure was justifiably *ryotwari*. But he equated the right of collection of revenue as equivalent to the exercise of zamindari rights.[24] The small percentage paid to the collectors of revenue as the cost of management was held as a theoretical justification for not considering the prevalent system as ryotwari. However small the profits of the zamindars, they alone were held to have engaged for the payment of lump sum as revenue and made their own arrangements for its distribution among the cultivators.

Since all political authority was concentrated under the regency administration in the Political Agent, it was easy to displace the *mustajjirs* (*ijaredars*) who could now derive no support from the traditional political structure. The reinstatement of the ex-zamindars was a deliberate act of policy to fulfil some political objectives since the British believed that a coterie of state officials and their relatives had deprived the earlier zamindars. The entire edifice of grievances of zamindars against the *ijaredars*, built up so assiduously by Raw and his fellow officials, was purely imaginary. He had been very sure about the taking away of a large number of villages in Bari tehsil from the zamindars and giving them to the *ijaredars*. But to his disappointment, genuine claimants who had been dispossessed came forward only for 2 out of 23 villages in the tehsil.[25] For the rest there were either false or no claimants.

All the *ijaredars* who had enjoyed that position for less than 30 years were replaced by the zamindars, old or new. The zamindars who wished to be reinstated were given back villages on payment of the amount of original arrears paid by the *ijaredar* plus the cost of improvements effected by the latter. The restoration of the zamindars was done in a manner so as to make their authority over the peasantry more absolute than what it had ever been earlier. The state demand in respect of villages settled with the zamindars could not be enhanced during the continuation of the settlement. The zamindars were given the right to eject, before April 1913, all tenants with less than two years of tenancy in 1907 when the settlement operations had begun, in a particular plot of land; the latter were thus reduced to the status of tenants at will. The fixity of tenure and rent, available to the tenants earlier, was considerably cut down. Not content with the restoration of the erstwhile zamindars, Raw wanted a sympathetic treatment of the zamindars during the years to come. Many of the zamindars had forgotten the art of management of their estates. The restoration of the zamindars had been decided upon even before the settlement operations had begun. Raw confessed candidly that one of the compelling motives behind the revenue settlement was the 'restitution of as many as possible of 100 *khalsa* villages to the zamindars.[26] The new zamindars replaced the existing *ijaredars*; they were conferred certain extra privileges. The prevalent 'modified' zamindari was changed into a 'pure' zamindari system by depriving cultivators of all rights in land and by conferring additional rights and concessions on the new intermediaries.

These extra concessions had to be substantial enough to be attractive. The British, first of all, reduced the significance of the phrase 'ownership of the soil' by the state. It was called a 'mere formula'. If the state was the owner of the soil, the zamindar was declared the perpetual lessee paying lease money.[27] This was contrary to the notion enforced by the British in other states of the region. Secondly, the zamindars were entitled to make their own arrangements for breaking up the fallow land and to take the entire assets there of until the next settlement, subject to the payment of the fixed jama. The state ownership of all trees was also relinquished. As a measure of further protection of the rights of the zamindars in case of default by some cosharers, it was provided that the state demand from a cosharer could be recovered from another without his consent only as a last resource. The solvent cosharers were given the freedom to refuse to pay the share of a defaulter for a certain period. It was only when the arrears could not be realised even by the sale of defaulter's share, that action could be taken against other cosharers. This was a protection which had not been available to the cosharers at Mewar, or Alwar or Bharatpur. Joint responsibility, protected by these conditions was 'readily accepted by the zamindars'.[28]

It was not considered enough to have brought forth a class of zamindars for the future; Raw thought of restoring all such zamindars as had been dispossessed during the last 30 years. A rule was therefore laid down that the *mustajjirs* who have been in possession for a period of 30 years and above were made zamindars; all such *mustajjirs* as had been in possession for less than 30 years were displaced if the zamindars came forward to claim possession. A class of landowners, which had been thrust on a *ryotwari* state by a British summary settlement earlier and which had been virtually driven out by the state itself, was rethrust on the state by the British revenue settlement. In course of time, the tenants and cultivators were exploited by this zamindari class which had now been given more secure rights.

A Revenue Code was compiled to safeguard the rights of the zamindars in future. The Code prohibited sale of land; disallowed a mortgage for more than 20 years. It further laid down that any suit pertaining to rights in land shall be heard only by a revenue court. Land rights may not be sold in execution of a civil court decree; if the decree has to be executed, it should be done through a revenue court who may put the holder of the decree in possession of a part of the debtor's land. In case a zamindar has defaulted revenue payment, his share may be sold out rather than the whole village may be given to a *mustajjir*.[29]

The creation at Bharatpur and the resotration at Dholpur of the intermediary class of zamindars was achieved by expressing a theoretical concern for the 'record of rights' of the cultivating community. The concern was expressed not for preserving the existing rights but for creating something which, according to the officers, did not exist. By arguing the need for more definite and specific rights, they changed the entire structure of land relations by creating a new 'record of rights'. At Dholpur this process went two steps further in changing the prevalent order. Both - the zamindars (who were neither proprietors of land nor even farmers of revenue) and the cultivators (who had security of tenure and were very much in demand) - found their positions suddenly transformed, by the 'record of rights'. This 'record' not only bolstered up the 'rights' of the zamindars but also deprived the tenants of all rights which they had enjoyed since times immemorial. It was plainly confessed that the 'record of rights' was used 'to put on record what we (the British land revenue settlement officers) have accepted' or 'what we conceive to have been in the past' as the respective rights of the state, the zamindars and the tenants.[30] The zamindars in Dholpur were given the right to eject tenants within a certain period. This was a major innovation. The tenant was left completely at the mercy of the zamindar and all such rights as he had enjoyed, had been taken away at one stroke.

In the light of the above, Raw's claim that he gave 'fixity of tenure and rent to practically every tenant' was a figment of his imagination. He had only succeeded in creating a rivalry between the displaced *ijaredars* and the new enthroned zamindars, but had left the entire cultivating tenant community at the mercy of the zamindars. This led to far reaching consequences in the social life of the state and ushered in an era of peasant exploitation the like of which had been non-existent earlier.

The device of 'record of rights' was also used to dismember joint ownership of land at Alwar and Bharatpur. Both these states had experienced a number of settlements after 1850 under the supervision of British officers. O'Dwyer, the Settlement Commissioner for Alwar and Bharatpur, did not hesitate to call the various earlier land revenue settlements as 'shortlived makeshift assessments, none of which , since the summary settlement (of 1855), has been based on anything approaching a regular system or made by an official possessing any special acquaintance with revenue or settlement work'.[31] A new concern for 'record of rights' was expressed to justify a thorough change of the prevalent system of land tenure. This concern for 'record of rights' meant neither a record nor a preservation of existing rights and tenures in a manner better than before. There was no ambiguity among the village peasantry either about the nature of ownership or of liability to pay revenue; litigation on this account in the states was practically absent. The 'record of rights' which took Dwyer four years to complete, was a device to bring about a subtle transfer of land ownership.

The scope and nature of Dwyer's 'record of rights' was revealed when he laid emphasis on the preparation of *Khatauni* (the cultivation register) and *khewat* (account of proprietary holdings); the earlier normal practice was to prepare only a *khasra* containing the field numbers with the amount of revenue payable by each field. He was keen that the *khewat* should trace the geneological tree of the owner which would help in finding out the real form of joint tenure - whether it was joint by shares or by possession. In case of a different geneological tree, the joint ownership could be easily dissolved. The proprietary holdings could then be defined and subordinate cultivating holdings could be easily located.

Dwyer launched his offensive against the prevalent tenures by declaring that the old tenures were 'in a state of chaotic confusion'; clear tenures and definable rights were declared to be missing though it was not so. Although he explained the finer nuances of ownership rights in the state, yet he wanted 'to create specific and definable rights in land'. The prevalent forms of land tenure were[32]:

1. *Zamindari khalis*:

   Land held by a single owner.

2. *Zamindari bilijmal (gol ijmali)*:

   Land held jointly by a body of owners. Here the owners were nominally jointly responsible for state revenue but they help separate possession of land for long and could not be disturbed therein. In practice such estates were really *Bhayachara*, for separate possession formed the basis of separate ownership.

3. *Pattidari*:

   Land partitioned and held according to shares ancestral or customary.

4. *Bhayachara (gol kabzawar)*

   Land held by possession. In these estates, a partition had originally taken place and that formed the basis for the partition of common lands. Contemporaneously, possession was important and original allotment of share was not considered significant.

5. A combination of two or more of the above.

   The *pattidari* and *bhayachara* forms were again sub-divided into (i) complete and (ii) incomplete forms. In the former the whole area was held in severally and in the later some area was still kept joint (*shamilat*). What appeared confusing to Dwyer was the fact that '*gol*' (undivided/joint) tenure covered all estates in which a legal partition had not taken place formally. Even in estates where separate possession had prevailed for generations, the zamindars did not consider it a sufficient basis for separate property rights till it had been legally partitioned. They enjoyed all the advantages of a partitioned estate and yet adhered to the concept of joint ownership. Another instance of Dwyer's 'chaotic confusion' was that many estates—admittedly joint or held by shares—distributed the state demand according to the possession of each owner and sometimes at the same rate for both—owners and cultivators. Such estates, though held jointly, had all the advantages of separate holdings.[33]

Dwyer launched a strong attack on the prevalent concept of 'joint' ownership of land. He called it as 'most natural and workable form during an early or backward stage of agriculture'. His aim was to 'create specific and definable rights in land'; in other words to reduce the areas under joint ownership of all types. He justified his policy by arguing that individual rights would 'increase the value of land' and would provide an attractive area for the investment of capital. Thus Dwyer argued that the two processes of creating definable rights in land and of enhancing the value of land were complementary goals to be achieved by re-defining the various forms of land tenures. He waxed eloquent on the merits of separate ownership, considered it not only the inevitable outcome of agricultural development but also largely its cause. The greater merit of the settlement operations, according to him, would be to give an 'enormous stimulus' 'to the development of separate ownership'.[34] He believed that the old tenures prevented the process of transfer of land. Hence he decided that where the owners differed about the type of tenure enjoyed by them, separate occupancy of owners, if of a considerably duration, should be recognised as separate ownership. When he learnt that the famine of 1877-78 had forced the cultivators in Alwar to abandon separate ownership and to fall back on joint ownership to take advantage of limited sources of irrigation, he used fairly strong language to condemn this development calling it 'pernicious'. Little appreciating the helplessness of the cultivators, he held this tendency responsible for encouraging co-sharers to abandon cultivation and to put land under pasture.

He hypothesized that the most prosperous estates were those in which separate ownership was most developed and the owners had the spur of individual gain as an incentive to industry. He ridiculed the joint estates of Thakurs and Saiyyids which were held to be immensely poorer by comparison. Individual ownership, he was well aware, must lead to inequality, discontent, litigation and frequent over reaching of the weak by the strong. He confessed to have encouraged this process through the land revenue settlement because joint ownerships were held responsible for arresting agricultural progress. There could not have been a more brazen confession of the attempt to wreck the social order through forcible encouragement to individual ownership of land even though it generated greater insecurity.

In accordance with the approach, Dwyer introduced the principle that separate possession of long standing in individual holdings should be taken as the basis of proprietary rights; land held according to shares was held as joint (*shamilat*). The result was that it anticipated 'partition by at once recording the area long held in separate possession as the property of the holder'. Thus joint zamindari, mixed pattidari and imperfect or mixed *bhayachari* estates were partitioned without legal suits. It was a major and a very far reaching change, contrary to all past traditions. At one stroke Dwyer divided 1423 out of 1456 estates in Alwar and 1206½ out of 1353½ estates in Bharatpur. The following table (No. 2.3) gives the relevant statistics.

Thus 97.7% and 89.1% estates in Alwar and Bharatpur were divided with one stroke of administrative decision by Dwyer. He hastened this process by providing that in case of resumption of the estate of a defaulter, the state would resume, not a share of the whole estate in proportion to the liability of the defaulter/deceased, but the actual area of which he (the defaulter), was in possession. Once this was done, the proprietors would become more conscious of their rights in the estate.

TABLE: 2.3*

Type of Tenure of Estates

State	Tehsil	Zamindari		Pattidari		Bhayachara			State Property	Total
		Pure	Joint	Pure	Mixed	Per.	Imper.	Mixed		
Alwar	Kishangarh	1	15		39			94 ½		149 ½
	Ramgarh	3	14		10			84		111
	Govindgarh	1	13		11			23		48
	Lachmangarh	1	41		53			23		118
	Tijara	3	43		121			32		199
	Bahrod	2	12		100	2		14		130
	Mandawar	-	16	1	86	1		8		112
	Katumbar	-	22		36			12		70
	Rajgarh	2	50		21			35		108
	Alwar	2	50 ½	1	71			33		157 ½
	Bansur	4	26	3	89	3		8		133
	Thanaghazi	3	67		25			25		120
	Total	22	369 ½	5	662	6		387 ½		1456

* For Alwar based on Dwyer's Assessment Reports : Eastern Tehsils, p. 40; Northern & Southern Tehsils, p. 59; Central & Southern Tehsils, p. 59

(Contd)

(*Table* 2.3 *Contd.*)

State	Tehsil	Zamindari		Pattidari		Bhayachara			State Property	Total
		Pure	Joint	Pure	Mixed	Per.	Imper.	Mixed		
Bharatpur	Gopalgarh	1	9	10	37	3	78	-	-	138
	Pahari	-	1	4	12	16	55	-	-	88
	Kama	3	11	-	46	-	55	-	3	118
	Deeg	2	24	-	58	-	33	-	7	124
	Kumher	-	15	31	40	9	17	-	7	119
	Akheygarh	-	9	7	62	4	-	-	1	83
	Bharatpur	4	39	4	31	1	38	26	10	153
	Nagar	2	37	-	13	-	22	7	-	81
	Rupbas	3	25 ½	2	35	-	11	-	1 ½	78
	Oochain	1	18	15	47	-	9	-	6	96
	Biyana	-	33	14	91	3	26	-	2	169
	Bhusavar	1	20	7	108	1	8	-	4	149
	Total	17	241 ½	94	580	37	352	33	41 ½	1396

For Bharatpur based on O Dwyer's Assessment Reports : Northern Tehsils p. 41; Central Tehsil, p. 42; Southern Tehsils, p. 52

The Meos and the Jats who held land under either *bhayachara* or some sort of joint ownership were led to repudiate 'shares' for possession. Dwyer was conscious of the transformation he had brought about. He felt exultant because he had succeeded in giving 'great stimulus to separate ownership' as a result of the settlement operations. He confessed that he had made the people 'anxious to have their rights defined by partition'.[35] This process was held to be favourable to individual enterprise and agricultural development. The land revenue settlement destroyed the cohesive spirit among the agricultural community by an administrative measure. Joint ownership of land was practically abolished; multiplication of proprietorship and fragmentation of land holdings was encouraged.

Dwyer had not abolished the restrictions on the transfer of land to non-agriculturists; he had thus not facilitated investment of capital by all classes in land which had been declared to be one of the main objects of land settlement. Non agriculturists were not allowed to easily acquire land; hence land did not and could not acquire value. The rates of mortgage and sale of land amply proved it. He had succeeded in breaking the old land tenure and also the cohesiveness of the agricultural community. New social tensions between agriculturist and non-agriculturist sections of the society which had been created in the Punjab were let loose at Bharatpur, and, by the middle of the 20th century, a new social divisiveness which had been non-existent earlier, had become apparent.

II

The second part of structural engineering was concerned with changing the nature and character of local functionaries at the village level. Smith, chosen to prepare a justification of land revenue settlement in one of the most conservative and populous states of Rajasthan, had the perceptive ability to locate the second major factor sustaining the sturdy and independent peasantry. It lay in the close cooperation between the state functionaries at the village level—*patels, lambardars* and *patwaries*—and the cultivators. These functionaries were responsive to the difficulties and problems of the peasantry. Smith was loud in their denunciation, not because of any statistical data about their dishonesty but because of his fundamental 'a priori' belief that " spotless integrity is no more a distinguishing characteristic of the Udaipur state than of any other part of India".[36] He did not take much time to reach the conclusion that 'the system is vicious in every way, full of openings for every kind of fraud and embezzlement'. Wingate did not agree with Smith about the prevalence of corruption; he said that if the ryots cannot be induced to do a thing, no pressure would be put on them; from the independence of the people and of the officials, the *ameens* must find Mewar a comparatively barren field.[37] Smith advocated the absolute necessity for reorganisation and reconstitution of the offices of *patel* and *patwari* who were held to have supported the cultivators in their passive resistance movement of 1875 in Mewar. He emphatically denied the need to introduce a new official; all that was necessary could be accomplished through the instrumentality already available in the majority of villages. He was thus inconsistent with a purpose. The change to be brought about was in the nature of tenure and functioning of the officials at the local level. He wanted that these officials should be independent of the goodwill of the cultivators. "The appointments should be made valuable; their tenure should be certain, and dependent on conduct alone...".[38]

He considered the harmonious and cooperative working between the tax collector and the tax payer to be equivalent to the prevalence of bribery and made it to be primarily against the interests of the state. He could not visualise the basic harmony of interests between the state and the revenue paying peasantry. He had a preconceived notion that the summary revenue settlement of 1871, introduced on British advice, could not have been wrong; if the peasantry revolted against it, the fault lay with the local officials who did not suppress it. Wingate found fault with the settlement and its revenue demand was considered excessive.[39] But such was the preconceived bias of Smith that he blamed the local officials for the peasant movement. Similar approach was echoed by Abbott at Jhalawar. In his settlement of 1882-85, he had raised the overall revenue demand by 6% though in some areas its incidence was higher by 28%. This was done at a time when the prices of opium and food grains had fallen by 39% and 28% respectively. In the days of falling prices of agricultural produce, the enhancement of land revenue demand was bound to be oppressive; but Abbott found fault with the *patels* and other subordinate officials of the revenue department for having engineered peasant dissatisfaction against the land revenue settlement.[40] Both Smith and Abbott, in an effort to defend unsound and oppressive settlements opposed by the peasantry, found a scapegoat in the local official machinery. It betrayed an attitude of refusing to accept that the British settlement officers could have made a mistake.

The main function which the local functionaries had performed for generations in the past was concerned with the determination of state share of the produce. This required an intimate knowledge of agricultural operations and the ability to form a correct estimate of the standing crop since the normal method of determining the state land revenue demand was through *banta* (division) or *lata kunta* (an approximate estimate). In the post settlement scenario, this ability was no longer needed. The state demand had been determined on bases other than the field produce. It was generally a soil rate, varying with the availability of irrigation sources, or else a crop rate for cash crops like opium. The tenure of the local functionaries was mainly hereditary. Tod found the *patel* to be enjoying his land in perpetuity, free of rent to the state except a small triennial quit rent and the liability to pay two war taxes. The office was originally elective but became hereditary with the passage of time. The *patel* was 'primus inter pares', the constituted representative of the commune, and as the medium between the cultivator and the government, enjoyed benefits from both. Besides his *bapota* and *serona* (2½ % of produce) he had a remission of ¼ or 1/3 of the rent for such extra lands as he might cultivate in addition to his patrimony.[41] In all states, the posts of *patel*, *patwari* and *lambardar* were inherited by the son of the incumbent; in some states, the concessional land was inherited by all the sons while the emoluments were enjoyed by the person who performed the duties of that office. The hereditary character of the posts had continued because the ownership of land had been hereditary and was not subject to frequent changes.

The work of land revenue realisation in the post settlement period in each state required a fundamentally different approach on the part of the local revenue officials. They had to realise it irrespective of the crop yield of the peasant, regardless of the fact that he was or was not in a position to pay it. The officials concerned had to develop indifference towards, instead of harmony with, the peasantry in realising land revenue after each harvest. The problem of arrears, so prominent in the post settlement era, was not so serious in the past, because the peasant paid a portion of the produce. The produce factor was irrelevant in the post settlement era. The revenue settlements succeeded in breaking the close relationship between the peasant and the local functionary because a sympathetic understanding of the problems of the peasantry was not required. In the crisis of 1875 in Mewar, the local officials had projected the problems of the peasantry; they had been told that the government decision would be conveyed after the return of the Political Agent from Bombay. They came to realise the attitude of the political power towards the problems of the peasantry and adjusted themselves to the changing trends.

The land settlements, in the post 1870 period, had made land ownership right terminable by the state on nonpayment of land revenue. The inheritable and inextinguishable land ownership had been virtually reduced to an occupancy right which could be enjoyed so long as the state demand of land revenue had been paid. The joint ownership of land / zamindari rights had been terminated in more than 90% cases in Alwar and Bharatpur. Keeping record of the changing ownership right, either by inheritance, subdivision or non payment of government land revenue, became fundamentally important for the successful implementation of the land revenue settlements. This was a new responsibility which had to be discharged by the *patwaris* and *kanungos.*

The new emphasis on the record of rights was thus a ready stick to beat the local officials. Even in Ajmer Merwara, the AGG, alongwith the settlement officer, was complaining in 1908 that the record of land rights had not been well kept. O'Dwyer spoke of a chaotic and confused state of affairs regarding land records. The type of land records which the settlement officers required were not kept because *the same had not been needed.* Ownership had been hereditary and did not change easily. It was only after land ownership became a commodity of which the peasantry could be deprived by the state that the record of land rights became important. The settlement officers strongly criticised the local functionaries for their inability to maintain the type of records now needed which was the result of their not being literate enough to be of use to the new system now introduced. The example of Alwar is significant. Dwyer issued instructions for preparation of a complete record of rights during 1896-1900. A number of landowners who had migrated out during 1877-78, rushed back to get their land rights recorded. Meanwhile some of their lands had been allotted to such other persons as had come forward to cultivate and pay the revenue. Even for tenants, the record of rights became important since Powlett had, in 1876, provided for 'occupancy rights' to such tenants as had cultivated and paid at owner's rates for 15 (later reduced to 10) years and had no *patta*. The claims of both, the proprietors and occupancy tenants, depended on evidence from the *patwari's* papers. The *patwaris* being hereditary, did not realise the importance of recording the temporary incumbents/cultivators; in some cases the names of owners, long since dead, had continued on their registers.[42] O'Dwyer thus realised that the *patwaris* and other local officials could, by not recording the changes in ownership and cultivation of land, easily nullify the structural changes which were being introduced by the British policy. This realisation led him to adopt a stiff attitude on the need to change the local officials.

The generally hereditary character of the *patels, patwaris, lambardars* and *kanungos*, the mainstay of the land system in the past, appeared to the British settlement officers as its greatest defect. They wanted detailed information not only about the crops grown, the fertility of the soil and the sources of irrigation but also about the process of inheritance. All this had to be put in charts and statements according to a definite plan. Hence the settlement officers laid great emphasis on literacy of the local officials.

It may have been at the back of the mind of some settlement officers that the survey staff, rendered surplus in British India, after the completion of settlement work in different provinces, could be provided an opportunity of employment in the Indian states. This notion persisted depsite the fact that the land survey and measurement papers at Alwar, prepared by the *amins* and *munsarims*, borrowed from adjoining British provinces, were not found to be quite reliable. Dwyer had dropped the scheme of a wholesale change of the local functionaries because it would have posed the problem of lack of local cooperation in the settlement work. Wingate had reported widespread distrust of settlement work and still greater boycott and noncooperation by inhabitants of Sadri pargana. He had to import even chaindrawers from outside when he was unable to attract local people to work for him.[44]

The settlement officers' main object in talking about the shortcomings of the local functionaries and yet retaining them was to make them realise that they should 'look to the state government and not to the village' for their position and status. Smith initiated the process of enhancing the authority of the pargana *hakim* who was, in course of time, invested with all authority which formerly lay with the *patel* and the village community. He confessed that his object was to render the cultivator so helpless that he 'should never have the power to impede the state in its efforts to bring under cultivation something of the vast area of magnificent soil which the self styled owner either refuses or is unable to bring under the plough himself'.[45] The settlement rules, framed by Wingate, vested authority and power in a representative of the state and disinvested all other functionaries of authority to decide. The underlying assumption was a basic disharmony of interests between the village peasantry and the state administration. This was a totally different approach from the pre-settlement period and was reflected in the new settlement rules which gave elaborate, extensive, almost unlimited powers and discretion to the pargana *hakim*; the *patels* and *patwaris* were now made, instead of the village community's, his local representatives. The *hakim* was strengthened at the cost of the autonomy of the rural community and the *bapi* rights of the peasant, both of which withered in course of time. This was what the settlement officers meant by the strengthening of the state machinery.

The nature of duties expected of the local officials was now fundamentally different. The settlement officers used to find fault with the existing system and the local incumbents. They did not explain that they were asking them to perform basically different functions. By finding fault with the prevalent system, they appeared to be reforming the system while the reality was that the nature of functions and the role of the local functionaries had been changed in accordance with concepts completely foreign to the old order. Smith, with his high moralising attitude, presumed that the settlement of 1871 must have caused 'loss of much of their influence and nearly all their illegitimate profit'. He had put forward the idea of reorganisation of all the local officers 'on a fresh and efficient basis'.[46] In the post settlement era, the local officials were completely freed from the control of the peasantry.

The land revenue settlement officers first devoted their attention to fundamentally alter the service conditions and recruitment of that functionary in the local land revenue machinery who was having a dominant status and authority in the state concerned. Any generalisation by the name of a functionary would be inaccurate because the same functionary did not carry the same weight in different states. The *kanungo* at Alwar was more powerful than his namesake at Bharatpur; the *lambardar* at Bharatpur was more influential than at Alwar; the *patel* was more powerful at Udaipur and Kota, he did not exist at Alwar and Bharatpur. The *patwari* in Tonk was very powerful but not so at Udaipur or Bharatpur. The Mandlois were important only at Jhalawar, and the Mehtas existed only at Karauli. The settlement officers changed the security and independence bred in the hereditary officers. The attack was on their 'hereditary' character outwardly but it was really on their independence and lack of awareness to serve imperial interests. Later on 'loyal' and 'competent' incumbents would be allowed to secure entry for their heirs; but it would be a favour and not a right. The hereditary character would be maintained but only after the incumbents had developed the 'rights' attitude to the imperialists.

In Mewar the *patel* was the most influential functionary in the village. Smith blamed him for inciting the presant revolt of 1875; he therefore misrepresented his status and position and went to the extent of misquoting and misrepresenting Tod in a significant manner. Tod had written: "Who dared complain against a *patel*, the intimate of *Pathan* and Maratha commanders, his adopted patrons", Smith misquoted: "The patel was the intimate of Pathan and Maratha commanders, his adopted patrons". By dropping the question mark, by changing an indefinite article 'a' by 'the', the whole meaning had been changed.[47] He knew that the *patel* was 'still the representative and headman of the village'; he was referred to in disputes, and was 'the person through whom orders addressed to the community are carried out'. But he represented him to be 'a mere ordinary cultivator paying rent for land he held like the rest'.

Smith had indulged in misrepresenting the past; what he wanted to achieve in the future, he projected it in the past. His contention that the pargana officials held the area under their charge in a tightened grip was amply disproved by the difficulty in restoring normalcy in Mewar during 1818-1870. The administrative failure of the state was a sufficient rebuttal of tightly controlled pargana administration.

Wingate accepted in his 1881 report that 'to punish *patels* was to court disaster and failure'. He had set before himself the goal of success in introducing the land revenue settlement by winning the confidence of the *patels*. Punishing even misguided *patels* would have been a mistake he could never rectify.[48] For this very reason, the *patel* was made ineffective for the future by strengthening the pargana *hakim* who was made the appointing authority for the *patel*. Normally, the *patel* was to be appointed for life; but if there were more than one family having a right to serve as *patel*, the tenure would be 5 years. The *Hakim* was naturally given the power to remove a *patel* but a report would have to be sent to the state government. The *patel's* emoluments were decided on the basis of a certain percentage of the revenue from the area under his jurisdiction.

The *pargana hakim* was made a more powerful official in the new set up. Some of his new powers may be enumerated in order to form a picture of the extent of his authority.[49] He alone had the power:

1. to allot waste land in any village or any land abandoned by a cultivator or by a co-parcenor;
2. to recommend condonation of arrears of revenue from a new *assami* who had agreed to cultivate abondoned land by an earlier *assami*;
3. to let out land in the beds of tanks or rivers and to fix the rate of revenue for the same;
4. to certify unserviceable wells and to permit their being re-made;
5. to recommend cases for temporary suspension of revenue demand;
6. to accept payment of revenue by a person other than the cultivator.

The creation of an all powerful *hakim*, controlled by the state, unresponsive to the needs of the village community and uncontrolled by the revenue payers was the most important change in the official machinery at the local level which had been brought about by the land settlement. It boded ill for the healthy autonomous and self reliant village community of the pre 1870 period.

The *Lambardars*

The *lambardar* or headman in a village was a hereditary officer who was responsible for collecting the state revenue demand. He was normally succeeded by his eldest son if the latter was not disqualified or embarrassed by being seriously in debt. If the eldest son were disqualified, next surviving son or an agnate upto the fourth generation, would succeed. If a *lambardar* was seriously indebted or had been guilty of a crime whose effects will fall on his family or had been imprisoned, a new *lambardar*, out of the co-sharers, would be selected, preference being given to next of kin in order of relationship. If he were dismissed for negligence, his next of kin will succeed him.

In Ajmer the *lambardar* was a subordinate revenue official. It was his duty to keep accounts of the common receipts and disbursements, to give information of crime, to furnish supplies when called upon and to carry out all lawful requisitions of the government.[50]

An enquiry into the *lambardari* system was undertaken in Bharatpur and Alwar. It was found that no *lambardars* had been appointed in *maafi, inaam,* and *chauth* estates and hence there was no machinery for realising state *jama* or other state dues from them. A considerable number of self appointed *lambardars* were also found out; they reduced the emoluments of the *lambardars.* All these self appointed *lambardars* were removed since they had no just claim to the office. A number of *lambardars* were found to be shirking their duties thinking that others would do it for them; they were removed on grounds of unfitness due to minority, old age, misconduct, inefficiency, etc.. The *lambardars* who were found in excess, were appointed to *maafi, inaam* and *chauth* villages for the first time. The *lambardar* was thus transformed from an ex-officio zamindar or a co-sharer to a paid employee of the state. This was achieved by giving a new definition to '*hakk mokaddami*'. This *hakk* had been considered in the past equivalent to zamindar's status and rank, but now it was considered as wages for duty of collection of land revenue. The *lambardar* was now made answerable for his actions, and was given the sole responsibility for collection of revenue; the *patwari* was completely excluded from this responsibility. The policy of removal and transfer was also accompanied by retrenchment of the *lambardars.*[51]

TABLE: 2.4

State	Year	No. of in 1895	Lambardars reduced by 1900	New appointment	Total	Average jama to be collected by each Lambardar
Bharatpur	1901	7415	2664	617	5368	Rs. 400-00

Full figures of retrenchment at Alwar are not available but in 60 villages, 174 *lambardars* were retrenched. Bharatpur had witnessed a 36% retrenchment in the total strength.

The reduction in status and autonomy of the *lambardars* was accompanied by an enhancement in their emoluments in Alwar and Bharatpur where they were otherwise important.

They had been paid a certain percentage of the assessed sum for each village. The cess levied for the purpose was called differently. At Alwar it was called '*mujrai*'; at Bharatpur it was called '*hakk mokaddami*'. *Mujrai* varied from 2 to 3%; '*hakk mokaddami*' ranged between 2.5% to 5%. The '*hakk*' originally represented the percentage of profits which the state remitted in favour of the owners or their representatives at the time of making the payment. The 1898-1900 settlement had allowed one third profit to the owners hence this '*hakk*' was held to belong not to the owners but to the *lambardar* for his services in and responsibility for collecting the state demand. After the land revenue settlements, his emoluments were sought to be made uniform. At Alwar, the rate of *mujrai* was fixed at 3% on the total amount of land revenue; he was also paid 2% of the amount of *malba* (village fund). At Bharatpur a uniform 3.12% *hakk mokaddami* was fixed but this income was not enough. Hence 1.56% *malba* was also to be distributed among the *lambardars*.[52]

At Kota, Butler found a general breakdown of the village system in the state as a result of 'the decay of the *patel* or village headman'. The *patels* had ceased to receive sufficient emoluments under the old system; they did not pay the *nazrana* required at the accession of the new Maharao. The result was that at the time of settlement of 1904-09, a *patel* was found only in 164 out of 1191 villages in Kotah. The situation was slightly different in the reverted territories from Jhalawar where the *patels* were paid 5% on the collections. Butler reduced this commission to 3%. The amount of *nazar* to be paid to the ruler was made an annual feature; only the amount was fixed at

Rs. 1 for *patels* collecting Rs. 1000 or less; for the others it was Rs. 2 to be paid to the ruler when on a tour or else forwarded through the *Nazim*. The post was not made hereditary. The change brought about a basic transformation in their functions; they now looked to the state for their emoluments and lost their healthy independence and social leadership of the village community. The government justified the change as preventing embezzlement in the collection of revenue and giving a direct interest in extending cultivation. Butler was not averse to make the *patel* hereditary but he wanted 'experience of the new system' to be gained by him before this concession could be granted.[53]

At Alwar the reorganisation of the *kanungos* was the important problem because they were the highest of the three functionaries at the local level. They had been able to pull many strings at Alwar when Powlett first mooted a change in their powers and functions in 1876. They were unable to do so during 1898-1900 because of the regency administration.

The fundamental objection which Dwyer raised was that the office had become absolutely hereditary and the emoluments paid to the original incumbent were shared by all his descendants even though only one person worked as *kanungo*; others were either in service within/outside the state or were carrying on trade. There were 71 working *kanungos* though the income was shared by 250 shareholders. The system was indefensible; the resources allotted for the *kanungos* were sufficient but the return to the state was minimal since even the incumbent *kanungos* did not take their duties seriously because the other 179 shareholders received as much for not doing the job as they received for doing it. The system could have been improved by depriving the non-*kanungo* shareholders of the emoluments. But that would not have brought the *kanungos* round to adopt a proper frame of mind to 'supervise' the working of the land revenue settlement. He had got it announced before the beginning of the settlement operations that unless the *kanungos* acquainted themselves thoroughly with the settlement work, they would have no claims to appointment when the system would be reorganised. Some *kanungos* were deputed to the settlement office for training but a large number of them held aloof. Dwyer had thus seen the reluctance of the *kanungos* to change easily. He therefore decided to overhaul the establishment completely.[54]

The restructuring programme focussed on changing the hereditary character of the post and the practice of dividing the emoluments among all the shareholders. Therefore, it was notified that the *kanungo* emoluments, whether in cash or rent free or favourably assessed lands, were not to be considered as personal or hereditary but only as remuneration for services rendered to the state as *kanungo*. The existing incumbents would be given an opportunity to prove their merit and fitness for the job when selections for *kanungos* would be made. Newly appointed *kanungos* would be paid out of the existing total funds meant for them; any balance, if the state thought proper, might be divided among the hereditary *kanungos* as before.

The *kanungos* were subjected to a written and oral examination at which 37 out of 100 passed; out of the failures, 30 were given another chance to improve their performance. They were told to supervise the work of the *Patwaris* and help in the preparation of correct records.

Dwyer utilised the post land revenue settlement reconstruction not only to change but also to snap the links of the *kanungos* with their past heritage. The hereditary incumbents were made salaried servants of the state. They were cut off from their co-sharers. *Kanungos* in services were quick to realise their dependence on British goodwill. They had experienced the change when they saw that their emoluments had been changed with ease by Dwyer. Out of 71 working *kanungos*, 67 were ultimately absorbed and accommodated.

The Patwari

The *patwari* was the lowest official at the local level; the land revenue settlement officers aimed at strengthening the control of the state and weakening that of the village community over him. This was necessary because his role was being transformed to serve imperial interests. While earlier he performed functions of only local relevance, now he had to fulfill imperial objects by the compilation of statistical data about cultivation and the crops grown. This object could not be achieved till the local officials willingly cooperated.

The *patwaris* were generally a hereditary body partly paid in cash and partly by concessional land. The states levied no special cess on this account. This may be contrasted with Ajmer administration which imposed a *Patwari* cess @ Rs. 6.88% in 1874, raised to 10% in 1887. In almost every state, including Ajmer district, the *patwaris* were drawn generally from the trading classes. Smith had made critical and adverse remarks on this account; but Whiteway said that 'as a rule they make good *patwaris*'.[55] In states where the office was not hereditary, the claims of the son or heir of the incumbent were nearly always taken into account whenever a vacancy occurred.

Since maintenance of record of land rights, survey and measurement of land were fundamental to the new revenue settlements, emphasis was laid on literacy and competence to understand survey and mensuration. These were considered as basic qualifications for successfully performing the duties of a *patwari*. During the course of land survey and settlement operations, opportunity was provided to the existing personnel to get acquainted with the process; later on examinations were conducted and the successful were given certificates of proficiency. Old and aged *patwaris* were advised to send their sons or heirs for training; in case the heir passed the test, he was given preference in appointment. Pears imposed a restriction on the appointment of a *Patwari* unless he passed an examination in surveying, mensuration and prescribed system of keeping accounts. If he failed to pass, he shall have to pay for a properly trained assistant. Another device adopted was to reduce the number of *patwaris* in the states concerned. Dwyer and Pears had brought about the following reduction in the strength of the *patwaris* in the state under their charge.[56]

TABLE: 2.5

State	Year	No. of patwaris	No. reduced	New appointments	Total
Tonk	1887-1892	327	86	-	241
Alwar	1895-1901	466	146	121	441
Bharatpur	1895-1900	624	215	95	504

The above table summarises a lot of change through numbers. The absolute reduction in the number of *patwaris* was only 5.36% at Alwar but 19.2% at Bharatpur and 26% at Tonk. The impact on the patwaris, hereditary so far, may be easily visualised. The insecurity generated by the process of reduction was accompanied by the demoralising impact of dismissal on grounds of incompetence. One-third personnel had been changed at Alwar and Bharatpur during a short span of a couple of years. With a view to mollify, the emoluments and conditions of service of the patwaris were improved. Formerly, there was one grade for all *patwaris*; now different grades—three at Alwar, four at Bharatpur and Karauli—were introduced. The grades generally varied from Rs. 7 to Rs. 11. In Alwar three grades of Rs. 7, 8 and 9; in Bharatpur 4 grades of Rs. 8, 9, 10 and 11; in Karauli four grades from Rs. 7 to 10 per month were introduced. The *patwaris* may have been encouraged to work harder for promotion to higher grades; but this only served to sever the links and dependence on village community and to enhance their subservience to the government which alone could promote them to a higher grade. The grades were as follows[57]:

TABLE: 2.6

State	Year	Average Salary	Grades of service	Average area per patwari (in Bighas) Land area	Cultivated area	Average revenue demand per patwari (Rs.)
Alwar	1895	Rs. 5.75	1	4984	3100	4462
	1901	7.80	3	5264	3274	5154
Bharatpur	1895	7.75	1	5300	2400	3330
	1901	9.50	4	6330	3812	4704
Karauli	1908	7.25	3			
	1912	8.50	4			

The emoluments of the *patwaris* in the states were not low as compared to Ajmer. In 1867 in Ajmer they were paid from Rs. 6.66 to Rs. 10 per month; by 1887 these ranged from Rs. 11 to 18 per month. They remained underpaid at Beawar and Todgarh though in Ajmer tehsil they were well paid.

The *patwaris* in Tonk were very powerful and influential. They had, at different times, taken lease of certain villages and themselves acquired concessions for settling new hamlets on waste lands. The process of curtailment of their powers was begun by abolishing the hereditary character of the post. The stock argument was the necessity to pass an examination in surveying and maintenance of accounts. In accordance with the conditions at Tonk it was considered necessary to redistribute the area of circles in their charge and the circle to a land revenue demand of Rs. 6000. After limiting the circle, the *patwari* was asked to reside permanently within his circle in the interests of proper management. The *patwari's* duties were defined rather elaborately and a detailed list of charts and records to be maintained by him covered full 13 pages (Appendix B). The *patwari* was excluded from undertaking the responsibility of revenue collection. He was now confined to keeping records and slips of revenue demand and noting payment and attesting receipts. The division of work at the local level tended to reduce the total authority of each individual functionary.

Certain guidelines had been laid down for future. The *patwari* should be able to read and write both Hindi and Urdu languages. The practice of appointing a minor son to the post was done away with. The heirs and descendants of a dead *patwari* were to be given priority only when fully qualified. The existing *patwaris* who had not yet obtained certificates of proficiency for survey work, would be subjected to repeated examinations till they qualified themselves. Any *patwari* who either himself did not attend or did not send his heir to the *patwari* school (established for three months in a year) would lose his lien on appointment.

The justification put forth for enhancement of salary was 'the extra work' which was to be exacted from the *patwaris* under the new system. The state, by maintaining a continuous system of land records and agricultural statistics, could derive financial and administrative advantages and hence the extra expenditure was only reasonable remuneration for the duties performed.

Appendix-B

A *patwari* was required to maintain the following records:

1. The field map: It was a copy of the settlement map of the village in his charge; its annual correction 'shall be an essential part' of his duty. When the corrections became numerous, the *patwari* was to get a clear tracing of the correct field map.

2. The *Roznamcha* or diary: He shall have to enter briefly each day the name of the village in which he had been engaged and the work he had done or the reason why he had done no work. If he had been engaged in field inspection, he shall record the same giving field numbers. The list of events which shall have to be recorded occupied one full page.

3. The *Khasra* or field book: It will have the following components:

(a) *Milan khasra* or comparative statement of area:

It was an abstract record in which the information about village area was to be filled in 19 classified columns: e.g.

(i) each holding's area to be noted -

Under crops

Not cropped but under cultivation

Out of cultivation.

(ii) Area not included in individual holdings. The columns were:

Groves, tree, forests, scrub jungle and grass, under water, hill and rock, occupied by roads.

(iii) Area double cropped.

(iv) Details of irrigation -

Sources and area irrigated from each source.

(v) Number of irrigation wells (*kachha* and *pucca*).

(vi) Number of ploughs, plough cattle, number of irrigation tanks.

(b) *Kharif Jinswar* (crop-wise details).

(c) *Rabi Jinswar* (Crop-wise details).

(d) Hot weather *Jinswar* (Summer crop details).

4. The *Jamabandi.* It had two types of separate statements:

(a) Statement showing increase and decrease of irrigated area.

(b) Statement showing increase and decrease of cultivated area (unirrigated).

Each of these statements had fifteen columns each.

The *Jamabandi* had 37 columns pertaining to each individual *Khatedar*. Two copies of the Jamabandi were to be prepared, 1 kept in the Tehsil for 3 years and thereafter sent to the State for record.

5. *Rasid Bahis.* The patwari was to ensure that each khatedar shall have a rasid bahi in which entries had to be made in his presence. It had 17 columns, showing details of payments and arrears if any left. The *patwari* was to record in his cash account all sums credited in *rasid bahis.*

Notes & References

1. Foreign, General A, March 1871, nos. 3-4, para 216
2. R.A.R., 1875-76, p.3
3. Review of Famine Relief Operations in the Native States of Rajputana and Ajmer Merwar 1905-6, p.44 (published 1907)
4. G.S.L. Devra: Rajasthan ki Prasasnik Vyavastha, pp. 214-217; Tod: Annals and Antiquities of Rajasthan, vol.1, pp.572-573
5. M.F.O'Dwyer: Final Report on the Settlement of the Bharatpur State (1901), p.65 (later cited as Final Report of Bharatpur)

6. The population statistics are from the relevant censuses. Special census had been held at Alwar and Bharatpur in 1872 and 1867 respectively. R.A.R., 1871-72, pp.190-191 and R.A.R., 1873-74, p.173
7. A. Wingate: Proposal for the Settlement of the Jat Pergannahs of Meywar (1885), p.10 (cited later as jat Pergannahs Report).
8. R.A.R., 1871-72, pp. 204-206
9. Smith came to Mewar on February 22, 1878 and before the end of May 1878 he had submitted his report. Foreign, Revenue A, October 1879, nos. 1-17
10. W.H. Smith: Report on the Revenue System of Meywar (later cited as Report of 1878), para 124
11. Ibid. para nos. 60 and 61
12. Ibid. para nos. 55, 56
13. Ibid. para no. 60
14. A. Wingate: Settlement Report upon the Sadri Zillah of the Meywar State (1889), para nos. 66 and 69 (cited later as Sadri Report).
15. A. Wingate: Jat Pergannahs Report, para nos. 22 and 49
16. Letter of Morrison to Nixon, no. 112, dated 31.12.1856 cited by O'Dwyer: Assessment Report for the four Northern Tehsils of Bharatpur (later cited as Northern Tehsils Report), Introduction, p. xvi, para 33
17. Letter of Lawrence, AGG, to Nixon, no. 41, dated 17.1.1857. Cited by O'Dwyer: Northern Tehsils Report, Introduction, p. xvii, para 34
18. Letter from Lawrence to Secretary, Government of India, dated March 4, 1857. Cited as above, Ibid.
19. M.R. O'Dwyer: Final Report of Bharatpur, p. 36
20. R.A.R. 1873-74, pp. 154-155
21. O'Dwyer: Northern Tehsils Report, Introduction, p. xvi
22. Ibid., paras 176-178
23. Umacharan Mukhopadhya: Report on the Land Settlement of the Dholpur State (1894), p. 55
24. W. Raw: Final Report of the Revision of Settlement of the Dholpur State (1909-1912), p. 15
25. Ibid., pp. 25, 28
26. Ibid., p. 27
27. Ibid., p. 17

28. Ibid.
29. Ibid. pp. 49-50
30. Ibid., pp. 17, 18
31. M.F. O'Dwyer: Assessment Report of the four Central Tehsils (cited later as Central Tehsils Report), p. 28
32. Northern Tehsils Report, pp. 40-42; Central Tehsils Report, pp. 42-43; Southern Tehsils Report, pp. 52-53
33. Ibid.
34. M.F. O'Dwyer: Assessment Report of eastern Tehsils of Kishangarh, Ramgarh, Govindgarh and Lachmangarh of Alwar (later cited as Eastern Tehsils Report) pp. 39-40
35. Ibid.
36. Report of 1878, pp. 18-19
37. Wingate's Report of 1881. Foreign Revenue A, May 1881, no. 6 paras 25 and 50
38. Report of 1878, p. 28
39. Jat Pergannahs Report, pp. 4, 7 and 8
40. H.B. Abbott: Land Settlement Report of Jhallawar, p. 74
41. Tod: Annals, vol. 1, p. 580
42. M.F. O'Dwyer: Final Report on the Alwar Settlement, pp. 58 and 109
43. Eastern Tehsil Report, Introduction, p. ii
44. Wingate's Report of 1881, pp. 3, 15
45. Report of 1878, p. 15
46. Ibid., p. 28
47. Ibid., pp. 12-13
48. Wingate's Report of 1881, pp. 3-4
49. Jat Pergannahs Report, Settlement rules, Sections 5, 19, 29, 36, 46
50. J.D. La Touche: Report on the Settlement of the Ajmer and Mhairwarra Districts, 1875 (cited later as La Touche's Report), pp. 142-143
51. Final Report of Bharatpur, pp. 105-107
52. Northern Tehsils Report, p. 90; Central Tehsils Report, p. 84; Final Report of Bharatpur, p. 105
53. M.S.D. Butler: Final Report of the Second Settlement of the Kotah State (cited later as Butler's Kota Report), p. 46

54. O'Dwyer: Final Report on the Alwar Settlement, p. 116 and Appendix C
55. R.S. Whiteway: Report on the Settlement of the Ajmer Merwara Districts, p. 15
56. Final Report of Bharatpur, p. 52; Final Report on the Alwar Settlement, p. 52; T.C. Pears: Report on the Revenue Settlement of Tonk, Pt.I, p. 81
57. Final Report on the Alwar Settlement, pp. 52, 113; Final Report of Bharatpur, p. 51
58. Pears: Report on the Revenue Settlement of Tonk (later cited as Tonk Report) pt.III, pp. 55-67

3

Resource Crunch and Revenue Settlements

The states in the region experienced, during 1840-70, a great resource crunch; its intensity varied according to the geographical location of the concerned state. The resource crunch was the result primarily of the diversion of transit trade passing through Rajasthan as a result of certain policy decisions, in the post 1818 period, to promote British commercial and colonial interests. The prosperity of the larger states, including the sparsely populated Jaisalmer, was dependent on income from the brisk transit trade along three different trunk routes passing through the region. One connected north western India and central Asia to the west coast. This route bifurcated at Bhawalpur and passed either through Pokaran, Jaisalmer, Barmer, Umarkot to Hyderabad (Sind) or through Bikaner, Nagore, Pali, Palanpur to Ahmedabad. A second route from Agra in the East ran either through Bharatpur, Amer, Ajmer, Bhilwara, Chittor, Udaipur, Doongarpur or through Alwar, Amer, Ajmer, Pushkar, Pali, Palanpur to Ahmedabad. A third route connected northern and north western India with central India passing through Hanumangarh, Nohar, Reni, Rajgarh, Rewari, Amer and thereafter bifurcated into two alternative routes - either through Ajmer, Bhilwara Chittor to Ratlam or through Malpura, Sawai Madhopur, Bundi, Kota, Jhalrapatan to Ujjain.

The East India Company administration had evolved, during 1805-15, a policy of discriminating against goods not of British origin; it had also imposed duties on goods passing from the frontiers of native states into British territory at the highest rates i.e. 4 times the general rate charged upon British goods.[1] This heavy transit duty diverted the transit trade along routes within British Indian territories only and adversely affected the income of various states. A systematic account of the income from transit duty to the different states of the region is not available but some idea can be formed by figures given by Tod and by a recent work on Trade and Commerce in the 18th century[2].

	Amount of Income	Period, if and
Jaipur Town	Rs. 19235	4 months 13 days (1732)
Jaipur State	Rs. 18354	1 month (Feb. 1763 A.D.)
Jodhpur Town	Rs. 35101	1 year (1778 A.D.)
Jhalrapatan Town	Rs. 15544	1 year (1804 A.D.)
Nagore	Rs. 50001	1 year (1784 A.D.)
Tod's Figures are:		
Jodhpur Town	Rs. 76000	For one year
Pali Town	Rs. 75000	For one year
Nagore Town	Rs. 75000	For one year
Phalodi Town	Rs. 41000	For one year

After the conquest of Sind and Punjab, the British government found it convenient to abolish the internal transit duties. It was soon followed by the laying down of a trunk rail route between Bombay and Delhi which did not pass through this region; another trunk route (B.B. & C.I. Rly) passed through a minimum part of south eastern Rajasthan. The transit trade of the region could not be revived.

The need to integrate the markets of Indian states with British provinces required the abolition of all custom duties on the import and export of foodgrains in the states. This opportunity came with the famine of 1868. The AGG called a meeting of the rulers or their representatives at Ajmer and, on grounds of alleviating the suffering of the famine stricken, persuaded them to abolish all such duties.[3] Ramsingh of Jaipur earned the goodwill of the British by abolishing them permanently; others abolished them for the duration of the famine. Soon afterwards the construction of the Delhi-Ahmedabad metre gauge railway line began. The passage of the railway line through the states undoubtedly led to a serious shortfall in revenue income since they had agreed to renounce their right to impose transit and customs duties on goods carried by the railways; in the cases of some, the loss was heavy. Jaipur experienced by 1875-76 a 'considerable falling off in the customs receipts as compared with those for the period prior to the introduction of the Rajputana Railway. The resource crunch for Sirohi and Dungarpur was even heavier. Sirohi, by 1877-78, had suffered a very serious reduction of revenue by the loss of transit duties. Dungarpur, by 1886-87, found its income from transit duties reduced to 1/3rd on account of diversion of road traffic to railways. The loss to Jaipur was not considered of much significance by the British; but they tried to compensate Dungarpur by a land revenue settlement when the regency administration was established in 1905-6; they suggested to Sirohi to market the timber wealth of its forests through the railways and to utilise the land cleared of forests for cultivation.[4]

The seventies and eighties of the 19th century were the decades when the British civilising mission was at its peak. The Mayo College had been established and the different states were 'persuaded' to contribute funds to the construction of state houses for the residence of their princes and wards. The various states contributed 11 lacs of which the following were important[5].

Jaipur	2.00 lakhs	Jodhpur	1.78 lakhs
Kota	1.64 lakhs	Udaipur	1.44 lakhs
Jhalawar	1.00 lakhs	Bikaner	0.86 lakhs
Alwar	0.80 lakhs	Bharatpur	0.69 lakhs

The imperial outlay was only 5.69 lakhs.

During these decades the expenditure on public works (roads, buildings and schools), construction of allopathic dispensaries, was encouraged. Competition among the ruling princes was generated by some public recognition - conferment of a title on the ruler or an enhancement in the number of salute guns. The format of the annual administration report by the AGG and the Political Agents underwent change. The political events within the states normally got a shorter coverage; the details for public works were given greater prominence. The diversion of funds to newer areas, however laudable, implied the withdrawal of support from other areas. The states were forced to search for means to maintain their establishments.

Another development during these two decades (1870-90) was the beginning of an emphasis on bringing the ruling princes into closer contacts with the imperial authorities. Visits by the Viceroys, Prince of Wales, Duke of Connaught and other dignitaries became more frequent. From Mayo onwards, every Viceroy made it a point to visit Mayo College and some of the leading states in the region. The bigger states, which could bear the expenses, were encouraged to invite the Viceroy for a visit to the state. The ruling princes were advised to attend imperial Durbars, to see off the outgoing and to receive the incoming Viceroy. The number of formal ceremonial durbars in the states - the installation of the ruler, the receipt of a letter of thanks by the Queen Empress on some event of importance, the celebration of golden and diamond jubilees of Queen Victoria - began to increase. This was in sharp contrast to a reduction of formalities on the visits of fellow rulers to other states. The ceremonial remained important; only the person and the occasion had changed. The expenses connected with these events can not be easily quantified because they were camouflaged under various heads; where it could not be done, it was shown as extraordinary expenditure.[6]

The year 1875-76 illustrated the heavy expenses involved in such visits by the Viceroy and Prince of Wales. Mewar which had a surplus of 30 lacs in 1862 when it came under dominant British influence for more than two decades, spent 5 lacs for receiving Northbrook and exhausted the entire surplus in receiving Prince of Wales. The arrangements, during the visits of both these dignitaries at Jaipur, for their reception were 'surpassingly grand'; the municipal reception alone costed Rs. 2,56,712.00. Jodhpur had been given a loan of 24 lakhs in August 1875; this ensured 'magnificent' reception of both the dignitaries in November, 1875. Tonk was in financial difficulty; it was given a loan of Rs. 1.5 lakhs to accord a welcome to Prince of Wales at Agra.[7] A few years later Tonk was held responsible for its extravagance; the state had to kneel down on account of its financial bankruptcy.

The states which were for many years at a stretch notoriously in debt were Kota, Tonk and Dholpur. Jodhpur in the seventies and early eighties, Bikaner in the seventies; Alwar and Bharatpur for short duration, remained in debt. However, the Annual Administrative Reports for three consecutive years—1869-70, 1870-71 and 1871-72 depict the following states in debt:

1869-70 Karauli, Pratapgarh, Bundi, Tonk, Sirohi, Shahpura.

1870-71 Mewar, Kota, Bikaner, Jaipur, Tonk, Dholpur, Banswara, Dungarpur, Pratapgarh, Kishangarh, Sirohi, Karauli and Khetri.

1871-72 Alwar, Sirohi, Kota, Tonk, Karauli, Dholpur.

The increase in the number of visits by the imperial dignitaries enhanced invisible expenditure on presents to be made on such occasions. Not only were these occasions in addition to social festivities of marriages and births in the families and relations of the chiefs but the nature of presents and gifts on these occasions acquired significance. Ostentatious gifts had come into vogue. A competition for adopting a western style of life and for making purchases in European shops had begun. This style of life percolated down. A majority of the feudal nobles in every state were deep in debt. The archival records of every state have a section dealing with the indebted jagirdars. The states themselves slipped into debts. Every annual administrative report, after 1875, mentioned the names of about 8 to 10 states as being in debt. The cases of Kota, Bundi, Jodhpur, Dholpur, Tonk, Bikaner, Banswara, Karauli were frequently mentioned. The pervasive indebtedness of states and their nobles was a new phenomenon.

The states now experienced increasing shortage of resources; the bigger the state, the greater the financial squeeze.[8] The cumulative impact of drain of resources in the form of tribute paid after 1818 and the maintenance of contingents and armies was increasing. The loss of transit duties, an important source of income, combined with the drying out of profit by salt and opium trade had tightened the crunch on resources. The rulers were now easily amenable to the suggestions that additional resources could be mobilised by exploiting the 'virgin soil waiting to be cultivated'.[9]

The Political Officers were motivated to change the land revenue settlements only during the regency administrations primarily because the fundamental changes to be brought about in the prevalent system were not possible when a ruler was actually running the state administration. J.C. Brooke, the AGG, after his visit to central Rajasthan in 1870-71, felt that the states of Tonk, Alwar, Bharatpur, Dholpur, Karauli and Jaipur could produce much more valuable crops than they actually did. The main hindrance, in his opinion, was that there was an absence 'of a settled method of revenue management', which discouraged proprietors, farmers and the ryots from cultivating anything except ordinary grains.[10] He thought that large tracts in these states were capable of producing opium, sugarcane and tobacco. He wanted the Political Officers to give advice to the rulers on the subject of revenue management on convenient occasions. British control over the management of revenue and expenditure increased in the post 1870 period; the states were encouraged to produce articles of export for the consumption of the British provinces which could send in exchange clothes and metal vessels and articles of native luxury. This influenced the revenue rates for certain crops in the new land revenue settlements, e.g. cotton in unirrigated lands was taxed lower than bajra and maize (Mewar); rates for tobacco were lower than for wheat or sugarcane.

The states experiencing resource crunch had cut down some of their establishments out of their helplessness. It was the British perception that the states' income from land revenue should be increased so that they could be persuaded to spend on newer items of expenditure on durbars and receptions as also on items of imperial preference, particularly means of communication which connected major towns and cantonments and opened up the interior of the state for trade and commerce. In the post 1870 period whenever a state was in financial difficulty and came under British control, it was told to effect economies in its traditional expenses; the extra expenses on public works were not cut. The departments which had to suffer retrenchment were concerned with the employment of local artisans and craftsmen.

The settlement officers, in their keenness to project their settlements to be liberal and lenient, asserted that the rulers in Indian states were keen to extract a far greater land revenue from their subjects than the British did in their Indian provinces. This was an ex-parte assertion and was made deliberately to cover their regressive land revenue settlements. Dwyer quoted Powlett's observation who quoted Impey that the rulers wanted maximisation of land revenue.[11] None of them cited from action done or letters written by the rulers betraying this desire. It is noteworthy that there were three generations of 18 rulers in as many states of Rajasthan during 1818-1900. Why did the British not allow even one of them to enhance land revenue demand to prove their contention? When in 1930 Bharatpur got the earlier settlement revised by one of its own officers and granted more concessions for failed crops and menials, the final report had to be whetted and cleared by a British officer from Punjab.[11a]

The district of Ajmer Merwara put forth example of another type. Here the work of tank construction for irrigation virtually came to a standstill after 1860. Dixon had shown that whatever amount had been spent on tank construction and repair, had been paid many times over during his lifetime. Nothing fresh was being done to enhance tank irrigation after 1860. During 1870-74, it was decided that the money spent on tank construction, more than a generation ago, should be put as capital expenditure and the irrigation revenue be shown as return on the capital.[12] The tank maintenance was limited to 20 times the annual revenue from it. The result was that talabi irrigation area went continuously down as the following statistics show[13] Table 3.1.

Two different standards were thus apparent. In Indian states, the land revenue demand was enhanced by British officers 'because the (minor) rulers wanted it'; in Ajmer the money spent on irrigation which had been paid over 600% during 1846-69 was shown as capital expenditure in the post

1874 period. In the latter case the attempt was to project as if money was being spent on tank irrigation and maintenance.

TABLE: 3.1

Area under tank irrigation (acres)

Tehsil	1849	1874	1887	1908
Ajmer	9165	8365	8328	7361
Beawar	7992	7690	7259	5093
Todgarh	2406	2406	2700	2127
Total	19563	18461	18287	14581

Mewar is an apt illustration to expose the fallacious contention of the British officers that the land revenue settlement was carried out at the desire of the rulers. The state administration was practically under British control after 1862 for about 25 years. In 1869-70, the British thought of introducing a systematic revenue settlement even when they knew that the prevalent system of revenue collection was very popular and there were very few complaints. They also knew that there was great opposition to land settlement in the state. In 1870-71 they accepted that the agricultural population was very well off and there was an absence of litigation and disputes. Being the suzerain authority, they introduced a summary settlement even though they had failed to find any lambardars to come forward to accept the responsibility of realising the revenue demand. They remained content with a ryotwari settlement. There was a successful passive resistance movement in 1875 against the summary settlement. Wingate reported total non-cooperation by the peasantry in his survey and measurement work in 1881.[14] He had to stay for more than a decade to introduce the settlement in the state. Abbott faced opposition at Jhalawar which was ignored.[15] Butler took more than 4 years to bring about the land settlement at Kota; there was some opposition but the settlement continued.[16] At Karauli, Raw received objections by the thousands; the people had to accept the heavy revenue demand.[17] These examples of opposition to the 'liberal and lighter' assessment should not have been there if the rulers had been keen to impose a far heavier settlement.

The accession of 2 year old Jaswant Singh in 1853 at Bharatpur provided the first opportunity to the British to undertake a land revenue settlement. In August 1855 Lawrence and Nixon completed a summary settlement for the state. The revenue demand, though based on the average collections of the past 10 years, was reduced by 10 to 14% in different tehsils. It was done to provide a greater margin of profit to the new intermediaries, the zamindars, who were sought to be created for the first time. Since the creation of this intermediary class could not brought about, the rationale for reduction of the revenue demand disappeared. The land revenue settlement was revised three times during the regency administration - 1858-59, 1862-63 and 1868-69; each time the revenue was enhanced by 10.26%, 6.9% and 8.5% respectively.[18] The last settlement was done when the state was in the grip of a famine. The Political Agent, in his reports for 1868-69 and 1870-71, had suggested an enhancement by 2 lakhs in the revenue due to increased irrigation facilities.[19] When power was handed over to the ruler in 1869, he was prevented from changing the land revenue settlement.[20] The settlement was enhanced by 7.5% in 1871-72 pending a 10 years' settlement. This enhancement was justified by the Political Agent at the time. The 10 year regular settlement was made in 1873-74 enhancing the revenue by another 8.5%. Even this last was justified by the Political Agent on grounds of enhanced irrigation and masonry wells.[21] Excepting the last one, all earlier revisions had been done by the British officers. When the settlement became due for revision in 1883-84, the ruler reduced the demand by 9.8% on account of mass migration out of the state after the stoppage of salt manufacture. It was further marginally reduced in 1884-85. The settlement was revised in 1890-91 for a 15 year term. But the Government decided on a thorough revision of the whole settlement in 1895; Dwyer enhanced the revenue demand during 1897-1900 when the land under cultivation was going down as the population of the state was also declining.[22]

TABLE: 3.2

Revenue Demand at Bharatpur (1855-1900)

Settlement Year	Total revenue Demand	Area under cultivation	Population of the State
1855-56	Rs. 1406922		
1858-59	1551261		
1862-63	1666154		
1868-69	1807688	740000 acres	743710 (1867)
1871-72	1940973	(1867)	
1873-74	2105724		
1883-84	1898890		645540 (1881)
1884-85	1879810	(1896-97)	
1898-1900	2055621	533392 acres	640330 (1891)

Alwar experienced five different land revenue settlements in the later half of the 19th century under the direction of British Political or Settlement Officers. All these had been introduced at a time when the state had, either on account of the minority of the ruler or on account of revolt against the ruler, come under regency administration presided over by the Political Agent. The revenue demand was enhanced, not at the desire of the ruler, but of the British officers to fulfil administrative goals set by them. The average revenue realisation, during the 10 years prior to the establishment of regency administration (1849-59), had been Rs. 14,11,740 per year. In fact during the last 5 years of the above period, it had averaged Rs. 13,59,750 per year.[23] This revenue realisation was held by Capt. Impey, the Political Agent, to have impoverished the people. The five revisions of land revenue demand were all in an upward direction[24].

TABLE: 3.3

Revenue demand at Alwar

Settlement Year	Total revenue demand	Percentage of increase on the 1854-59 average
1859	Rs. 14.29 lakhs	5%
1862-72 (average)	17.19 lakhs	26.5%
1872	18.89 lakhs	40.2%
1876 (16 years) (Variable)	20.19 to 20.84 lakhs	48.56% 53.26%
1897-99	22.73 lakhs	67.1%

The revenue demand had increase by 48.56% during a period of 17 years, 1859-76. Capt. Impey had talked of oppression of the cultivators during 1850-59; he forgot it when he enhanced the revenue demand by 19.6% in 1862; Powlett also enhanced it by another 17% in 1876. The argument now advanced that the British had enhanced the revenue demand because the peasantry in Indian states had been accustomed to a much heavier burden in comparison to the British provinces, was another variant of the earlier view. This argument, like the earlier one, was based on ex-parte justification. The British looked for a minority administration to undertake a revenue settlement. There is enough evidence to show the incorrectness of the contention that the ruler wanted a much higher assessment. Mangal Singh (1876-92) did not charge *neota* (marriage cess) at his marriage because the burden of Powlett's settlement was very heavy. The burden of extra cesses in British administered Punjab was 20% over and above the revenue demand while it was only 3% in Alwar.[25] Bharatpur gave much larger concessions to the peasants when it revised the settlement in 1930-31.

The oppressive settlement imposed by the British settlement officers were projected as liberal by putting forward the argument that the state in the pre-settlement period used to take the whole rental minus an allowance of 2 to 5% paid to the *lambardars*. The British argued that they were taking only 2/3rd of the rentals. This was a misleading argument because 1/3rd had been left to the new intermediary (*biswadar* at Alwar, zamindar at Bharatpur) which had been non-existent earlier. The land settlements had to provide for the maintenance of the new class created by them. The argument of taking 2/3rd rentals only, should have meant lighter taxation if the state had been taking the whole rental earlier. But the land revenue demand had been enhanced by more than 65% in Alwar on the average collections of 1854-59; this demand was 2/3rd of the rental paid by the cultivators. It simply meant that cultivators paid 65% more land revenue to the new intermediaries.[26] The government demand had, in real effect, been raised by 223% during 1859-99 as the figures in Table 3.4 show.

The land revenue settlement in Tonk was undertaken under very special circumstances. Not only was the state passing through a very difficult financial situation, but the peasantry was also experiencing considerable hardship on account of a fall in the price of opium - the major cash crop of three out of six parganas in the state. While the state might persuade a settlement officer to enhance the revenue demand, the peasantry almost required a moderate assessment, keeping in view the general fall in prices of agricultural products. Captain Pears, the settlement officer, was aware that the cultivators paid a share of the produce when a crop was raised and nothing on uncropped land in half the state.[28] He found, after detailed survey, that very low rates were sufficient to bring the demand of a village up to what it was under share-cropping assessment.[29] The survey was commenced on 1st Feb. 1887 and continued till 12th December 1891 in different parganas. The settlement began on different dates in the various parganas: Nimbahera (1890-91), Pirawa, Chabra, Sironj (1891-92) and Aligarh and Tonk (1892-93). Pears was convinced that the

TABLE: 3.4

Alwar State Revenue Demand in the years

	1854-59	1859	1862	1872	1876	1897	1899-1900
State	1359750	1465615	1753425	1889002	2011128	2084481	2273486
Biswa dars	nil	483653	578630	623370	663672	678879	750250
Net payment by culti- vator	1359750	1949268	2332055	2512372	2674800	2772360	3023736
Higher by % Base 1854 % =	100	143%	171.5%	184.7%	196.7%	203%	222%

Bharatpur State Revenue Demand in the years[27]

	1855	1859	1862	1873	1890	1900-02
State Demand	Rs. 1406922	1551261	1666154	2105724	1909766	2108509
Zamindar's share	—	—	—	—	—	1054254
Net payment by cultivators	1406922	1551261	1666154	2105724	1909766	3162763
Higher by % with 1890 as base year						65.6%

settlement should be for a term of 20 years during which there should be no enhancement of revenue. He felt that a majority of the cultivators were impoverished since the fall in opium prices was not accompanied by a corresponding reduction in assessment. He affirmed that the light assessment, proposed by him for a term of 20 years, would ultimately lead to a substantial increase in land revenue later on.[30] To what extent did the settlement achieve the goal of a light assessment in view of falling opium prices? An answer may be found in the settlement itself, and particularly in the revenue demand which had been raised by 10.2% on the demand of 1886-87.[31]

TABLE: 3.5

Tonk Land Revenue Demand During 1874-1892

Year	Revenue Demand	Jagir resumed	Total
1874-1885 (Average)	915434 (Average)		915434
1885-86	856593		856593
1886-87	851888	4000	855888
1887-88	853885	34000	887885
1888-89	902562	40000	942562
1889-90	881760	50000	931760
1890-91	916407	50000	966407
1891-92	939000	50000	989000

The first land revenue settlement of Kota had been undertaken by Munshi Durga Prasad at a time when the state was under British superintendence and control. It began in 1876-77 and continued at a leisurely speed till 1884-85. The soil classification, the introduction of a uniform measuring chain, if not for the entire state, at least for some Nizamats, and the reclamation of waste lands were some gains of the settlement. The revenue demand had been enhanced by 5.5%.[32]

The reversion to Kota of a few parganas in 1899 (Shahabad and central Jhalawar) from Jhalawar was held to justify a fresh land revenue settlement; but the real reason was the loss suffered by the state government on account of allowing a discount of 14 to 18% on the revenue demand to the peasantry. This had become necessary in view of allowing a similar discount on Kota/Jhalawar rupee after the Imperial currency became the legal tender in the state during 1901-02. The Kota maund had also been replaced by the imperial maund in the ration of 40:37. The state wanted to be relieved of the burden of allowing the discount to the peasantry after the introduction of imperial currency. The falling price of opium and foodgrains necessitated a fresh determination of state land revenue demand. The state also faced financial problems because of a decline in land under cultivation; the population of the state had also fallen by 24% during the decade 1891-1901.[33]

TABLE: 3.6

Year	Cultivated Land area Piwat	Korwan	Total	Year	Population
1884-85	144414	1853496	1997910	1891	718771
1907-08	112594	1650650	1763244	1901	544879

The piwat area had fallen by 22% and the *Korwan* by 10.9%; there had been a decline of 11.7% in the total area under cultivation. And still the land revenue settlement raised the revenue demand in the Kota region in terms of imperial rupees. In other words the land revenue demand had been raised. The relevant figures were.

Year	Kota revenue demand (realised)	Revenue from the areas reverted to Kota	Total
1884-85	1439180	551564	1990744
1908-09	1903749	553473	2457222

Butler claimed that he had raised the revenue demand only by 10% but he compared the figures of the year before his settlement. In fact the revenue demand had gone up by 32.3%

apparently but really by 80% keeping in view the currency difference also. He was aware that the assessment was a high one and laid down five conditions for its stability.[34] These were: (1) the rates imposed can be paid only from a reasonably good crop; (2) the rates can only be borne by land cultivated; untilled land must be removed from the *khatas* with reasonable liberality; (3) the wild animals must not be allowed to ravage the crops; (4) the revenue department must be maintained in its present state of efficiency; and (5) the assessment on *chahi* lands depended on the continued cultivation of the poppy or some equally valuable crop.

Dholpur was one of the few states in Rajasthan which had the benefit of a land settlement by a local officer; his settlement happened to fall in between two land revenue settlements undertaken by British officers. The first was a summary settlement by W.H. Smith in 1877-78, the second was a regular settlement by Umacharan Mukhopadhyaya during 1892-94, and the third settlement by W. Raw in 1912. Raw had come with a determination to introduce the zamindar class. He used very disparaging remarks for the abilities of Umacharan and, called his work 'imaginary', and the whole attempt at revision as 'farce'.[35] This criticism was understandable because Raw was re-introducing the old intermediary class which had been replaced by *ijaredars* during 1894-1908. The revenue demand was enhanced considerably by Raw.

TABLE: 3.7

Expanding Revenue Demand at Dholpur[36]

S. No.	Year of Settlement	Amount of Demand	Remarks
1.	1863	Rs. 648616	
2.	1872	Rs. 693135	
3.	1878	Rs. 731885	5.6% higher than the previous demand
4.	1891	Rs. 822184	12.3% higher than the previous demand
5.	1911	Rs. 990787	20.5 higher than the 1891 demand

The revenue demand had thus been increased by 42.9% during a period of 40-years. Taking the figures as they have been given by the different settlement reports, the 1891 report claimed 34602 acres more cultivation than the figure of 1878, and 6% more irrigation.[37] There had been a large scale resumption of mafi lands. In 1884-85, 5445 acres had been resumed.[38] The 1911 report gave the following figures.

TABLE: 3.8

Year	Cultivated area (bighas)		Total
	Irrigated	Dry	
1875	116292	306669	422961
1891	172972	299247	472219
1910	141567	293625	435192

Raw had found that the irrigated area had gone down by 18.16% and the total area under cultivation had declined by 7.84% and yet he enhanced the revenue demand by 20.5%.

Jhalawar did not have sound financial position from the very beginning. By 1847 it was indebted to the British Government to the extent of Rs. 2.67 lakhs. No sooner was it paid, the state again became indebted to the tune of Rs. 25 lakhs by 1858. The loan could be paid only after 9 years of regency administration (1875-84) which witnessed a 10% rise in revenue demand in two phases: 4% by the summary settlement and 6% by the regular settlement. This increase in revenue demand was made at a time when the price of the principal cash crop, opium, fell by 39% and of foodgrains by 28%. The relevant figures were[40]:

Year	Revenue demand	
1878	Rs. 1275729	
1879-80	Rs. 1330245	Summary settlement (4.27% enhancement)
1884-85	Rs. 1405968	Regular settlement (5.7% enhancement on the summary settlement demand)

Supposing that the peasantry paid 50% produce by way of land revenue, (converted in cash at the rates of 1878) the incidence of taxation now came to mean that it paid Rs. 55/- as revenue (after 10% increase by the two settlements made during the regency administration) on the same produce which earlier fetched Rs. 100/- but now fetched only Rs. 61/- in case of opium and Rs. 72/- in case of foodgrains. The incidence of revenue demand had increased to 90% of the produce in opium growing areas and 76% in other areas, though only 10% enhancement had been made. Further 86% of the irrigated area had been devoted to opium cultivation where the fall in prices was 39%. The cultivation of this commercial crop thus did not leave a margin of more than 10%; the foodgrains production left a margin of 24% only. Opposition to such an oppressive land settlement would be natural, though Abbott accused the local officials connected with the fixation and collection of land revenue for having engineered opposition to the settlement. He even argued that the 'equitable' distribution of revenue under the new system had led to opposition by the relatives and friends of the corrupt officials. Opposition to a land settlement which did not leave even subsistence to the cultivators was natural; but the settlement officer misrepresented it as a manoeuvre by the local officials.[41]

The examples from different states have been given to show that the British settlement officers were interested only in enhancing the revenue demand. The irrigated/cultivated area may have gone down in Dholpur, Kota, the population may have declined in Bharatpur, the prices may have declined but the revenue demand was increased everywhere.

The British administration in Ajmer Merwara was faced with widespread misery and indebtedness among the peasantry as a result of its land revenue policy. The land revenue demand had been raised by Dixon to a level which was not crossed during the next half century despite three revisions. By 1870 it had resulted in a massive destruction of peasant prosperity which led the government to direct La Touche, to 'find out those villages in which an appropriate demand had been collected' and to assess the rest accordingly. He was asked to fix a revenue which 'village *could* pay for a series of years with some degree of certainty and ease'.[42] It was a fair confession that its half a century of direct revenue administration had succeeded in bringing about peasant impoverishment.

However, a policy decision by the Government, to charge a water rate on all lands irrigated from tanks in the district, was to introduce a new complicating factor. The settlement officer was instructed to assess water revenue of the tanks separately and to add it to the land revenue. The total revenue demand for the whole district was reduced in 1874 from Rs. 356231 to 305183 (14.3%). It was further argued that there had been a 30% rise in the prices of food grains during the last few years and hence the incidence of taxation would not be more than ¼th of the gross produce. A scheme of classification of water tanks into five categories and fixation of different rates was the main contribution of this settlement.[43] The tanks were categorised on the basis of their irrigation potential:

(i) First class tanks were those which irrigated both the kharif and rabi crops.

(ii) Second class tanks provided water for rabi sowing and one watering for rabi crops.

(iii) Third class tanks provided water for rabi sowing when they did not irrigate the kharif crops.

(iv) Fourth class tanks provided water for rabi sowing when they did not irrigate kharif crops due to good rainfall.

(v) Fifth class tanks did not have enough water even for kharif but rabi could be sown in their beds.

The water rate for the first class tanks was fixed; for others it was variable in order to cover up the yearly fluctuations in irrigated area. The water rate would increase/decrease if the irrigated area was less/more than the expected area. The settlement was sanctioned for 10 years.

The decade 1874-84 was, except for the famine of 1877-78, of comparatively good years when contrasted with the earlier decade. There was not much occasion for evaluating the consequences of the variable water rate. The Government felt that the settlement had been moderate and the district had made progress. Therefore Whiteway was appointed to get thoroughly correct maps and records prepared and to establish a proper system of maintaining the records up to date. He was instructed to assess all increase of cultivation at the dry rates of the last settlement and not to assess the increased well irrigated area at well rates; to allow no enhancement of revenue except on grounds of increased cultivation or of improvement in irrigation works constructed at government expense.[44] With definite liberal instructions not to venture any material enhancement and not to assess the well-irrigated areas at well rates, it could have been expected that Whiteway would make an equitable settlement. But these instructions could not achieve the goal because of the changed system of maintaining a water revenue account separately. Lupton considered that the greatest defect of Whiteway's settlement and his irrigation rules was that they aimed 'too much at the stability of the annual water revenue demand'.

The fundamental change introduced by the Government of opening a capital account for tanks and of maintaining a water revenue account separately was largely responsible for the failure of Whiteway's settlement. It had aimed 'too much at the stability of the annual water revenue demand'.[45] In Ajmer tehsil he had calculated Rs. 73045 as revenue on 18237 acres of well lands and Rs. 35348 on 9263 acres of *talabi* lands. The *chahi* and *talabi* area actually irrigated over a period of 15 years (1893-1907) was 15,560 and 6018 acres respectively. Thus (18237 - 15560) i.e. 2677 acres of *chahi* and (9263 - 6018) - 3245 acres of *talabi* lands had paid irrigated water rates for barani cultivation.[46] For the two decades (1887-1907) the average revenue collection of Ajmer tehsil had fallen short by (Rs. 165625 - 140005) = Rs. 25620 which was virtually equal to the water rate for (2677 + 3245) = 5922 acres @ Rs. 4.06 (= Rs. 24043/-).* All claim of an equitable land revenue settlement was futile when 21.5% land paid *chahi* and *talabi* rate for dry cultivation.

TABLE: 3.9
Assessed Ajmer Merwara

		Land area (in acres)				
District	Year	chahi	talabi	abi	Barani	Total
i. Ajmer Merwara	1874	18553	8365	7746	74256	108920
ii.	1887	18237	9263	10996	85956	124452
iii. Average of 15 years cultivation:	1893-1907	15560	6018	5597	69994	97169
Difference between ii and iii		-2677 17.2%	-3245 -53.9%	-5399 -96.4%	-15962 -22.8%	-27233 -28.06%

Whiteway's approach to the problems of the peasantry was that it was accustomed to live from hand to mouth. The surplus in good years was spent easily; it borrowed in bad years and rarely managed to pay off the debt and its accumulated interest.[47] He disclaimed all intention to fix revenue demand at a lower level which may be easily paid even in bad years because, he argued, in times of widespread famine, suspensions or remissions would still be needed. He introduced crop rate on some first class tanks and, by introducing variable assessment of water rate on all classes of tanks, increased the total assessment marginally by Rs. 20,646.00 or 6.7% on La Touche's settlement.[48] His variable system of assessment proved so harmful and generated so much of opposition that it had to be changed during the continuation of the settlement itself.[49] The assessment proved so ruinous that the Government had to direct Lupton to avoid the variable system unless it was impossible to propose a fixed assessment.

Lupton, appointed in 1907, was asked to undertake a complete revaluation and reassessment of land and water revenue of all the *khalsa* lands. He submitted his report on land and water revenue in 1908 and his settlement report in 1910. Whiteway had enhanced the irrigated land areas considerably. Lupton found the land under cultivation to be much less than it was in 1887. The revenue demand was reduced by about 6.4% when the irrigated land area had gone down by 16.7%; the *barani* area had marginally increased by 2%. The revenue demand continued to be heavy:

TABLE: 3.9A

Revenue Demand By Various Revenue Settlements in Ajmer Merwara[50]

Tehsil	Dixon's Settlement 1854	La Tough's Settlement 1874	Whiteway's Settlement 1887	Lupton's Settlement 1910
Ajmer	183669	170076	165625	157776
Beawar	95502	72769	71872	71238
Todgarh	77060	62338	61430	50820
Total	356231	305183	298927	279834

The Mechanism Of Revenue Enhancement

The various revenue settlements in different states and Ajmer Merwara were subtle exercises in enhancing revenue demand from the peasantry. This was done in a manner which apparently appeared fair and objective though it was basically partisan and regressive. The essence of the method lay either in devising a classification of land or in evolving a principle which could theoretically justify enhancement of land revenue demand. The land classification could be categorised either.

(i) on the basis of natural classes ((i.e. quality of soil); or

(ii) on the basis of artificial classes (i.e. on the basis or irrigation).

The first justified enhancement of revenue by promoting inferior soil to a superior category; the availability of irrigation facility was not relevant. The second consisted in laying down a new definition of what could be considered irrigated land. By this method a larger area was determined to be irrigated by a well. A new definition of what could be considered as irrigated lands - irrigated in the year or irrigated during the last few years. Both these methods were part of the process to justify enhancement of revenue. There were various facets of these methods.

a. The *sairaba/dahri* lands at Bharatpur and Alwar respectively were re-defined so as to include *barani* land under irrigated category. This was done by adding *sabiqa* and *barishi* categories to it.

b. The area irrigated by a well was enlarged, and the wells not in working order, were supposed to be in working order. Brackish, bitter or oily wells were considered as capable of irrigating normally which they were not. A *sabiqa* category was added here also.

c. Another variant was to fix variable water revenue for tank irrigation. It was done at Ajmer where the farmer had to pay more money for getting lesser quantity of water. The object was to have a stable water revenue.

d. Classification and sub-division of well known categories was undertaken so that fixation of land revenue at a higher level may appear to be rational and justified. There were 30 different sub-classes of soil at Alwar and Dungarpur, and the determination of rates for each particular area of land was more or less dependent upon the arbitrary judgment of the officer concerned.

Some illustrations of the above principles in operation are being given below to explain their practical impact.

The enhancement of revenue demand by means of changes in soil classification may best be seen in operation at Alwar.

The soil of the state had been classified into three broad categories - *chiknot, mattiyar* and *bhur*. *Chiknot* is clayey loam, richest natural soil requiring more working and irrigation than any other. It is rarely manured. *Mattiyar* is ordinary loam, more easily worked than *chiknot*. It is improved by manure. *Bhur* is sandy having less clay and more sand than *mattiyar*; it is suitable for lighter crops. O'Dwyer was, if left to himself, against 'any classification according to the quality of soil'.[51] But he could not abolish the classification because it had been started by his predecessor; he, however, cut down the number of varied subdivisions of each category. He had departed from the past classification so as to increase the area of *chiknot* and *mattiyar* soils at the expense of *bhur* and thereby justified an enhancement of revenue demand. He knew that the quality of soil does not change easily; he also confessed that all new cultivation was in the poorest soils.[52] This should have increased the extent of the *barani* and *bhur* cultivation only. But the result of his classification was that the area of *chiknot* and *mattiyar* soils increased while that of the *barani* soil decreased by more than one lakh *bighas* in the state. The detailed measurements of the different tehsils has been given in a separate appendix (No.C); the gist of the difference in measurements of the two settlements is give here:

TABLE: 3.10

Soil Classification (Alwar)

Year	Chiknot	Mattiyar	Barani	Total
1876	164479	695041	512755	1372275 Bighas
1898	176554	806814	409397	1392765 "
Difference	+ 12075	+111773	-103358	+ 20490
	or 7.34%	or 16.5%	or - 20%	or 1.5%

O'Dwyer knew that soil classification 'was a most useful guide' specially when carried out honestly under one man's guidance. Despite his taking four years to carry out the settlement, he did away with the subdivision of each class of soil in his subsequent reports of eight tehsils though he retained it in the four tehsils (eastern) which had been surveyed first. His apparent objection was that it created too many categories since each class was subdivided into *chahi, dahri* and *barani* according to the source of irrigation for the crops. The real reason was that a detailed classification restricted his freedom to manipulate an increase in the total revenue demand.

The table giving a comparative statement of soil areas in the different tehsils reveals the extent of injustice perpetrated on the peasantry. In the four eastern tehsils of Kishangarh, Ramgarh, Govindgarh and Lachmangarh, the increase in the total area was a paltry 5697 bighas (1.4 %); but the area of *mattiyar* soil had been increased by 63120 bighas (32.3 %) and that of *bhur* reduced by 55506 bighas. The *chiknot* area had also been reduced by 1926 bighas. In the five tehsils of Tijara, Mandawar, Behror, Rajgarh and Katumber, the total area under cultivation had decreased by 589 bighas, but the area of *mattiyar* soil and increased by 44170 bighas and that of *chiknot* by 2181 bighas. The *bhur* soil area had been reduced by 46940 bighas. In the three central and southern tehsils of Alwar, Bansur and Thanaghazi, the total area under cultivation had increased by 15383 bighas and the *bhur* area had gone down by 912 bighas. Of this total of 16295 bighas, 11820 (68%) went to *chiknot* and 4475 (32%) to *mattiyar* categories.

This is contrary to the contention of all settlement officers that the best soils were already cultivated; if there was any extension of cultivation, it was and could only be, in poorer soils. It means that *bhur* was promoted to *mattiyar* which in turn was promoted to *chiknot*. The peasant was taxed at a higher rate because the quality of land had been upgraded. Thus even though the total cultivated area in the state increased by a mere 20490 bighas (1.5%), the land revenue demand could be substantially increased because of increase in *chiknot* and *mattiyar* soil areas. The variations in soil classification help us to understand the phenomenon of 'increasing revenue demand with reducing soil rates'. The rates for *mattiyar* or *chiknot* could be lowered when *bhur* soil was classified as *mattiyar* and *mattiyar* in turn was promoted to *chiknot*. The change in the character of soil had been brought about because all political power was in the hands of the British administrators.

This was the essence of a regressive land settlement. Poorer soil was taxed at a higher rate and better soil was taxed at a lower rate. The owners of *chiknot* and *mattiyar* soil were given relief because the soil rate had been reduced; but the owner of *bhur* soil were now subjected to heavier taxation because it had been promoted to *mattiyar* soil.

Another thing he did was similar to what he did at Bharatpur. He increased the *dahri* area by 25336 bighas from 92427 to 117763 bighas or 27%. It was not that the new area had been inundated or flooded and therefore it was logical. What Dwyer did was to give a new definition of *dahri* and *dahri sabiqa*. The *dahri* area was treated as a single class at the last settlement. It was now divided into two classes: *dahri hal* and *dahri sabiqa*. *Dahri hal* was defined as land ordinarily inundated and actually done within the last five years; *sabiqa* was land sometimes inundated but not within the last 5 years. The definition of *sabiqa* meant that *barani* land was now categorised as *dahri sabiqa*. Out of a total 117763 bighas, 44% (51352 bighas) was land which had not been flooded for the last 5 years and yet it paid *dahri* rate which included water charges for rain water never supplied.

While advocating the need to revise the 1876 settlement at Alwar, Jennings had emphasized increased irrigation in 23000 bighas and enhanced cultivation of 43000 bighas as a justification for it.[53] Dwyer found at Alwar that the anticipated enhanced cultivation did not materialise. He had therefore to find justification for enhancing the revenue demand in the states of Alwar and Bharatpur. Besides altering the area of natural classes of soil, he devised a method by which the irrigated area could be enhanced in both the states. He introduced a new category of *sabiqa* (past or earlier). This category was added to *chahi* and *sairaba/dahri* lands. In earlier settlements, this category was part of *barani* and not of irrigated land area. Similarly, the *chahi* land area at Bharatpur had been considerably reduced after the Salt Agreement of January 1879 which had prohibited salt manufacture. Not only did it lead to a large scale migration out of the state during the next half century, but it also led to deterioration in the quality of well water as also of soil on account of greater salinity. Dwyer found that a far greater number of wells had become brackish and bitter and their capacity to irrigate had gone down considerably. The well statistics alongwith the *chahi* irrigated area have been given in Table No. 3.11.[54]

The number of masonry wells and laos in working condition had done down by (11135+15184) - (10474+13304) = 2680 or 10.2% but the chahi cultivated area had gone down by (366437-355801) = 10636 bighas or 2.9% during 8 or 9 years. This was the difference between the settlement of 1890 and Dwyer's settlement, introduced during 1897-1899 in different tehsils in a phased manner. All things remaining the same, the *chahi* irrigated area should have been reduced proportionately by 10.2% or 37376 bighas. In other words (37376-19636) = 26740 bighas were assessed at *chahi* rates by arbitrarily enhancing the area irrigated by masonry wells/*laos* and by including *chahi sabika* in *chahi* area. This was justified by citing example of the irrigation capacity of a well in Punjab or Mathura. These examples were inappropriate because the irrigation capacity of a well in Bharatpur or Alwar had no comparison with those of Punjab or even of Mathura. He knew that the irrigation capacity of a well differed from tehsil to tehsil even in a group of tehsils in the same state. The area presumed to be irrigated by a masonry well in different tehsils of Bharatpur was as follows[55]:

TABLE: 3.11

Chahi Irrigated Area and well Statistics

Bharatpur Tehsil	1890 Masonry wells working	1890 Masonry wells not working	1898-99 working	1898-99 not working	Masonry 1890	Laos 1898-99	Chahi area (bighas) 1890	Chahi area (bighas) 1898-99 hal	Chahi area (bighas) 1898-99 sabiqa	Total Chahi Area
Gopalgarh	498	131	362	321	685	486	13363	10078	3065	13143
Pahari	251	118	198	186	118	335	6911	5401	3150	8551
Kama	354	55	378	58	516	597	14833	10916	8305	19221
Deeg	792	147	884	125	1072	1199	24361	24888	10944	35832
Kumher	827	165	827	163	1204	113	41038	26163	14638	40801
Akheygarh	975	92	893	146	1456	1348	40788	28508	7623	36131
Bharatpur	936	380	942	340	1569	1350	36665	24677	16242	40919
Nagar	481	175	471	140	603	545	12611	9853	2305	12158
Rupbas	676	274	641	391	931	813	15314	8414	4621	13035
Oochain	1331	70	1174	266	1758	1555	37953	23980	8026	32006
Biyana	1934	—	1777	106	2541	2249	52671	39051	7879	46930
Bhusawar	2080	32	1927	294	2731	2714	69929	43162	13912	57074
Total	11135	1639	10474	2536	15184	13304	366437	255091	100710	355801

Bharatpur Tehsils

Area irrigated per	Gopalgarh	Pahari	Kama	Deeg	Kumher	Akheygarh
masonry well	16	14	12	6	16	18
kachha well	10	9	8	4	11	12
	Bharatpur	Nagar	Rupbas	Ochhain	Biyana	Bhusawar
masonry well	14	16	11	15	15	17
kachha well	10	8	4½	9	9	9

These figures and averages given by Dwyer were far in excess of the capacity of a normal well - masonry or *kachha.* This may be seen by a comparison of the area irrigated according to the above table and the actual irrigated area which was assessed though never irrigated:

The total irrigated area according to the expected irrigated area was 1½ times more than the area assessed as irrigated. (Table No. 3.12) But even the assessed irrigated *hal* area was more than could be irrigated by the wells. The evidence is the cropped area which was much less than the assessed irrigated area. It was even 2.6% less than the *chahi hal* area[56] (Table No. 3.13)

The percentage of cropped chahi to assessed chahi area varied from 57 to 88; this was an indication of the limit to which the assessed area could be irrigated. Besides the over assessment of the irrigation capacity of a well/*lao,* another reason for the shortfall in the cropped irrigated area was the growing salination of wells in the state and decline in the quality of water of the wells. A great number of wells were becoming brackish, bitter and oily which could only provide a second irrigation to rabi crops or could irrigate in alternate years. The quality of well water, in tehsil groups, is given in Table No. 3.14.[57]

TABLE: 3.12

Area irrigated by wells in accordance with Dwyer's estimate. In Bharatpur state during 1898-1900

Tehsils	Masonry wells & Laos x area	Area Irrigated	Kacha well Irri-Irrigated area	Total Irri-gated area	Total Assesed chahi hal area
Gopalgarh	341+486 x16	13552	3460	17012	10078
Pahari	198+335 x14	7462	1530	8992	5401
Kama	378+597 x12	11700	4320	16020	10916
Deeg	884+1199x 6	12498	2640	15138	24888
Kumher	827+113 x16	15040	2045	17085	26163
Akheygarh	893+1348x18	40338	8505	48843	28508
Bharatpur	817+1350x14	30338	7085	37423	24677
Nagar	458+545 x16	16048	944	16992	9853
Rupbas	641+813 x11	15994	1289	17283	8414
Oochain	1174+1555x15	40935	1092	42027	23980
Biyana	1777+2249x15	60390	6719	67109	39051
Bhusawar	1927+2714x17	78897	6527	85424	43162
Total				389349	255091

(irrigated area is 1.52 times more than assessed area)

TABLE: 3.13

Assessed and Cropped Irrigated Area

Bharatpur Tehsils	Irrigated Area Assessed	Irrigated Area Cropped	Percentage of cropped to assessed area
Gopalgarh	13143	10399	79
Pahari	8551	5663	66.2
Kama	19221	11115	57.8
Deeg	35632	24904	69.5
Kumher	40801	26170	64.1
Akheygarh	34131	26842	78.7
Bharatpur	40919	25452	62.2
Nagar	12154	9895	81.4
Rupbas	13035	8352	64
Oochain	23980	17559	73.2
Biyana	43862	38691	88
Bhusawar	54641	42752	78.2
State Total	340070	247794	72.8

TABLE: 3.14

Tehsils	Masonry Wells Total No.	Quality of Water: Sweet	Brackish	Bitter & oily
4 Northern tehsils	1822	916	381	525
4 Central tehsils	3133	1268	599	1266
4 Southern tehsils	5519	4172	528	819
Total	10474	6356	1508	2610
Percentage		60.7	14.4	24.9

Thus only 60.7% working wells were of sweet water. By applying the same percentage to working masonry laos (Table 3.11) only 8075 out of 13304 laos would be of sweet water. The percentage of wells which had been brackish or oily or bitter in 1890 is not available; therefore any comparison would be a wild guess. Dwyer himself had noted that the number of wells not working had increased tremendously. One of the reasons responsible for this development was the wells becoming brackish.

Thus there were now two positive factors which turned against extension of *chahi* cultivation: i. The number of working masonry wells and *laos* had gone down by 10.2% in absolute terms; ii. of this reduced number, only 60.7% wells could be utilised for regular irrigation. This could be very harsh for the owners of *chahi* lands. But Dwyer introduced a new category of soil - *chahi sabiqa* - (land irrigated by wells within the last 4 years). Thus land area which could be irrigated by brackish wells in alternate years or after a gap of 2 years came in this category. It was assessed at about 50% rate and was exempted from paying full *chahi* irrigation rate permanently. The *sabiqa chahi* category had served two useful purposes: (i) it provided a cover to the falling area of *chahi* cultivation; (ii) it enabled Dwyer to cover up a concession to *chahi* land owners. A substantial part of chahi land was subjected to lower revenue demand.[58] (Table No. 3.15)

Dwyer had marginally enhanced the rates of *chahi hal* but cleverly moderated it with *chahi sabiqa* and put forth an average *chahi* rate. By comparison with the settlement of 1890, the *chahi hal* rate had been lowered in two and enhanced in one tehsil substantially and marginally adjusted in 9 other tehsils. But the *chahi* land owner had been given a major relief.

Similarly at Ajmer, Whiteway introduced a variable system of assessment by which all land area in a village was converted into dry units by multiplying the *abi, talabi* and *chahi* acres by 2.5, 4.5 and 6 respectively, in accordance with the difference between their land revenue rates.[59] e.g. Village 'A' had a total of 222 acres land of different types: 124 *barani*, 40 *abi, talabi*, and 50 acres of *chahi* cultivation and paid a revenue of

Rs. 350/-. Now under the new system, the village would have (124+40x2½+8x4½+50x6) 560 dry unit acres. The revenue demand of Rs. 350 would be divided by 560, thus giving Rs. 0.62½ per acre. In a good year the cultivation would extend and the rate would come down; the reverse would happen in a bad year. The net result of this variable assessment was that the dry land had been subjected to a heavier taxation in years of scanty rainfall. The justification was that the market price of commodities was higher and the cultivator got greater profit. The argument was only theoretical because a large section of the peasantry ploughed the fields for its maintenance and not for sale in market.

TABLE: 3.15

Rate of assessment of chahi land in Bharatpur state

Tehsil	Rate Per Bigha in 1890 *Chahi hal*	Rate Per Bigha in 1897-99 *chahi hal*	Rate Per Bigha in 1897-99 *Sabiqa*	Average *chahi* rate in 1897-99
Gopalgarh	Rs. 2.46	Rs. 2.75	1.50	Rs. 2.44
Pahari	2.08	2.25	1.50	1.97
Kama	2.45	2.25	1.25	1.87
Deeg	2.29	2.12	1.25	1.90
Kumher	1.81	2.00	0.97	1.62
Akheygarh	2.21	2.25	1.72	2.13
Bharatpur	1.90	2.12	1.12	1.75
Nagar	3.06	2.00	1.50	1.90
Rupbas	3.16	2.75	1.50	2.31
Oochain	2.65	2.50	1.25	2.33
Biyana	2.53	3.00	1.50	2.52
Bhusavar	2.44	2.69	1.19	2.42

II

Regressive Taxation Of Land

A study of the various land revenue settlements in different states of Rajasthan in the later half of the 19th century (particularly in the post 1870 period) helps us to understand the operational aspects of a changed land revenue policy. It not only delineates the prominent changes brought about here but also provides an insight into the nature of changes brought about by it in the other provinces under direct British administration in India. These changes were fundamental and transformed not only the entire gamut of factors and relations of agricultural production but also affected the prevalent prosperity among agricultural classes.

The pre-1870 agricultural scenario was based fundamentally on inheritable right of land ownership which could not be extinguished except on serious political revolt. Even if families got divided in course of time, the form of joint ownership of land was retained (Alwar and Bharatpur) though separate possession was recognised. The percentage of dependence on agriculture was much less. The change which came over the region is reflected in an ever increasing dependence on agriculture with land area under cultivation not increasing proportionately. The number of ploughs in Ajmer Merwar in 1836, as noted by Edmonstone was 3485; it multiplied approximately eight times by 1884 to reach 27088. The population of the district had not increased in the same proportion. In 1908 the number of ploughs had come down to 20068 although there had been a 3.51% growth in population during 1881-1901. Agriculture had ceased to be attractive as a means of livelihood; people adopted other occupations which were available. A census of the population of Alwar was taken on April 10, 1872; out of a population of 778, 596 only 376, 245 were dependent on agriculture (i.e. 48.32%). The 1911 census put the percentage of population supported by agriculture in the state at 64.7%.[1]

Another element in the pre settlement agricultural scenario was that the state collected land revenue as a tax on production and not as rent for using land. Since the nature of land revenue demand was a tax on production, it was a share of the produce. The state was patriarchal and sympathetic to the peasant and hence aimed at leaving enough to the cultivator for meeting his family requirements. The state was interested in evaluating the production of the cultivator; the role and function of the local officials was to help in determining the state share.

All this was changed by the settlements carried out by British officers in Ajmer Merwara in the pre-1870 period, and in the states of Rajasthan, in the post-1870 period. The changes were significant, but more significant was the fact that these were deliberately contrived. Some of the settlement officers had no sympathy with the cultivator, had a very low opinion of his character and work habits and expressed the same in no uncertain terms. Some observations of the different settlement officers are being given below which help us to understand the objects they set out to achieve.

Dixon, in justification of having fixed the highest revenue demand, wrote[2]

> To have settled the rent at a lower amount would have called for the exercise of little exertion on the part of the people. Our policy has been to obviate idleness or to keep the people as closely employed for their immediate benefit as to check any desire in their minds to return to their pristine habits of irregularity.

La Touche was equally frank about the incidence of land revenue demand in Ajmer Merwara. He confessed[3]

> ... in ordinary years it would appear they (the cultivators) have just enough to live on and no more ... the assessment is certainly not light yet it would have served no good end to have reduced it further. The people are accustomed to pay a heavy assessment, and, if suddenly relieved by too much, would be demoralized ...

Whiteway even abandoned the idea of a lighter assessment. He wrote[4]

> The theory that the revenue should be fixed lightly, that in bad years it might be paid from the savings of the good, has not been found to hold water. Like peasantry all over the world, the zamindar lives from hand to mouth, he spends his surplus in good years and when hard times come, he is driven to borrow, and rarely afterwards manages to clear off the load of debt and accumulated interest.

Lupton, far more reasonable in evaluating the British land revenue policy, agreed that the application of suspensions and remissions was very demoralizing in its effects upon the cultivators. He conceded that the only remedy was to pitch the assessment low. Even he prevaricated[5]

> An assessment, with reference to bad years..., has not been found by experience elsewhere, I believe, to be a real kindness to the cultivators. On the contrary an enlargement of their credit equally generally results in an enhancement of indebtedness.

Smith had clearly revealed his object to be to restrain the ryot from impeding the state to 'bring under cultivation something of the vast area of magnificent soil which the self styled owner either refuses or is unable to bring under the plough himself'[6]. His was the first report about a Rajput state where the British were very keen to establish a land revenue settlement. His confirmed opinion was that 'the system is vicious in every way, full of openings for every kind of fraud and embezzlement...'[7].

Wingate, after 3 years of questioning and travelling wrote[8]:

> With a peasantry who, however industrious by force of circumstances, are prone to consider sitting still the highest good, the first result of too low an assessment would be to reduce the area cultivated, and the ultimate issue that the whole would be sub let.... Their first impulse is to idleness and prodigality.

He realised that the assumption of the prevalent theory of assessment in the states of the region was that every cultivator should have a certain quantity of food grains for his family to live on. His judgment was that 'the poor or lazy pay less than the rich or industrious'. His basic contention was that the possession of land involved the duty of cultivating it; rigid enforcement of a moderate assessment on the land, not on the crop, was, according to him, the true secret of agricultural activity.[9] This was a completely new departure from the prevalent practice, and it turned out to be the real secret of impoverishment of the cultivating peasantry.

With an emphasis on the duty of the cultivator to cultivate and his obligation to pay revenue, the policy of marginalisation of the poor cultivators had been adopted with a theoretical justification. By imposing a heavy tax on land itself and bracketing dry lands with *gorma* and manured lands within a specified area, Wingate had ensured that only the rich would benefit. The poorer cultivators, in the course of a few years, became tenants on the fields of the richer ones; the mahajan began to consider land as a source of investment which it was not, prior to this change in policy.

The emphasis on the duty of the cultivator to cultivate land was part of *a priori* view about him, that he considered sitting idle as the highest good. Wingate thought that lower assessment would have resulted in the reduction of area under cultivation as also in the lowering of the effort to grow a minimum crop. In case of lower assessment, it was argued, the 'whole land would be sub-let and the original owners would cease to cultivate'. This opinion about the average cultivator led the land settlement officers to increase the burden of taxation on inferior lands.

The essence of the regressive taxation was that the better land was subjected to lighter and the inferior land to heavier land revenue demand. The most reasoned out advocacy of such a principle was made by Wingate while introducing land settlement for the first time in Mewar. He ridiculed the older system of land revenue assessment since that was based upon produce rather than upon possession of land[10]. Wet (irrigated), manured and dry lands were subjected to different rates on account of the difference in the gross produce of these lands. The assumption of the prevalent theory of assessment was that every cultivator should have a certain quantity of foodgrains for his family to live on. Wingate, for reasons of his own, chose to attribute this difference in the produce of different fields to 'careless cultivation'. Instead of realising the limitations of irrigation and manure, he closed his eyes to see the obvious and put forward a new approach to land settlement and related questions. He argued that if a cultivator, by careless cultivation of 10 bighas, got 20 maunds food for his living, he would not cultivate carefully a lesser area. Wingate ignored the hard realities of shortage of irrigation facilities and the inferior quality of a large portion of land in the state; he went on to say that 'the poor or lazy pay less than the rich or industrious'. He cited the example of three fields of equal area—wet and manured, dry and manured, and only dry—whose production was in the ratio of 5:4:3. On the principle of 50% produce of the first two and 1/3rd of the third field, he showed that the three paid in the ratio of 2½, 2 and 1. Thus in case of a production of 50, 40 and 30 maunds, they paid 25, 20 and 10 maunds to the state. This, he argued, was calculated to 'cripple a country, to hinder the rich from investing in land and the poor from making any effort, to encourage idleness and repress industry'.[11] It was tantamount, in his words, 'to pounce on the well-to-do with heavy rates and let the poor off easily'. He felt that if a poor man had 5 bighas and manure for 2, it is better that he should give up the 3 bighas to a man who can fully use them. His way of thinking was that by poor crops on the 3 bighas, the poor man had starved the country to the extent of 30 maunds every year (@ 10 maunds per bigha of manured land). He called it false pity for the man who had lost the means of utilising the lands he had inherited or possessed.

The ultimate result, according to him, was that 'the country lost the produce and the state the revenue'. This approach was sufficiently indicative of his attitude to the cultivator in general.

He did not answer the questions: Where were the irrigation facilities to convert *barani* into *peeval* lands? Where was the manure to increase the productivity of soil? And, more importantly, where was the additional man-power to cultivate extra land? Wingate, apparently logical, was without solid basis since the man power in the state did not increase during the next three decades.

Wingate claimed that the main feature of the settlement in the five Jat parganas was that it equally distributed the wet rates and lightened the burden on dry lands and poor soils. Comparing the settlement rates with the earlier ones, Wingate claimed that the rates for wet and dry lands had been reduced.[12]

Table 3.16 apparently sustains the claim of Wingate about the lowering of land revenue demand on both types of lands. However, a closer look at the detailed Table 3.17 of land area and land revenue rates in the two broad categories of land, reveals that the areas of each were changed so drastically that the incidence of revenue demand operated lightly on better and harshly on inferior quality soils. The revenue rates of each soil category were by comparison lowered, so that the real extent and nature of regressive land taxation remained hidden from the public eye. The new measurement of land in the five Jat pargannahs of Mewar is shown in Table No. 3.17.[13]

TABLE: 3.16

Assessment Rates (old and new) in Mewar

Pargana	Wet Land Rates						Dry Land Rates		Total Area in Bighas	
	1874			1885			1874	1885	1874	1885
	Peeval	Gorma	Average	Peeval	Kabil	Average				
Rashmi	7.00	2.69	5.30	6.13	2.72	5.70	1.47	1.17	31917½	37140
Galund	6.00	3.50	5.66	4.87	2.09	4.66	0.76	0.71	12217½	13000
Pottah	5.69		5.69	5.51	4.25	5.30	1.74	0.74	5356¾	9079½
Sarra	6.32	2.94	4.70	4.73	2.36	4.32	1.01	0.61	20809	29391
Relmangra	6.78	2.65	5.38	5.19	2.20	4.73	0.78	0.49	18441½	24170
									88741¼	112780½

TABLE: 3.17

Settlement of 1885 in the 5 Jat parganas (Mewar)

Pargana	Year of Settlement	Wet Land (In Bighas) Peeval (Irrigated)	Wet Land Rate Per Bigha	Wet Land Gorma/Kabil Manured Irrigable	Wet Land Rate	Dry Land (In Bighas) Mal	Dry Land Rate per Bigha	Dry Land Rankad	Dry Land Rate per Bigha	Total Area In Bighas	Total Area Rate per Bigha	Amount of Land Revenue
Rashmi	1874	6957½	7.00	4487¾	2.69	9883	1.94	10579¼	1.05	31917½	2.87	94890.00
Average rate		11455 @ 5.30				20462 @ 1.47						
	1885	9657	6.13	1392	2.72	26091	1.17			37140	2.68	98239.00
Average rate		11049 @ 5.70										
Galund	1874	3364½	6.00	713½	3.50	4773	0.76	3366½	0.40	12217½	2.31	30888.00
Average rate		4078 @ 5.66				8139 @ 0.61						
	1885	4983	4.87	392	2.09	7625	0.71			13000	2.43	32800.00
Average rate		5375 @ 4.66										
Potlah	1874	2851	5.69			2505¾	1.74			5356¾	3.87	28841.00
	1885	3227½	5.51	649¼	4.25	5202¾	0.74			9079½	2.69	26500.00
Average rate		3877 @ 5.30										

(Contd.)

(*Table 3.17 Contd.*)

Pargana	Year of Settlement	Wet Land (In Bighas)				Dry Land (In Bighas)				Total Area		Amount of Land Revenue
		Peeval (Irrigated)	Rate Per Bigha	Gorma/ Kabil Manured Irrigable	Rate	Mal	Rate per Bigha	Rankad	Rate per Bigha	In Bighas	Rate per Bigha	
Sarra	1874	5184¾	6.32	4781	2.94			10842	1.01	20809	2.77	61947.00
Average rate		9967 @ 4.70										
	1885	8690½	4.73	1840¾	2.36			18859¾	0.61	29391	1.94	61000.00
Average rate		10531 @ 4.32										
Relmangra	1874	6858½	6.78	3503½	2.65	471		7608¼		18441½	3.37	67828.00
Average rate		10362 @ 5.38				8079 @ 0.78						
	1885	8979	5.19	1081	2.20	14110	0.49			24170	2.31	61000.00
Average rate		10069 @ 4.73										
Total	1874									88254	3.13	276413.00
Revenue	1885									112777	2.43	275088.00

It is significant to point out that though the total land under cultivation, now brought under revenue assessment, had been increased by 24523 bighas (28%), the total revenue demand had been lowered by Rs. 1325. This did not lead to a reduction in the general rate of land revenue demand. What had been done was that the demand on the cultivated *peeval* and *gorma* lands was lowered; the inferior class of land was subjected to a heavier rate and fresh untaxed land had been brought in the tax net. The irrigated land area had been enhanced by 10322 bighas but the rate per bigha had been lowered in every pargana. The land revenue rate of *peeval* land was reduced by 12.4% and 18.8% in Rashmi and Galund parganas, by 25 and 23.45 per cent in Sarrah and Relmangra parganas respectively; in Potlah pargana, the reduction was only by 3.16%. The *gorma* area had been reduced by 8130 bighas and all of it had gone to *peeval* category.

The land revenue rate had been reduced for the best kind of *peeval* (irrigated) land in accordance with Wingate's basic idea behind the settlement viz., the rich have to be given relief so that they were able to invest in land either by way of addition to irrigation or to inputs of manure. The reduction of assessment was implemented in a very subtle manner so that the reality of heavy assessment on the poor lands may not be apparent on the surface. The land revenue rates for every class of land—*peeval, gorma, mal,* and *rankad*—had been reduced so that the land settlement may be acceptable to the peasantry. But in reality what had been done was to change the category of inferior lands by upgrading them so that a larger area of land was brought to the higher category of soil. The real beneficiary were the owners of irrigated land. The benefits to the richer peasants and the oppression and marginalisation of the poorer farmers were both camouflaged. The impoverishment of the common farmers brought about by the land settlement was later on thrust either on their social customs or on their lethargy and inactivity. The real mechanism of settlement changes is being explained with the help of some tables.

TABLE: 3.18

Regressive Taxation in Mewar
Peeval (irrigated) Land (bighas)

	Rashmi	Galund	Potlah	Sarra	Relmangra	Total Area
1874	6957	3364	2851	5184	6858	25214
1885	9657	4983	3227	8690	8979	35536
Difference + -	+2700(38%)	+1619(48%)	+376(13.2%)	+3506(67%)	+2121(31%)	+10322(40.9%)
Diff. inland revenue (rate) In Rupees	-0.87(12%)	-1.13(18%)	-0.18(3%)	-1.56(25%)	-1.59(23%)	

Wingate repeatedly said that there had been no increase in irrigation sources since the time of Maharana Swarup Singh who died in 1861. Where from did the increase in *peeval* land area come? It came largely from *gorma* (manured) land which had been assessed earlier at a much lower rate and was now classified with *peeval* lands and subjected to higher land revenue. A look at the table, given below, of *gorma* land show that in Rashmi, Sarra and Relmangra, the increase of *peeval* land was on account of transfer of *gorma* to *peeral* category.

TABLE:3.19

Gorma Land (bighas)

	Rashmi	Galund	Potlah	Sarra	Relmangra	Total for 4 Parganas
1874	4487	713	—	4781	3503	13484
1885	1392	392	649	1840	1081	4705
Difference	-3095 (68.9%)	-321 (45%)	+649	-2941 (61.5%)	-2422 (69%)	-8779 (65%)
Land Rev. difference (Rs.) (Table 3.16)	+.03 (1%)	1.41 (40%)		-.58 (19%)	-.45 (17%)	

As compared to 1874, the *gorma* land had been reduced by 3095, 2941, 2422 bighas in Rashmi, Sarra and Relmangra parganahs respectively. In Potlah, the *gorma* area had increased by 649 bighas because there were no figures available for 1874. The decrease of *gorma* lands in Rashmi, Galund, Sarra and Relmangra and its increase in Potlah were examples of taxing inferior lands at a higher rate and were thus two sides of the same process. If there was *gorma* land, a substantial part of it was included in the *peeval* category; if there was no *gorma* land, mal land area was brought to the *gorma* category. Thus more land was brought in the higher categories and was subjected to heavier assessment. The rate of land revenue per bigha was reduced but inferior land was classified as superior land though irrigation and manure facilities had not increased during the last two decades. The peasants who owned richer and better lands were given some relief in revenue demand. The idea behind the pre-settlement land revenue policy was to ensure a sustenance to the poorest farmers by reducing the government demand on inferior lands; the richer lands were subjected to heavier rates of taxation as they could pay. Wingate set out to change all this. The *gorma* land which was assessed at a lower rate, had been reduced by 8779 bighas or 65%. Thus although the rate of land revenue for *peeval* lands had been reduced, 2/3rd of *gorma* land was subjected to heavier rate of assessment by being included in the *peeval* category.

In the Galund pargana on the south of river Banas, Wingate increased the *peeval* area by 1300 bighas. This was done partly by increasing the average area irrigated by a *seja* well, partly by including 321 bighas of *gorma* land to the *peeval* category, and partly by including a large tract of black soil, reserved for growing fodder earlier into irrigated lands, as it could grow wheat. He argued that fodder for cattle could be easily brought by railways to Nathdwara. This was the only parganah where dry land area came to be reduced by about 500 bighas because *peeval* area had increased and more land was not available. In Potlah 1026 bighas of irrigated land were added and 2700 bighas of new dry lands had been brought under assessment for the first time (Table 3.17). In Sarra more than 3500 bighas of *gorma* land, formerly assessed at Rs. 2.94 were brought to the *peeval* category and assessed at Rs. 4.73 per bigha. There was an increase of 8000 bighas in the dry land area. In the Relmangra parganah (which had led the revolt of 1875) the *peeval* area was increased by 2100 bighas of *gorma* land which was now subjected to heavier taxation; 6000 bighas of *barani* land were brought under revenue assessment.

Wingate's claim for reducing the land revenue demand may be looked at a bit closely. In *gorma* lands, if inferior lands were not brought into it, the rates of land revenue were either marginally raised as in Rashmi or were marginally reduced by Rs. 0.45 in Relmangra for political reasons and only Rs. 0.58 in Sarra because 600 bighas had been brought into this category; but if inferior lands were brought to the *gorma* category, in a larger measure, the revenue for it was substantially lowered though for the cultivator it was much higher than what had been paid earlier. e.g. in Galund, the rate was slashed by 40% because it was inferior land which had been brought to this category, the old *gorma* had gone to the *peeval* category.

Dry Land (Table 3.17)

Here *mal* and *rankad* areas were bracketted together and a common rate was evolved for them. The total area of these lands had been increased by 21860 bighas (43.7%). This new area, mostly in the *rankad* category may have been cultivated earlier but had not been subjected to any tax.

A large part of these lands were meant for growing *kharif* and fodder crops. Large areas of such lands were left uncultivated by rotation and no one had bothered to measure them or to subject such lands as gave a *kharif* crop to more than a nominal taxation. In the five parganas, a total area of 50027 bighas of land was subjected to land revenue in 1871 at different rates ranging from Rs. 0.40 to 1.94 per bigha. In 1885 a total of 71887 bighas was brought under revenue assessment at rates ranging from 0.49 to 1.17 per bigha. The land area had thus been increased by 21860 bighas.

Wingate's claim that the main feature of the settlement was to lighten the burden on dry lands and on poorer soils was a tall claim because burden had been imposed on lands which did not pay any land revenue earlier.[14] The rate of land revenue had been kept low to persuade people to accept the change; yet the rate in the new settlement depended on the amount of land brought for the first time under the revenue net. In Rashmi, the rate was Rs. 0.12 more than the old rate for *rankad* land because only 5600 bighas had been brought in the revenue net. 9883 bighas of *mal* lands were given relief. But 10579 bighas of *rankad* land was subjected to heavier revenue and 5629 bighas (26091-20462) of dry land which did not pay any revenue earlier had to pay Rs. 1.17 per bigha. In Galund it was equal to the old rate for *mal* since very little fresh land had been brought under assessment. In fact 3366 bighas of *rankad* land was charged at Rs. 0.71 per bigha in place of Rs. 0.40. In the three remaining parganas of Sarra, Potlah and Relmangra, 8017, 2697, 6031 bighas respectively had been added; therefore, the rate for dry lands was reduced substantially. The process of subjecting new land to revenue assessment had to be accepted by the peasantry. Once the land had been assessed, the bait held out for cultivators was that they were free to grow any crop they liked since it was land and not crop which was the basis of revenue demand. This led to devoting lesser area to fodder crops. The shortage of fodder crops and the reduction of land under lucerne grass was to prove very destructive of human life and cattle during the famine of 1899. This area now paid a land revenue of Rs. 16378. Further, 21553 bighas of *rankad* land in four out of five parganas had been paying revenue at lesser rates; this was now subjected to a marginally heavier tax. The extra income of Rs. 16378 plus the over all reduction of Rs. 1325, i.e. Rs. 17703 had been gifted in relief to the owners of wet lands. The cultivators of inferior lands had been taxed to provide relief to the cultivators of better lands.

The essence of the policy of regressive taxation at Bharatpur lay in the new revenue rates for *sairaba* (flooded) lands. The northern tehsils of the state were flooded by Ruparail stream; the southern tehsils were flooded by Banganga and Gambhiri. Dwyer, for the first time, divided the *sairaba* into *sairaba hal, sairaba sabiqa* and *sairaba barishi* at Bharatpur. In the earlier settlement, the first category only existed; the second and the third were included in the *barani* area. Dwyer defined *sairaba hal* as land flooded and actually inundated; *sairaba sabiqa* as land 'sometimes inundated and actually inundated within the last five years though not in the year of assessment'. *Sairaba barishi* was land lying at the foot of the hills and advantaged by hill drainage.[15] Dwyer projected the classification as an improvement since he devised different rates for the *hal, sabiqa* and *barishi* categories. But the reality was that he taxed *barani* land (which had not been inundated) as *sairaba sabiqa* at a rate which included some water rate also. The rate was 'intermediate between the rates for *sairaba hal* and *barani*'. He knew that the system was unjust to the peasantry but he pretended to justify the policy change by casting aspersions on the integrity of the state administration. The end result was that *sairaba sabiqa* had to pay for 5 years for rain water which it received once in five years. The rates for *sairaba sabiqa* and *sairaba barishi* were 33 to 50% higher than those for *barani* lands. The area of *sairaba sabiqa* and *barishi* is given below to explain the implications of the change as contrasted with the figures of 1890.[16]

TABLE: 3.20

Sairaba and Barani Land (Bharatpur)

Tehsil		Hal	Sabiqa	Barishi	Total	Barani	Total Sairaba and barani
Gopalgarh	1890				84254	50087	134341
	1898	60755	33974	5538	100264	59332	159596
Pahari	1890				32243	63555	95798
	1898	1400	36152	10405	47958	55961	103919
Kama	1890				29780	79841	109621
	1898	109	23641	11576	35326	85338	120664
Deeg	1890				98	101479	101577
	1898	23	7846	14665	22534	102017	124551
Kumher	1890				399	75743	76142
	1898				364	98529	98893

(Contd.)

(Table 3.20 Contd.)

Tehsil		Hal	Sabiqa	Barishi	Total	Barani	Total Sairaba and barani
Akheygarh	1890				240	77446	77686
	1898				432	90593	91025
Bharatpur	1890	8211	1260	60	9531	54823	64354
	1898	15039	4054	-	19093	69722	88815
Nagar	1890				3	70126	70129
	1898	1596	392	237	2225	85465	87690
Rupbas	1890				13124	23107	36231
	1898	4972	11401	250	16623	51668	68291
Oochain	1890				18217	46811	65028
	1898	31798	14447	480	46725	44602	91327
Biyana	1890				18411	63479	81890
	1898	12556	3602	1827	17985	76556	94541
Bhusawar	1890	4162	943		5105	91000	96105
	1898	8498	253		9114	103708	112822
State	1890				211405	797497	1008902
Total	1898	136746	135762	44978	317486	923491	1240977

Looked at comparatively, the *sairaba hal* area had come down by 35% ; the area had been increased by an equal '*sabiqa*' area; by adding the *barishi* area, the total *sairaba* had increased by 50%. The revenue rates of the three types of *sairaba* land depended on the increase or decrease of the area.[17]

The *sairaba hal* rates were lowered in central tehsils where the *sairaba* was negligible; it was enhanced at Bharatpur where the area had increased. The *sairaba sabiqa* and *barishi* had been earlier charged at *barani* rates and by comparison, the rates had been enhanced by 60 to 73% in the northern and 24 to 30% in the central tehsils and Nagar. But in the southern tehsils of Oochain, Biyana and Bhusavar, it was enhanced by 38, 125 and 53 per cent in case of *sairaba sabiqa* and by 55, 86 and 53 per cent in the case of *barishi* respectively. This enhancement of land revenue demand was a retrograde step because *barani* soil had been made to pay 33 to 50% higher revenue rates which included water charges for rain water or for floods which may occur once in 5 years. Could a more regressive land taxation be devised anywhere? The oppressive nature of a land revenue structure which included water charges for the next four years after the year in which nature had been bountiful enough to provide water can only be visualised. On the one hand Dwyer had been strengthening the state authority; on the other he was not trusting the state machinery to levy water charges when actual water had been supplied. He justified his retrograde step by taking cover under the plea of zamindars' lack of trust in the local administration which he had thoroughly restructured himself. The new intermediaries, created now for the first time, could not have done so. He was in fact subjecting the poorer peasantry to heavier taxation.

TABLE: 3.21

Sairaba Land Revenue Rates in Bharatpur

	Tehsil	In 1890 Hal Rs.	In 1897-99 Hal Rs.	Salika Rs.	Barishi Rs.	1897-99 Sairaba Average Rs.
Northern	Gopalgarh	2-08	2=25	1=50	1-50	1-95
	Pahari	1=59	2=00	1=37	1-37	1-39
	Kama	1=45	2=00	1=25	1-25	1-25
	Deeg	—	2=00	1=19	1-12	1-14
Central	Kumher	1=41	—	0=71		
	Akheygarh	1=33	1=00	—		
	Bharatpur	1=33	1=50	1=12		
	Nagar	0=72	0=94	0=94		
Southern	Ruphas	1=69	1=62	1=25	1-25	1-32
	Oochain	1=75	1=75	1=00	1-12	1-52
	Biyana	1=61	1=62	1=37	1-12	1-55
	Bhusavar	1=72	1=50	1=12	1-12	1-47

The retrogressive policy was implemented in another manner. In 1890 a total of 797497 bighas was *barani* land in Bharatpur. Out of this, 135762 and 44978 bighas of *sabiqa* and *barishi* lands respectively were subjected to a higher revenue demand (Table No. 3.20). The *barani* area was enhanced by the addition of 306734 bighas of fallow land by classifying the latter as *barani*. This had been charged at nominal rates earlier. Dwyer thus perfected the art of claiming extension of agriculture by changing the natural class of soil both at Alwar and Bharatpur. The difference was that at Alwar he could not find land to be added to the cultivated area. He had to remain content by transferring *bhur* land area to *mattiyar* quality and by enhancing the revènue demand. He abandoned soil classification at Bharatpur; he had wanted to do the same at Alwar also but could ṅot do so because his predecessor Colvin had approved it. At Bharatpur, no such classification had been done by any of his predecessors. He therefore found it easy to shift *barani/bhur*, new fallow/to *sairaba sabiqa* and *barishi/barani* respectively. The peasantry was thus burdened by a heavier land revenue for cultivating inferior quality land area. The percentage of cropped area revealed the helplessness of the *barani* cultivator who had to double crop his land whatever it was worth. Some statistics of the croped area reveal the state of helplessness of the peasantry.[18]

TABLE: 3.22

Cropped Area in *Sairaba* and *Barani* Lands in 1898-99

Tehsil	Sairaba Area	Barani Area	Total	Percentage of Cropped area	
				Sairaba	Barani
Gopalgarh	67900	108094	175994	67.7	182
Pahari	1515	111809	113324	3.2	199
Kaman	25178	114983	140161	71.3	134.7
Deeg	23	142178	142201	.1	139

Kumher	368	116231	116599	101	117.9
Akheygarh	443	102913	103356	102	113.6
Bharatpur	15633	91439	107072	81.8	131
Nagar	2219	95738	97957	99.7	112
Rupbas	5945	73052	78997	35.7	141.4
Oochain	38557	70110	108667	82.5	157
Biyana	15859	102838	118697	88.2	134.3
Bhusawar	9373	125197	134570	102.8	120.7
State Total	183013	1254582	1437595	57.6	135.8

The impoverishment of the agricultural masses was writ large in the Bharatpur State when statistical details of the cropped area in the various tehsils was looked at. While O Dwyer and the earlier Political Agents were making bold claims for the enhancement of *chahi* cultivation and consequent peasant prosperity, the pattern of cropped area gave a lie to it.

	% of total area	% of total cultivated area	Double cropped
Chahi	21.28	14.6	
Sairaba	20.96	11.6	
Barani	57.75	73.8 (+16%)	= 28%

The *barani* land could normally produce one crop—the kharif—and in that case also its maturity rate was on the average around 70%. The *rabi* crop matured in a far lower percentage and no record had been kept about it. The double cropping of a large area of *barani* land meant that the peasantry was forced to depend on *barani* agriculture, other sources of income having been closed to it. Only less than 15% cultivation had secured *chahi* irrigation; less than 12% depended on *sairaba* and could grow *rabi* crop only. *Barani* cultivation had multiplied when compared to earlier periods.

The new fallow area declined by 377150 bighas and all of it went to cultivation—*barani* and *sairaba*. The *sairaba* of Ruparel had declined considerably but Dwyer had charged *sairaba* rate from *sairaba sabiqa* also saying that when it was flooded the water rate would not be charged. This was regressive and impoverishing taxation.

The principle that the irrigated and better lands were to be provided relief while the lower quality irrigated lands were subjected to heavier taxation was implemented at Jhalawar very thoroughly. The highest rates for irrigated lands in central Jhalawar were substantially reduced while the lowest rates were equally substantially enhanced. The highest irrigated rates were reduced by a varying percentage upto 39%. In 6 tehsils it was reduced upto 15%, in 2 tehsils between 16 and 30%, in 5 tehsils it was reduced by more than 30%; only in two tehsils it was raised upto 5%. On the other hand the lowest rates in the irrigated category were enhanced in a big way; in 5 tehsils it was enhanced upto 100% ; in 8 tehsils between 100 to 200% ; in two tehsils by more than 200%. The difference between the highest and lowest average rates for irrigated category was thus reduced by lowering the highest average rate by Rs. 1.84 per acre and by increasing the lowest rate by Rs. 3.50 per acre. In the unirrigated category also, the highest rate was reduced in 3 parganas by 1-15%, in 8 parganas by 16-30%, and in 2 parganas by 30-50%, in one pargana of Taleti, it was reduced by more than 50%, and in Upreti pargana of Shahabad, it was raised by 10%. The lowest rates of unirrigated lands were enhanced in 2 parganas by 28-30% ; in the remaining 13 parganas it was reduced by a percentage between 16 and 76. The rates are given below[19]:

TABLE: 3.23

Jhalawar Land Revenue Rates

(Amount in Rs.)

Pargana	Former Rates				New Rates			
	Irrigated		Unirrigated		Irrigated		Unirrigated	
	Highest	Lowest	Highest	Lowest	Highest	Lowest	Highest	Lowest
Central Jhalawar								
Suket	16.48	3.45	6.71	1.41	13.73	7.72	5.03	0.90
Chechat	15.90	3.10	6.13	1.02	10.91	6.23	5.04	0.84
Asnawar	14.87	3.34	5.83	0.94	13.73	5.91	4.51	0.39
Dilanpur	14.12	2.60	5.87	0.65	13.73	6.63	5.03	0.45
Aklera.	15.46	2.74	5.35	1.19	13.72	6.76	4.48	0.28
Bakani	16.86	3.71	7.01	1.27	13.73	6.90	5.03	0.60
Patan	15.40	3.02	5.87	1.03	13.74	6.76	5.04	0.84
Manohar Thana	13.05	2.20	6.47	0.40	13.72	6.16	4.56	0.47
Chipa Barode	14.12	2.30	5.33	0.70	12.68	4.88	4.52	0.39
Distt. Chowmehla								
Pachpahar	24.52	2.23	5.00	0.71	22.08	5.53	3.67	0.91
Awar	36.10	4.03	5.79	0.76	22.08	6.44	3.00	0.41

(Contd.)

(Table 3.23 Contd.)

(Amount in Rs.)

Pargana	Former Rates				Present Rates			
	Irrigated		Unirrigated		Irrigated		Unirrigated	
	Highest	Lowest	Highest	Lowest	Highest	Lowest	Highest	Lowest
Dug	40.22	4.78	6.70	0.90	24.97	6.25	3.90	1.17
Gungadhar	21.40	4.35	4.30	1.07	22.08	5.53	3.67	0.47
Distt. Shahabad								
Upreti	12.83	0.78	2.63	0.62	8.41	2.89	2.89	0.26
Talati	12.37	0.64	8.23	0.52	8.12	2.60	2.59	0.18
Average rates for the three districts								
Central Jhalawar	15.14	2.94	6.06	0.96	13.30	6.44	4.80	0.57
Difference					-1.84	+3.50	-1.26	-0.39
Chowmehla	30.56	3.85	4.95	0.86	22.80	5.94	3.56	0.74
Difference					-7.76	+2.09	-1.39	-0.12
Shahabad	12.60	0.71	5.43	0.57	8.26	2.75	2.74	0.22
Difference					-4.34	+2.04	-2.69	-0.35

The above statistics show that if the lower rate was reduced by 100%, it was a relief of Rs. 0.20 to 0.70 per acre in the unirrigated category. The amount of money was not much; the relief given to the highest rates for irrigated lands was substantial. This relief was compensated by raising the lowest irrigated rates. Secondly the real nature of impact of new revenue rates was camouflaged by working out the average demand per cultivated acre. The regressive taxation, of relieving the burden on the rich and increasing it on the poor and not so rich cultivator was thus hidden as the following table shows[20]:

TABLE: 3.24

Regressive Taxation at Jhalawar

Pargana	Average Rate	
	Former	Present
Suket	Rs. 4-49	Rs. 4-45
Chechat	4-45	4-52
Asnawar	4-50	4-79
Dilanpur	4-65	4-32
Aklera	3-46	3 72
Bakani	5-43	5-51
Patana	4-45	4-57
Manohar Thana	4-01	4-29
Chipa Barode	3-40	4-10
Average for Central Jhallawar	4-24	4-46
Pachpahar	4-00	4-00
Awar	4-72	4-97
Dug	5-43	5-00
Gungdhar	4-39	4-02
Average for Chowmehla	4-55	4-38
Upreti	2-24	1-92
Talaiti	3-32	2-97
Average for Shahabad	2-61	2-29

The averate rates given above conceal the real change which had been brought about. The average result was an increase of Rs. 0.22 in central Jhalawar and a reduction of Rs. 0.17 and Rs. 0.32 per acre in Chowmehla and Shahabad. It would appear to be a minor adjustment or a 6% increase in the total demand of the state as claimed by Abbott. This was a virtual deception practised on the posterity.

Raw took 3½ years to complete the land settlement of a small state like Karauli (January 1909 - August 1912). Even when he knew that the revenue incidence was very high, he did not suggest any lowering of revenue demand because the finances of the state did not permit it. He was content to say that the general condition of the people 'did not indicate a *crying* need for an all round reduction'.[21] He therefore declared his object to be 'to redistribute as equitably as possible an undoubtedly high revenue'. His 'equitable' principle was: "Where the revenue of a village was excessive, it was invariably on the irrigated fields that a reduction was given".[22] As an illustration, the best land in the most highly assessed village had paid Rs. 37/- an acre earlier; it was now assessed at Rs. 28/- an acre. He conceded that the incidence of assessed revenue on land would not be easy even 20 years later with normal price rise.

In Dungarpur the land revenue settlement was revised a third time in 1924 when the state came under the regency administration. The old land revenue rates, fixed by the British in 1905, were not enhanced in 1915 when the settlement had been revised by the state ruler. In 1924 the settlement introduced excessive subclassification. The soil of the state had been divided into seven classes at the 1915 settlement - *chahi, digar, talabi, rohan, sirma, sukhi* and *rankad*. Five of these were already divided into three classes; now each was first divided into two classes and thereafter each was subdivided into five classes, three of which were made applicable to earlier villages and the last two were confined to Bhil villages, surveyed for the first time now.[23] Each of the five sub-classes was held to be 75% productive of the immediately preceding class.

Supposing than an acre of chahi A and B produced 10 and 8 maunds of foodgrains, the five sub-classes were supposed to produce on the following scale[24]:

		Chahi A	Chahi B
Sub Class	I	10.00 maunds	8.00 maunds
	II	7.5 maunds	6.00 maunds
	III	5.62 maunds	4.5 maunds
	IV	4.21 maunds	3.37 maunds
	V	3.16 maunds	2.53 maunds

This minute sub-classification was not based on experimental yields of various fields. It turned out to be a device to cover up the arbitrariness and unfairness of the determination of land revenue demand which was enhanced by more than 50% in some villages. The seven earlier classes of soil had now been broken up into 60 sub-classes with as many rates. The total revenue demand had been enhanced by 40.2% and the land area had been enhanced by 64% when the population had not increased proportionately. The population had increased by 19% over the figures of 1911; but this entire growth would be of the age group of below 10 years which could not have taken to agriculture.

While the rates for superior classes of *chahi* lands were maintained at the old levels or slightly reduced, the rates for all other categories were substantially enhanced. The following (table 3.25) shows that the rates for first and second sub-classes of *chahi* soil in Sagwara and Dungarpur were reduced or kept at the same levels; only the third subclass in Sagwara and first subclass in Aspur had faced enhancement in rates; the second and third subclasses in Aspur also had reduced rates. The same treatment was not meted out to other kinds of soils.[25]

TABLE: 3.25

Comparative revenue rates of 1905 and 1924 (per acre) in Dungarpur

Circle		Chahi 1905	Chahi 1924 I	Chahi 1924 II	Chahi Average	Chahi % enhancement	Sirma 1905	Sirma 1924 I	Sirma 1924 II	Sirma Average	Sirma % enhancement	Sukhi 1905	Sukhi 1924 I	Sukhi 1924 II	Sukhi Average	Sukhi % enhancement
Sagwara	I	6.60	7.60	5.70	6.65	+1	3.69	4.67	3.89	4.28	+16	2.92	2.38	3.84	3.11	+6.5
	II	4.98	5.70	4.16	4.93	-1	2.74	3.65	2.85	3.25	+18.6	2.38	2.60	2.36	2.48	+4
	III	2.33	4.15	3.13	3.64	+56	1.79	2.60	2.08	2.34	+30.7	1.54	1.82	1.56	1.69	+10
Aspur	I	5.33	7.27	5.47	6.37	+19	2.98	4.57	3.65	4.11	+38	2.47	3.12	2.60	2.86	+16
	II	4.83	5.47	4.15	4.81	-0.5	2.74	3.37	2.85	3.11	+13.5	2.38	2.35	2.07	2.21	-7
	III	3.81	4.15	3.13	3.64	-4.5	2.25	2.60	2.08	2.34	+4	2.00	1.82	1.56	1.69	-15
Dungarpur	I	7.69	8.31	6.25	7.28	-5.3	4.03	5.20	4.16	4.68	+16	2.99	3.65	3.13	3.39	+13.3
	II	6.40	6.25	4.67	5.46	-15	2.62	3.90	3.12	3.51	+34	2.29	2.85	2.35	2.60	+13.5
	III	3.90	4.67	3.65	4.16	+6.6	2.24	3.02	2.36	2.69	+20	1.82	2.07	1.83	1.95	+7.2

The enhancement of sirma and sukhi land revenue rates told a different story. In sirma land except in the third quality of Aspur circle, there was an enhancement of 13.5% to 20% in five classes and of above 30% in the three classes of the three circles, the enhancement ranged from 4 to 7.2% in three circles and 10 to 16% in four circles. The relevant point here is not the rate of enhancement or reduction; it is the fact that superior soil rates were not enhanced to the same extent to which inferior soil rates were enhanced. Dungarpur, a backward hilly state, was no exception to the general British policy of taxing the poorer classes of soil heavier than the better quality of soil. This was the essence of regressive taxation.

At Alwar the settlement of 1876 had been very harsh as conceded by the Government also. A large number of owners had abandoned their lands during the famine of 1877-78 and migrated out of the state. In 1897-99 when Dwyer began to record ownership rights, most of the owners rushed back to claim their hereditary lands. Dwyer was in real difficulty in deciding about their rights. Knowing full well the hardships caused by the last settlement, he was not willing to bear the odium of being responsible for depriving a large section of the intermediaries who had been created by the British themselves of their lands. He, therefore, by mutual agreement, persuaded the temporary owners to abandon in favour of the original owners.[26] But he realised that the hardships of the landowners had to be reduced. He therefore took recourse to a maze of classification and subclassification of lands which could cover up the real hardship. The three natural classes of soil - *chiknot, mattiyar* and *bhur*—were made into five classes, *chiknot, mattiyar* I & II, and *bhur* I and II. Each of the natural classes of soil were divided into artificial seven classes—*chahi* (permanent, *kacha,* temporary), *Dahri* (*hal, sabiqa, barishi*) and *Barani.* Rates for 35 different classes were to be provided theoretically. A detailed table for the four eastern tehsils is being given below to explain what had been done by Dwyer to enhance the land revenue demand and yet show as if not much hardship had been caused.[27]

TABLE: 3.26

Comparative Cultivated Area (Bighas) at Alwar

Tehsil	Year	Chahi	Dahri	Barani	Total
Kishangarh	1876	23568	12631	105597	141796
	1897-98	28293	15814	101348	145455
Ramgarh	1876	10529	28621	62769	101919
	1897-98	19575	28912	57920	106407
Govindgarh	1876	4648	1343	33769	39760
	1897-98	9549	1605	28522	39676
Lachmangarh	1876	16442	21869	74223	112534
	1897-98	21921	22311	69718	113950
Total	1876	55187	64464	276358	396009
	1897-98	79338	68642	257508	405488
					+ 9479 or 2.39%

The total area under cultivation in the four tehsils increased by only 9479 bighas (2.39%), from 396009 to 405488 bighas; but the revenue demand had been raised from Rs. 666429 to Rs. 730000, i.e. 9.5%. The rates of *chahi* lands were marginally raised or substantially reduced in all classes in the four tehsils except in Kishangarh *mattiyar* I. *Dahri* land was subjected to heavier rates in all natural classes except in Govindgarh and Lachmangarh *chiknoot*. *Barani* soil rates were enhanced in 3 tehsils in *chiknoot* and in 2 tehsils in *mattiyar* I; in the rest it was reduced.[28] (Table No. 3.27)

But this reduction had camouflaged enhancement of land revenue. The inferior *barani* soil had been promoted to the higher class (as explained earlier); even if the rate for the higher class was reduced, the land still paid at a higher rate.

TABLE: 3.27

Comparative Revenue Rates at Alwar

(Amount in Rs.)

		Chiknoot			Mattiyar I			Mattiyar II		
		C	D	B	C	D	B	C	D	B
Kishangarh	1876	3.37	2.16	1.66	3.07	1.77	1-82	2-71	1=46	1=03
	1897	3.44	2.31	1.75	3.44	2-37	1-37	2-62	1-62	0-87
Ramgarh	1876	3.35	2.76	1.93	3.49	2.45	1.66	3.33	1.94	1-42
	1897	3.31	2.81	2.00	3.56	2.69	1.62	2.69	2.06	1-12
Govindpur	1876	3.64	3.20	1.98	3.55	3.15	1.75	-	2-21	1-57
	1897	3.69	3.19	2.19	3.25	3.19	1.94	2.19	-	1-37
Lachmangarh	1876	3.37	1.80	1.58	3.21	1.61	1.25	2.87	1.22	1-00
	1897	2.94	1.87	1.37	3.25	1.81	1.37	2.81	-	0.87

(Contd.)

(Table 3.27 Contd.)

(Amount in Rs.)

		Bhur I					Bhur II			
		C	D	B			C	D	B	Total Average Per Bighas
Kishangarh	1876	2=73	1=41	0-81	Kishangarh	1876	3-06	-	0-61	1-48
	1897	2=69	1=75	0-62		1897-98	2-00	1-50	0-50	1-51
Ramgarh	1876	2-95	1-70	0-99	Ramgarh	1876	3-26	1-73	0-71	1-88
	1897	2-44	2-06	0-87		1897-98	2-00	1-25	0-50	2-08
Govindpur	1876	3-35		1-22	Govindgarh	1876	2-84		0-99	1-90
	1897	1-50		0-87		1897-98	1-44		0-62	2-18
Lachmangarh	1876	2-81	0-92	0-84	Lachmangarh	1876	2-95	2-00	0-68	1-56
	1897	2-56	-	0-69		1897-98	2-50		0-44	1-63

C = Chahi

D = Dahri

B = Barani

TABLE: 3.27A

Percentage of enhancement of rates

Tehsil	Chahi					Dahri					Barani				
	Ch	MI	MII	BhI	BhII	Ch	MI	MII	BhI	BhII	Ch	MI	MII	BhI	BhII
Kishargarh	+2	+12	-4	-1½	-35	+7	+35	+10	+25		+6	-25	-16	-25	-20
Ramgarh	-1	+2	-20	-17	-42	+2	+10	+6	+21		+3	-2	-21	-12	-30
Govindgarh	+1	-9		-55	-20		+1				+11	+11	-14	-30	-37
Lachmangarh	-13	+1	-2	-6	-15	-4	+12				-14	+10	-13	-20	-35

Ch=chiknoot; M-I=Mattiyar I; M-II=Mattiyar II; BhI=Bhur I; BhII=Bhur II

In table No. 3.27 in Kishangarh tehsil, even though the rates for *barani* of *mattiyar* I and II had been lowered to Rs. 1.37 and 0.87 per bigha, the *barani* soil still paid higher than the old rate which was Rs. 0.81 and 0.61 per bigha because *barani, bhur* I and II had been promoted to *mattiyar* I and II. In Govindgarh the rates of *barani* in *chiknoot* and *mattiyar* soils were enhanced; in Lachhmagarh only the rates of *mattiyar barani* were enhanced.

The different land settlement officers had put forth sufficient statistical information regarding Ajmer Merwara. The land under actual cultivation, the area irrigated by a well in ordinary years and in years of famine, the area cropped and the area assessed was very well known. When inspite of this information, the district administration ignored the real situation, it may be justifiable to say that there was an element of policy in persisting to enforce a regressive land revenue settlement. The taxation of a much larger area than was actually cultivated, levying water rate on land which was not irrigated, and measuring a much larger area of land as *chahi* or *talabi* were elements in the regressive land revenue policy pursued in Ajmer Merwara district. As early as 1884, Whiteway had found, after a survey of the irrigating capacity of wells in a famine year, that it was 1/5th of a normal year.[29] He reported the following facts:

Total No. of wells	Wells which irrigated over½	from½to¼	Under¼	Wells which did not irrigated
10907	1869	1963	1551	5524
	(17.1%)	(18%)	(14.2%)	(50.7%)

He reached the conclusion that in a famine year, only 1/5th or 1/6th of the revenue could be paid from the proceeds of the cultivation and to take more would be either to trench on savings or involve borrowing. Yet the administration continued to collect, as much as it could, the normal year's revenue demand in a famine year.

The impact of excessive land revenue demand in the province of Ajmer Merwara may be seen in some relevant statistics. The land under cultivation increased during 1874-1884, though the figures of 1887 were slightly inflated. But after 1884 there was a decline in cultivated land area. During 1884-1908, the land under cultivation had fallen by 7032 acres i.e. by 3.7% while the population of the district had increased from 4.6 lacs in 1881 to 4.76 lacs in 1901 (3.5%) and to 5.01 lakhs in 1911. Land had ceased to be attractive as a means of subsistence. Both La Touche and Lupton had observed the tendency on the part of cultivators to abandon fields and to rush to work as wage earning labourers on the railway tracks or on roads.[30] And yet La Touche, while introducing a land revenue settlement in Ajmer, was keen to show that the British claimed a much lower percentage or share of the gross produce than the Indian states' rulers. He calculated that the incidence of land revenue demand was about one-sixth of the gross produce or about one-fifth of the gross produce in an ordinarily good year. He conceded that 40% of the produce was the cost of production; he thus wanted to show that when the past governments took 50% of the gross produce, hardly little more than subsistence was left to the cultivators. By comparison he wanted to show that the land revenue demand under British administration was very low.[31] Having established this hypothesis, it was natural to postulate that the district progressed in material prosperity. When the district did not do so, the counter reply was that it was so partly because of the money lender's heavy rate of interest and partly on account of the social customs of the peasants which did not allow money to be accumulated.

What was the reality? The available data pertaining to land revenue settlement needs to be seen a bit more closely. La Touche had evaluated the gross produce of the farmers at the prevalent market prices on the basis of an assumed yield per acre. He did not give all the statistics but these were available in later reports. The data of land area assessed, actually cultivated, the actual and assumed yield of different kinds of soils, the market price and the statutory price at which the cash revenue was calculated have been complied below. La Touche did not allow various deductions which should have been allowed. Lupton pointed out that the cultivator got the price for his field products which varied on an average about 20% less than the market retail price.[32] Certain deductions were also to be allowed for payment to the menials, cartage and field labourers. The statistics for a 20 year period for the five circles of Ajmer tehsil have been complied below to give the picture as it was.

Lupton gave details of land cultivation in Ajmer tehsil and showed that in all the four categories of cultivation, the area assessed was more than actually cultivated.[33]

TABLE: 3.28

Land Assessed and 15 Years' Average Cultivation in Ajmer Tehsil (1892-1907)

Tehsil Circle	Land Area	Kinds of Soil Area (Acres)				
		Chahi	Talabi	Abi	Barani	Total
Ajmer	Assessed	5172	166	1226	16000	22564
	Cultivated	4169	163	1136	12988	18456
Gangwana	Assessed	3549	815	1438	21223	27025
	Cultivated	2857	512	892	18205	22466
Pushkar	Assessed	681	96	977	3565	5319
	Cultivated	915	61	802	3480	5258
Rajgarh	Assessed	4258	1839	1903	17827	25827
	Cultivated	3974	978	1229	15245	21426
Ramsar	Assessed	4603	6237	2014	27171	40025
	Cultivated	3645	4304	1538	20076	29563
Total Tehsil	Assessed	18263	9153	7558	85786	120760
	Cultivated	15560	6018	5597	69994	97169

TABLE: 3.29

Actual and Assumed Yield Per Acre in Ajmer Tehsil
(In Maunds)

	Ajmer		Gangwana		Pushkar		Rajgarh		Ramsar		District as a whole	
	Actual	Assumed	Actual	Assumed	Actual	Assumed	Actual	Assumed	Actual	Assumed	Actual	Assumed
Maize	7.56	12.5	9.45	13.0	10.24	14.0	8.44	13.50	9.43	12.00	9.00	13.20
Jowar	2.89	2.5	2.31	4.25	2.48	3.75	1.90	4.00	2.85	2.75	2.75	3.35
Bajra	3.82	2.5	4.11	4.25	3.34	4.66	3.13	4.00	2.16	2.75	3.5	3.60
Wheat	12.13	12.0	13.17	13.50	8.93	14.00	10.59	13.50	8.27	12.00	9.5	13.20
Barley	13.61	16.00	13.29	18.50	9.79	20.00	11.62	15.00	10.95	14.00	12.00	16.70

Source : Lupton : Land and Water Revenue Report (1908) pp. 67 & 71

While calculating the land revenue demand, a certain estimate of the produce of different kinds of soils was formed. The extent to which the estimate of the assumed differed from the actual yield would decide the harshness or liberality of the land revenue settlement.[34] The assumed and actual yield of various kinds of soils of Ajmer tehsil is given in table 3.29.

The estimate of assumed produce was accepted by Lupton in 1908 to have been very much on the higher side; he did give more realistic figures of assumed produce but the land revenue demand was not brought down proportionately. The incidence of land revenue demand became oppressive because of the following four factors.

(i) The assessed area was invariably greater than the cultivated area.

(ii) The assumed yield was greater than the actual yield.

(iii) The matured area was lesser than the sown area. The yield of the crop was variable depending on the general timing of rainfall.

(iv) The conversion of yield into money was done at a fixed rate which was far higher than the prevalent rate; it was also higher than the rate which was paid to the cultivator.

The operation of these factors may be analysed in some detail.

The Assessed and the Cultivated Area

Lupton had highlighted the fact that Whiteway had assessed 18237 acres of *chahi* and 9263 acres of *talabi* lands in Ajmer tehsil. During a period of 15 years (1893-1907) 15560 acres of *chahi* and 6018 acres of *talabi* lands were irrigated. Thus 2677 + 3245 acres of land paid at the rate of *chahi/talabi* lands when they were, if cultivated, growing only barani crops.[35]

The Matured And The Sown Area

The percentage of matured area differed in barani, talabi, abi and chahi lands considerably. Data regarding matured area in 55 villages in Ajmer district in irrigated and abi lands for 15 years (1892-1907) was compiled; similarly data for barani lands for the whole district was compiled by Lupton. The full data is given in Appendices D & E; its consolidated result is being given below.

Assessed And Matured Area In Ajmer District
1892-1907

District	Kind of Land area (in Acres)			
	Assessed	Sown	Matured	Percentage
Chahi		4518	4414	97.7
Talabi		1772	1681	94.9
Abi		1402	1296	92.4
Barani	85956	76483	54395	71 on sown 63 on assessed

Conversion Of Yield Into Money

The land revenue demand was fixed after an evaluation of the value of the gross yield of the assessed land. La Touche had evaluated it at the prevailing retail prices. Lupton compiled the price data for 20 years (1887-1907) and determined the price for conversion into money. (Table 3.30).

During this period of 20 years, the incidence of land revenue demand increased by a varying percentage for the peasants growing the three crops. (Table No. 3.30)

	Enhancement on account of fixation of a higher price for the crops			
Crop	By 0 to 25%	26 to 50%	51 to 75%	Above 76%
Maize	in 7 years	in 8 years	in 2 years	nil
Barley	in 7 years	in 9 years		
Wheat	in 11 years	in 6 years		

The advantage on account of higher prevalent price was available in 2, 2 and 1 years only to the growers of maize, barley and wheat respectively.[36]

TABLE: 3.30

Comparison of Actual and pre-determined Crop rates for Ajmer (1887-1907) Rupees per Maund

Year	Market Retail Price			20% less Price paid to the cultivator			Price applied to gross produce
	Maize	Barley	Wheat	Maize	Barley	Wheat	
1887-88	2.06	2.07	3.55	1.66	1.67	2.84	Maize=2.14
1888-89	2.77	2.43	3.31	2.23	1.95	2.65	
1889-90	2.08	2.04	2.84	1.68	1.64	2.27	
1890-91	1.90	2.18	2.96	1.52	1.75	2.37	Barley=2.31
1891-92	2.60	2.30	3.27	2.08	1.84	2.62	
1892-93	2.03	1.58	2.98	1.63	1.27	2.38	
1893-94	1.34	1.45	2.48	1.08	1.16	1.98	
1894-95	1.37	1.60	2.62	1.10	1.28	2.10	
1895-96	2.19	2.35	3.25	1.77	1.88	2.60	
1896-97	3.57	3.18	4.35	Famine year			
1897-98	2.57	2.04	3.22	1.71	1.72	2.58	
1898-99	1.83	2.09	2.83	1.47	1.68	2.47	Wheat=3.19
1899-1900	4.08	3.51	4.18	Famine year			
1900-01	2.13	2.15	3.29	1.71	1.72	2.63	
1901-02	2.56	2.53	3.23	2.06	2.03	2.58	
1902-03	1.91	2.38	3.09	1.53	1.91	2.47	
1903-04	1.53	1.83	2.76	1.23	1.47	2.21	
1904-05	1.65	2.25	3.18	1.32	1.80	2.55	
1905-06	2.92	3.11	3.62	2.34	2.49	2.90	
1906-07	2.29	3.48	4.85	1.85	2.78	3.88	

The Assumed and the Actual Yield

The figures of assumed and actual yields in Ajmer tehsil have been given in table no. 3.29. Though Lupton did talk of reducing the assumed yield to a more realistic level, yet he does not appear to have implemented the recommendation he had made in his 'Assessment of Land and Water Revenue Report'. The land revenue demand from the district should have come down considerably, if the realistic level had been implemented. The assumed yield was, in the light of the above figures, higher by 36.2% on all the five crops.

Thus the land revenue demand which was claimed to be about 11% of the gross produce or 38.37% of the net assets, had increased as follows:

	Land revenue enhanced by %
(i) Difference between assumed and cultivated area	Barani by 58% Chahi and talabi by 27.4%
(ii) Difference between assumed and actual yield	on an average by 36.2%
(iii) Difference between pre-fixed and current price	for 8 years by 26 to 50% for 7 years by 25% for maize growers by 51 to 75% in 2 years

The actual yield of chahi, talabi and abi lands have been given in table no. 3.29 the cumulative effect over a period of 15 years was an enhancement by 231%. (Table No. 4.4) The price factor had not been worked out in that table.

Appendix-C

Arbitrary Changes in Soil Classification at Alwar

ALWAR		Soil Classification			
Tehsils	Year	Chiknot	Mattiyar	Bhur	Total
Kishangarh	1876	19851	69480	52465	141796
	1898	20354	95956	29078	145389
Difference		+ 503	+26476	-23387	+ 3593
Ramgarh	1876	30513	38650	32547	101710
	1898	28095	62432	13527	104054
Difference		- 2418	+23782	-19020	+ 2344
Govindgarh	1876	3170	28130	8319	39619
	1898	3147	34220	1966	39333
Difference		- 23	+ 6090	- 6353	- 286
Lachmangarh	1876	30381	61888	20254	112523
	1898	30393	68668	13508	112569
Difference		+ 12	+ 6780	- 6746	+ 46
Total of 4 Tehsils		- 1926	+63128	-55506	+ 5697
Tijara	1876	nil	45107	121955	167062
	1898	nil	56017	113732	169749
Difference			+10910	- 8223	+ 2687
Bahrod	1876	nil	87528	71614	159142
	1898	nil	95893	63928	159821
Difference			+ 8365	- 7686	+ 679
Mandawar	1876	4999	71243	48745	124987
	1898	6465	80168	42670	129303
Difference		+ 1466	+ 8925	- 6075	+ 4314
Katumbar	1876	3082	70875	28761	102718
	1898	7825	83139	6847	97811
Difference		+ 4743	+12264	-21914	- 4907
Rajgarh	1876	15746	43816	8900	68462
	1898	11718	47522	5858	65098
Difference		- 4028	+ 3706	- 3042	- 3365
Total of 5 Tehsils		+ 2181	+44170	-46940	- 589

Alwar	1876	42941	110657	11561	165159
	1898	45715	108361	15238	169314
Difference		+ 2774	- 2296	+ 3677	+ 4155
Bansur	1876	4319	37432	102218	143969
	1898	6216	49724	99449	155389
Difference		+ 1897	+12292	- 2769	+ 11420
Thanaghazi	1876	9477	30235	5415	45127
	1898	16626	24714	3595	44935
Difference		+ 7149	- 5521	-1820	- 192
Total of 3 Tehsils		+11820	+4475	- 912	+ 15383
Total	1876	164479	695041	512755	1372275
	1898	176554	806814	409397	1392765
		+ 12075	+ 111773	- 103358	+20490
		+ 7.3%	16%	- 20%	+ 1.5%

The above data is based on Table no. 1 at the end of the three separate volumes of Alwar Tehsil assessment reports by M.F.O Dwyer.

Appendix-D

Statement showing Matured Barani Cultivation in Ajmer-Merwara (Khalsa Area) 1893-1907 AD

	Total Khalsa Only						
Year FASLI	Total area sown	Matured area	4 anna less area i.e., failed	Percentage of failed to sown area	Produce maunds	Average Produce in maunds on Sown area	Matured area
1	2	3	4	5	6	7	8
Area assessed	85,956	...	...	...	...	...	...
1,300	81,683	72,487	9,196	11.3	2,59,721	3.18	3.58
1,301	82,487	76,559	5,928	7.2	2,10,779	2.56	2.75
1,302	74,412	66,885	7,527	10.1	2,01,472	2.71	3.01
1,303	70,950	55,206	15,744	22.2	1,14,164	1.61	2.07
1,304	71,088	50,461	20,627	29.1	81,858	1.15	1.62
1,305	85,068	73,285	11,783	13.9	1,83,548	2.16	2.50
1,306	66,812	48,357	18,455	27.7	76,181	1.14	1.58
1,307	69,239	3,479	65,760	94.9	4,275	.06	1.23
1,308	82,091	78,036	4,055	4.9	3,98,339	4.85	5.10
1,309	83,766	17,972	65,794	78.5	37,223	.44	2.07
1,310	77,706	65,173	12,533	16.2	1,71,865	2.21	2.64
1,311	85,202	65.122	20,080	23.6	1,32,839	1.56	2.04
1,312	89,799	64,919	24,880	27.7	1,25,113	1.39	1.93
1,313	48,549	8,410	40,139	82.5	10,664	.22	1.27
1,314	78,394	69,578	8,816	11.3	2,10,856	2.69	3.03
Total	11,47,246	8,15,929	3,31,317	29	22,18,897	1.93	2.72
Average	76,483	54,395	22,088	29	1,47,926	1.93	2.72

Based on Lupton: Water Revenue Report, p.24.

Appendix-E

Statement showing Produce under each Class of Soil, District Ajmer, in 55 Villages.

Year (Fasli)	Chahi				
	Total sown area	Matured area	Produce	Average Produce on Sown area	Average Produce on Matured area
1300	3,721	3,475	40,854	10.98	11.76
1301	5,834	5,622	52,871	9.06	9.40
1302	5,673	5,598	60,790	10.72	10.86
1303	6,093	6,024	59,800	9.81	9.93
1304	6,178	6,137	62,220	10.07	10.14
1305	6,209	6,121	67,265	10.83	10.99
1306	5,336	5,301	49,438	9.28	9.33
1307	3,258	3,127	29,202	8.96	9.34
1308	3,462	3,433	49,311	14.21	14.36
1309	4,146	3,872	37,669	9.09	9.73
1310	3,725	3,717	41,686	11.19	11.22
1311	3,933	3,918	43,512	11.06	11.11
1312	4,027	3,870	31,736	7.88	8.20
1313	2,743	2,574	30,918	11.27	12.01
1314	3,431	3,424	48,650	14.18	14.21
Total	67,769	66,213	7,05,924	10.41	10.66
Average	4,518	4,414	47,062	10.41	10.66

(Contd.)

(Contd.)

Year (Fasli)	Talabi				
	Total sown area	Matured area	Produce	Average Produce on Sown area	Average Produce on Matured area
1300	1,194	1,179	11,199	9.38	9.50
1301	1,289	1,260	11,705	9.08	9.29
1302	2,703	1,813	16,180	5.99	8.92
1303	2,244	2,222	15,377	6.85	6.92
1304	2,156	2,146	19,547	9.07	9.11
1305	2,625	2,616	23,904	9.11	9.14
1306	1,833	1,826	16,782	9.16	9.19
1307	1,119	1,020	9,418	8.42	9.23
1308	1,810	1,807	19,726	10.90	10.92
1309	1,581	1,438	13,077	8.27	9.09
1310	1,649	1,622	13,399	8.13	8.26
1311	2,064	2,050	17,009	8.24	8.30
1312	1,291	1,279	8,400	6.51	6.57
1313	276	202	517	1.87	2.56
1314	2,748	2,740	39,537	14.39	14.43
Total	26,582	25,220	2,35,777	8.87	9.35
Average	1,772	1,681	15,718	8.87	9.35

Year (Fasli)	Abi				
	Total sown area	Matured area	Produce	Average Produce on Sown area	Average Produce on Matured area
1300	1,450	1,400	10,952	7.55	7.82
1301	1,663	1,634	10,509	6.32	6.43
1302	1,669	1,658	11,529	6.91	6.95
1303	1,675	1,561	8,310	4.96	5.32
1304	1,286	1,233	5,456	5.80	6.05
1305	1,483	1,408	7,599	5.12	5.40
1306	1,365	1,279	5,619	4.12	4.39
1307	742	607	3,896	5.25	6.42
1308	1,551	1,459	9,384	6.05	6.43
1309	1,250	1,068	6,030	4.82	5.65
1310	1,615	1,495	9,880	6.12	6.61
1311	1,611	1,448	7,912	4.91	5.46
1312	1,081	881	3,071	2.84	3.49
1313	752	522	2,804	3.73	5.37
1314	1,835	1,779	13,252	7.22	7.45
Total	21,028	19,432	1,18,203	5.62	6.08
Average	1,402	1,296	7,880	5.62	6.08

(Contd.)

(Contd.)

Year (Fasli)	Total				
				Average Produce on	
	Total sown area	Matured area	Produce	Sown area	Matured area
1300	6,365	6,054	63,005	9.90	10.41
1301	8,786	8,516	75,085	8.55	8.82
1302	10,045	9,069	88,499	8.81	9.76
1303	10,012	9,807	83,487	8.34	8.51
1304	9,620	9,516	89,223	9.27	9.38
1305	10,317	10,145	98,768	9.57	9.74
1306	8,534	8,406	71,839	8.42	8.55
1307	5,119	4,754	42,516	8.31	8.94
1308	6,823	6,699	78,421	11.49	11.71
1309	6,977	6,378	56,776	8.14	8.90
1310	6,989	6,834	64,967	9.30	9.51
1311	7,608	7,416	68,433	8.99	9.23
1312	6,399	6,030	43,207	6.75	7.17
1313	3,771	3,298	34,239	9.08	10.38
1314	8,014	7,943	1,01,439	12.66	12.77
Total	1,15,379	1,10,865	10,59,904	9.19	9.56
Average	7,692	7,391	70,660	9.19	9.56

Based on Lupton: Water Revenue Report, Appendix no. xii, p. 143.

Notes & References

1. C.J. Hamilton: Trade Relations between England and India (1600-1896), p. 228
2. Tod: Annals, vol. II, p.1117; B.L. Gupta: Trade and Commerce in the 18th Century, p. 228
3. C.J. Brooke: Report on the Famine of 1868, pp. 38-39. Foreign General A, March 1871, nos. 3-4
4. R.A.R., 1875-76, p.68; R.A.R., 1877-78, pp.37 & 237; R.A.R., 1886-87, p.98
5. Herbert Sherring: History of Mayo College, vol.1, pp. 30-31
6. Dholpur was given a loan of 4½ lakhs to undertake extraordinary expenses on the occasion of the visit of Duke and Duchess of Connaught in 1885 and to witness the military manoeuvres in February 1886 at Delhi.
7. R.A.R., 1875-76, pp. 38-39, 66-67, 72-73, 85, 112
8. The case of Mewar was instructive. The state had a surplus of Rs. 30 lakhs in 1862 when it came under the regency administration. By the year 1870-71 the annual budget showed a deficit of Rs. 43,555.00.
9. Each settlement officer talked of expansion of cultivation in virgin barani soil. All extension of cultivation in the last quarter of the 19th century was in barani soil. Smith and Wingate in Mewar and O'Dwyer in Alwar and Bharatpur laid great emphasis on this aspect of increasing cultivation. The point has been taken up later in the chapter for detailed discussion.
10. R.A.R., 1870-71, pp. 10-11
11. O'Dwyer: Report of Eastern Tehsils, Alwar, p.29; Report of Northern and Southern Tehsils, p. 42

11a. At Bharatpur the settlement of 1930 allowed deductions on three counts in a much greater measure than was done by the settlement of 1897-1900, pp. 48-50

Statement of Concessions for failed crops allowed at Bharatpur in 1930

Deductions allowed :	Settlement of 1930-31	Kama	Pahari	Deeg	Nagar	Bharatpur	Rupbas	Bayana	Weir	Nadbai	Kumher
		Percentage of crop by way of deductions.									
i. For Fodder:	1900	7	7	6	9	3	6	8	4	4	6
	1930	12	12	10	14	8	7	6	7		
ii. Menial Dues	1900	5	5	5	5	5	5	5	5	5	5
	1930	8	8	8	8	8	8	8	8	11	11
iii. Harvesting labour	1900	-	-		-	-	-	-	-		
	1930 for cotton: 1/10th; for all food crops 1/16th.										
iv. Failedcrops	1900										
	1930	8	4.8	7.2	8.9	11	10.4	11.95	4	10	15

The deductions of failed crops was on matured area and not on sown area.

12. The Government of India had asked the Ajmer administration to appoint a Committee to examine the question of opening a Capital and Revenue Account for older Tanks in Ajmer Merwara. The Government directed such an account be opened although the Committee had recommended against it. The amount of Rs.6, 17, 563.44 was to be shown as capital expenditure, and the water revenue was to be shown as return on the capital. Government of India, P.W.D., orders Nos. 148-51-A-1, May 29, 1874 (Government of India Orders on Accounts Tanks, Ajmer, 1875, pp. 1-8)
13. La Touche's Report, pp. 119, 123; Whiteway's Report, p. 16; Lupton's Final Settlement Report, Appendix III, p. 43
14. Wingate's Report of 1881, para 26 He wrote that the people distrusted the motives of the proposed settlement. (para 6) Even the chaindrawers had to be brought from outside the state.
15. Abbott: Land Settlement Report of Jhalawar, pp. 72-74
16. M.S.D. Butler: Final Report of the Second Settlement of the Kotah State, pp. 31-32
17. W. Raw: Final Report on the First Settlement of the Karauli State, 1909-12, p. 24
18. O'Dwyer: Final Report of Bharatpur, p. 37
19. R.A.R., 1868-69, pp. 125-126, 1870-71, p. 164
20. R.A.R., 1869-70, pp. 19-21
21. R.A.R., 1873-74, p. 155
22. Final Report of Bharatpur, pp. 5 and 83
23. O'Dwyer: Final Report on the Alwar Settlement, p. 32
24. Ibid., pp. 33-39
25. Report of Eastern Tehsils of Alwar, p. 83
26. Report of Northern and Southern Tehsils, pp. 103-105; Eastern Tehsils, p. 87; Central and Southern Tehsils, pp. 102-103; Final Report of Alwar, p. 39
27. Final Report of Bharatpur, p. 85
28. Pears: Report on the Revenue Settlement of Tonk, pt. 1, p. 24
29. Ibid., p. 36
30. Ibid., p. 49
31. Ibid., p. 62
32. R.A.R., 1884-85, p. 199

33. Butler: Kotah Settlement Report 1904-1909, p. 19
34. Ibid., p. 32
35. Raw: Dholpur Settlement Report, p. 31
36. Umacharan Mukhopadhyaya: Report on the Land Settlement of the Dholpur State, pp. 10, 11, 53; Raw: Final Report of the Revision of Settlement of the Dholpur State, 1909-12, p. 59
37. Umacharan Mukhopadhyaya: op.cit., p. 24
38. R.A.R., 1884-85, p.238; Raw: Dholpur Report, p. 52
39. Abbott: Land Settlement Report of Jhallawar, p. 75
40. Ibid., pp.78-85; R.A.R., 1879-80, p. 104
41. Abbott: op.cit., p. 74
42. La Touche's Report, para 252
43. Ibid., paras 259-264
44. Whiteway: Report on the Settlement of Ajmer Merwara District, p. 18
45. W.J.E. Lupton: Report on the Land and Water Revenue in Ajmer Merwara (cited later on as Water Revenue Report), p. 116
46. Whiteway: op.cit., p. 31; Lupton: Water Revenue Report. p. 92
47. Whiteway: op.cit., pp. 8-9
48. Ibid., pp. 32-33
49. Lupton: Water Revenue Report, Appendix III
50. Lupton: Final Settlement Report of Ajmer Merwara. Appendix X; La Touche's Report, pp. 122, 126
51. O'Dwyer: Eastern Tehsils' Report, pp. 15-16
52. Ibid.
53. O'Dwyer: Final Report on the Alwar Settlement, p. 69
54. O'Dwyer: Northern Tehsils' Report, p.11; Central Tehsils' Report, p. 20; Southern Tehsils' Report, p. 26
55. O'Dwyer: Northern Tehsils' Report, p. 14; Central Tehsils' Report, p. 21; Southern Tehsils' Report, p. 28
56. O'Dwyer: Northern Tehsils' Report, p. 59; Central Tehsils' Report, p. 58; Southern Tehsils' Report, p. 63
57. O'Dwyer: Northern Tehsils' Report, p. 12; Central Tehsils' Report, p. 21; Southern Tehsils' Report, p. 27

58. O'Dwyer: Northern Tehsils' Report, pp. 86, 87, 95; Central Tehsils' Report, pp. 81, 90; Southern Tehsils' Report, pp. 84, 95
59. Whiteway: op.cit., pp. 22-24

II

1. R.A.R., 1871-72, p. 192; Census of India, 1911, Vol.XXII, pt. 1, p. 216
2. Cited by La Touche's Report, pp. 131-132
3. La Touche's Report, p. 132
4. Whitway: op.cit, p.8
5. Lupton: Water Revenue Report, p. 16
6. Smith: Report of 1878, p. 15
7. Ibid., p. 18
8. Wingate: Jat Pergannahs Report, p. 20
9. Ibid.
10. Ibid., pp. 18-19
11. Ibid.
12. This and the next chart are based on statistics given by Wingate in his Jat Pergannahs Report, para nos. 52, 63, 73, 74, 82, 89, 90, 96 and 97
13. Ibid.
14. Wingate: Jat Pergannahs Report, p. 25
15. O'Dwyer: Northern Tehsils' Report, p. 9
16. The data has been compiled from the Report of Northern, Central and Southern Tehsils of Bharatpur, page nos. 57,57 and 62 respectively.
17. Compiled from the Reports of Northern, Central and Southern Tehsils of Bharatpur, page nos. 81 and 95; 81 and 90; 84 and 95 respectively.
18. Report of the Northern, Central and Southern Tehsils of Bharatpur, pages numbering 57-59, 57-58, 62-63 respectively.
19. Abbott: Settlement Report of Jhalawar, pp. 58, 63 and 68
20. Ibid.
21. W. Raw: Karauli Settlement Report, p. 12
22. Ibid., p. 36

23. Report on the Revision of the Settlement of the Dungarpur State, 1924, pp. 15-16
24. Ibid., p. 18
25. Ibid., Appendix no. XIII
26. O'Dwyer: Final Report of Alwar, pp. 44-45; Report of Eastern Tehsils, pp. 37-38; Report of Northern and Southern Tehsils, pp. 56-57; Report of Central and Southern Tehsils, pp. 56-57
27. O'Dwyer: Eastern Tehsils Report, p. 48
28. Ibid., p. 82
29. Whiteway: op.cit., p. 8
30. La Touche's Report, p. 83; Lupton: Final Settlement of Ajmer Merwara, pp. 20-21
31. La Touche's Report, para nos. 278, 280, 282 and 285
32. Lupton: Final Report, pp. 21-24
33. Lupton: Water Revenue Report, pp. 78, 81, 83, 85 and 87
34. Ibid., pp. 137-142
35. Lupton : Water Revenue Report, p. 14, and Appendix No. VIII & IX
36. op. cit., Appendix No. XIII, p. 144

4

Search For An Equitable Justification

The land settlement officers, from La Touche onwards, in their eagerness to show the incidence of land revenue demand to be lower than what it actually was, had adopted a three pronged strategy. The first lay in showing a larger area under cultivation than it actually was. This was done by including large tracts of *barani* fields as cultivated land. These *barani* areas were cultivated but they yielded crops for 2-3 years and then needed an equal time to regain fertility. The peasant used to cultivate some land in one year, other land in another year and came back to the original land after a gap of years as the situation demanded. He considered the land actually cultivated to be under cultivation; the British settlement officers included the entire cultivable area under the control and possession of the peasant as cultivated area. The peasant was not in a position to renounce such lands because that affected his capacity to cultivate. The result was that he paid for land the whole of which could not be and was not cultivated in any one year. This showed a larger area under cultivation and hence greater burden of payment of land revenue. The second strategy adopted was the change in the classification of soil—

either on the basis of quality or on the basis of irrigation. This classification method helped them to increase land revenue demand, and yet to claim that they were lowering the rate of land revenue when in fact they had enhanced the revenue demand. The third device adopted was to assume a higher yield of the crop per bigha which would, when multiplied by large numbers, make a great difference. The valuation of the crop at the prevalent market rate helped them to show a greater return to the peasant. La Touche had been able to show a comparatively lighter incidence of land revenue demand on the peasants by estimating the value of the crop in 1874 at the prevalent market rate. Dwyer adopted a variant of this device by disallowing certain legitimate expenses incurred by the peasantry. It was only in 1908 that Lupton allowed certain reductions from the prevalent market price. The operation of the first and second devices had been seen in the last chapter; the third device is being examined in this chapter.

The enhancement of land revenue demand was an act of policy pursued by the settlement officers uniformly irrespective of local considerations. However, after La Touche had highlighted in 1874 the fact that the settlement officers in Ajmer Merwara had neither employed 'the inductive or the deductive process' nor worked out rates of any kind to determine the land revenue demand for individual villages,[1] it became necessary for all settlement officers, in the post 1875 period, to put forward criteria for determining the revenue demand for different states to escape the criticism that it had been an assumed guess of the assessing officer. The justifications differed with each settlement officer. Sometimes factual data—like the growth of sources of irrigation, increase in cattle wealth, rise in prices of agricultural commodities and increase in land area under cultivation—were put forth as justification for increasing the revenue demand; at other times theoretical arguments—percentage of net assets, cash rentals or rentals in neighbouring jagir lands—were advanced to justify the enhanced revenue demand. Whiteway was directed to place the assessment upon a footing so that future revisions may be effected on that basis.[2]

The Government normally asked the local Political Officer to send an advance estimate of the likely results of the revision of land revenue settlements and the basis on which it was proposed to be revised. When these had been approved, the settlement officers were sent to achieve the targets settled in advance. A variation was when the Government did not approve of the anticipated enhancement but agreed to a new revenue settlement. At Alwar the Government did not approve of the estimated enhancement of revenue by 4 lakhs since the incidence of assessment in Alwar was already much higher than in the adjoining Gurgaon district of Punjab. When Dwyer did not find enough evidence to justify the expected enhancement, he raised the demand by 2 lakhs and set out to justify it.

The settlement officers, therefore, attempted that the land revenue demand fixed by them should appear to be rational and equitable. Various parameters of determining land revenue demand were discussed. In the final analysis, they argued that the interests of the state/ruler were in trust under their management and hence could not be sacrificed. The enhancement of the revenue demand was justified on some theoretical principle; some officers went to the extent of claiming that the enhanced revenue was a 'comparatively lighter' taxation.

The various criteria put forth to formulate an equitable revenue demand were the following[3]:

(i) to apply the all round average rate on cultivation of the last settlement to the present cultivated areas;

(ii) to apply the actual soil rates of last settlement to the present area;

(iii) to increase the (i) and (ii) in proportion to the increase in prices since the last settlement;

(iv) to take ¼th value of the gross produce of crops as sta share;

(v) to calculate the value of the owner's share of the produc (i.e. net assets) according to khatauni rents and to tak 2/3rd of this as state share;

(vi) to calculate the net assets according to the competitiv cash rents (assumed or corrected) and to take 2/3rd this as state share.

The application of the first criterion of all round averag rates of the last settlement was rejected because the rates we not equally pitched in all the tehsils and they did not take in account the increase in prices and in irrigated area. The secon criterion of actual soil rates of the last settlement were n applied because the soil classification were changed conside ably sometimes, e.g., in Alwar with a large addition to the are of superior soils. This had been brought about not on accou of improvement in the soils but of difference in classificatio Hence the old soil rates were not considered a safe guid Moreover the introduction of '*sabiqa*' category in *chahi* an *sairaba* lands and the inclusion of water rate in *sairaba sabiqa* an *barishi* lands had changed the basis of old soil rates. *Cha* cultivation had declined in Bharatpur and hence the rat would have to be adjusted. The application of old soil rat would have led to a very high nay oppressive enhancement Alwar and a significant reduction at Bharatpur. Both th developments would have been undesirable. The third crit rion of increasing the demand in relation to price rise w considered unfair because there had also been a rise in the co of production. It was further held to be unfair because son allowance should also be made for improvement in the stan ard of comfort. A more important reason for Dwyer for n accepting any of the earlier principles was that he had broug into existence a new class of intermediaries at Bharatpur whi had to be provided maintenance. The class of intermediaries Alwar had been created earlier but a definite basis for th nolument/profits of this class had not been laid down by owlett. This had to be done now. The fifth principle deended on the fourth and the sixth criteria was dependent on ish rents received by the owners.

Thus the six different criteria resolved themselves to two: 1 estimate of gross produce and claiming one-fourth produce ; land revenue; a determination of cash rents which would iable the settlement officer to form an opinion about the net ;sets and daim 2/3rd net assets as government revenue emand.

The cash rents paid by tenants were considered ' absolute id certain data'. When even that proved unhelpful in raising e revenue demand; the principle of evaluating the gross oduce of crops and taking ¼th as state share had to be relied oon. The gross produce of a field depended upon weather icertainties, quality of manure and irrigation; experiments ere conducted to reduce wide differences of opinion. The ita helping the process of formation of estimate and its value as presented with considerable dexterity and ingeniousness as to justify the enhancement. The criterion of cash rents d gross produce were mainly considered to determine the id revenue demand. The same are being examined in detail understand the process how both these were determined.

ish Rents

Dwyer had created a new class of intermediaries at Bharatpur d had sought to strengthen and formally recognise this class Alwar also. He postulated the theory that the class of ermediaries (called the zamindars) was entitled to one-third ofit margin out of the cash rents paid by the tenants to them io were called the owners. He went a step further and gued that the cash rents actually paid by the tenants to the mers included this margin. None of the earlier settlements Bharatpur or at Alwar had stated this principle; in fact there is no need to do so because an intermediary class did not exist at Bharatpur prior to 1897. Even at Alwar, Powlett had not defined the position of the intermediaries; he casually referred to the fact that he took 2/3rd of the net assets of owners. O' Dwyer set out to establish his postulate though he found no evidence of such cash rents, paid by the tenants-at-will, which might have included 1/3rd share of the owners' profit. The way he resolved this difficulty and proved his point was quite interesting and ingenious.

He set out to compile data pertaining to cash rents paid by the tenants-at-will, simultaneously advocating the view that the land revenue demand was 2/3rd of cash rents. The proportion of tenants-at-will paying cash rents was quite high; the occupancy tenants and tenants holding at favourable rents were not taken into consideration in this matter. The rents paid by the tenants-at-will fell into two categories: (i) at owner's rates and (ii) at other rates. The data collected about these tenants and their rents, at Alwar and Bharatpur, is given in (Table 4.1).[4]

Both types of rents in all tehsils had been recorded in the *khatauni*. Dwyer considered land revenue demand on the basis of 2/3rd cash rents as most equitable. When land revenue demand was worked out on that basis, it turned out to be about 20% less than the existing demand as given in Table 4.2. O' Dwyer said that this alone was sufficient to discredit the recorded rents.[5] The land revenue demand on the basis of 2/3 of recorded cash rents did not help him.[6]

Faced with this reality, Dwyer developed arguments to criticise the prevalent policy in both the states and to reject the recorded cash rents. He argued that the state government had prohibited profit rents from the tenants because Alwar, after 1877-78 and Bharatpur after 1879-80 had faced acute shortage of tenants, though for different reasons, to work on the fields

TABLE: 4.1

Percentage of Tenants-at-will paying at owner's and other rates (Alwar and Bharatpur)

Tehsils of Alwar	Percentage	paying at owner's rates	other rates	Tehsils of Bharatpur	Percentage	paying at owner's rates	other rates
Kishangarh	34.5	8.5	26	Gopalgargh	37.5	35	2.5
Ramgarh	31.7	22	10	Pahari	21.5	21	0.5
Govindgarh	38	32	6	Kama	31	15.5	15.5
Lachmangarh	32	16	16	Deeg	45	27	18.5
Tijara	37	14.5	22.5	Kumher	47.5	23.5	24
Bahrod	22.5	7.7	14.8	Akheygarh	55.5	6.5	49
Mandawar	33.6	9.6	24	Bharatpur	59	29	30
Katumbar	57	8	49	Nagar	40	32	8
Rajgarh	39	17	22	Rupbas	46	15	31
Alwar	50.4	20.6	29.8	Oochain	55	24	31
Bansur	39.6	14.9	24.7	Biyana	48	9	39
Thanaghazi	41.6	28.7	12.9	Bhusawar	58	9	49

TABLE: 4.2

State Demand and net assets by Cash rents (Alwar & Bharatpur)

Alwar Tehsils	Net assets	2/3 assets	Present Demand	Bharatpur Tehsils	Net assets	2/3rd assets	Present Demand
Kishangarh	237541	158360	213181	Gopalgarh	294323	196215	243040
Ramgarh	270068	180045	202512	Pahari	226155	150770	123717
Govindgarh	117934	78623	76411	Kama	201613	134424	138264
Lachmangarh	208255	136833	173754	Deeg	196664	110212	135446
Tijara	186182	124121	158903	Kumher	174140	116093	135743
Bahrod	299233	199489	194574	Akheygarh	176273	117515	139342
Mandawar	213387	142258	160739	Bharatpur	165460	110307	143603
Katumbar	170355	113570	159653	Nagar	94532	63021	90007
Rajgarh	161662	107775	156372	Rupbas	119258	79839	105855
Alwar	345771	230514	274665	Oochain	206001	137334	172705
Bansur	215602	143735	163304	Biyana	225394	150263	205972
Thanaghazi	201513	134342	150622	Bhusawar	256784	171189	236489
Total	2627503	1749665	2084690	Total	2336597	1537182	1870183
Excess Demand		+335025				+333001	

These rents had been attested by O' Dwyer's team which had been engaged in land settlement operations. Face to face with this reality, he went to the extent of alleging 'a general conspiracy to conceal rents' because if 2/3rd of the cash rents received by the zamindar proprietor was to be the basis of government revenue demand, the latter would have to be considerably reduced.[8] Unwilling to reduce government revenue demand in the face of the 'ascertainable data', he resorted to disbelieving these rents. He held the influence of the zamindars responsible for this concealment of rents. Not content with blaming the zamindars only, O' Dwyer put forward the theory of a profit rent being taken separately by the owner and held the state responsible for allowing this development. The state, according to him, was largely to blame for the present state of things. It may be of interest to add that all revenue settlements had been made by the British officers and the state administration had been under British control for various periods during 1858-1900. Such a practice could have developed or continued only because the British had allowed it to do so. A tradition was prevalent by which any rent, in excess of the state demand, shall have to be refunded by the owner to the state whenever it came to know of it. The revenue courts were preventing enhancement of cash rents. O' Dwyer decided that these practices, tending 'to obliterate one of the main privileges of ownership', should be abolished. It may be added here that tenants had been unavailable in both the states after 1878 and the owners were in need of them and not otherwise. In such a situation the owner's rates would be normal for payment by a tenant. The theory of the existence of this custom not having being known to the British who had been running the actual administration was the result of O' Dwyer's fertile imagination. His difficulty was frankly stated by him. "If we strike an arithmetic average of the cash rents of tenants paying at 'other rates' than owners in each tehsil, take 2/3rd as state share..." the result would be 'an enormous reduction of revenue'. Excepting the two tehsils of

Govindgarh and Bahrod, the reduction varied from 31% in Rajgarh to 11% in Thanaghazi, Bansur, Mandawar and Ramgarh. In Bharartpur excepting the two tehsils of Pahari and Kama, the revenue demand would have to be reduced in four tehsils by a percentage varying from 14 to 20 and in six tehsils by a percentage ranging from 20.5 to 30. Since the cash rents envisaged a lower demand, O' Dwyer's conclusion was a rejection of the recorded rents'. He, therefore, set out to find the real rents paid by the tenants. After a personal enquiry, he was satisfied that the actual rents deduced from certain selected villages were representative of the whole. The final rates which were supposed to be paid by the tenants cultivating at other rates were arbitrarily fixed at a figure which justified enhanced demand of revenue.

The Government of India had informed him in advance that "rent rates will be of comparatively small assistance in calculating the assessment" because the greater part of cultivation as well as the best lands were in the hands of the owners.[9] Despite this information, Dwyer held the view that the cash rents included 1/3rd profit of the owner and therefore they were one of the most objective criterion on which the demand of land revenue could be based.

Since the class of intermediaries did not exist at Bharatpur prior to 1897-99, how could the cash rents prevalent in the pre-1897 provide for 1/3rd profit rent to the intermediaries? At Alwar, Powlett had not carried out in 1876 any actual survey; he honestly confessed that he had arbitrarily supposed the cash rents to be giving 1/3rd profit to the land owners. He had recorded that the prevalent cash rents were low. Dwyer was caught in the web of a theory of his own making. He came out of this web by launching a virulent, though unjustified, criticism of the policies of the two state governments in the past. He argued that the past governments had allowed undesirable practices to develop. The owners, according to him, took a profit rent but did not allow any record of the same to be left.

The written agreements signed between the owners and the tenants did not mention profit rents and yet Dwyer argued that such rents existed. Dwyer conceded at Bharatpur that the fact of low rents was genuine and gave a few reasons for this development.

(i) The great agricultural depression that followed the famine of 1877-78 and the drought and scarcity of the closing years of the century (1894-1900) had kept the rents low.

(ii) The large scale desertion of owners and tenants in the post 1877-80 period in both the states resulted in large areas being left uncultivated. The government had to make efforts for temporary cultivation of the same on easy terms; low rents were offered to the cultivators.

(iii) The comparative scarcity of tenants-at-will and the absence of competition for land kept the rents low. The total population of Bharatpur state had been on the decline in the post 1881 period; in Alwar the abandonment of land by the owners and the temporary allotment of land to others was a major development during 1878-95.

(iv) The drought of the years (1894-1900) in Alwar and the increasing salination of well water in both the states, though considerably greater in Bharatpur than in Alwar, had resulted in increased cultivation of barani lands in both the states; this had kept the rents very low. Tenants who broke up fresh waste land were allowed very lenient rates, generally one-fourth of a rupee per bigha for a few years.

He knew that the recorded cash rents were genuine. He gave the following additional factors which had kept the rents low at Alwar.

1. Owners used to cultivate one another's holdings by way of exchange of plots;

2. relations of owners or old tenants, long settled in those lands, had acquired by prescription the privilege to hold at lenient rates;
3. tenants cultivating inferior lands and paying at owner's rates;
4. village menials cultivating at favourable rates in lieu of service to the owners.

Moreover Dwyer also came face to face with the fact that considerable area of land was held by privileged or lightly assessed tenants paying little more than the state dues and a large number of owners—ranging from 55 to 70%—cultivated the land themselves. It meant that profitable rents were not prevalent.

In his final report on Bharatpur, after the announcement of the settlement demand, he conceded that the prevalence of low rents 'as compared with the *jama* was a genuine fact' and accepted genuine reasons for the low rents.[10] Yet his desire to provide for the intermediary class created by him, was so great that it led him to reject the recorded cash rents everywhere.

But mere rejection of the recorded evidence was not enough; Dwyer had to find out "the true rents" paid by the tenants to the owners in order to sustain his theory that the intermediary proprietors retained 1/3rd cash rents. He undertook careful inquiry at some places himself and at other places through his subordinates; he succeeded in finding out some stray instances of very high fancy rates prevalent for some lands in some villages in a few tehsils.[11] The average deduced on the basis of these selected villages was considered appropriate to and representative of the whole regions of both the states. He and his subordinates cited a few random examples of high rents and enhanced the entire range of cash rents accordingly. (Table No. 4.3).[11a]

Another argument, advanced by Dwyer to justify higher state demand, was that the peasant proprietors retained the most fertile and best cultivated lands in their own hands; the

TABLE: 4.3

Recorded and Assumed rents at Bharatpur

Bharatpur Tehsils	Recorded rent		Khatauni recorded rents per Bigha				Ascertained and assumed rents per bigha			
	at owner's rate	at other rates	Chahi average	Dahri Hal	Dahri Sabiqa	Barani	Chahi	Dahri Hal	Dahri Sabiqa	Barani
Gopalgarh	1-56	1-28	2-28	1-88	1-61	1-10	2-44	2-25	1-50	1-00
Pahari	1-25	-	3-06	3-02		1-87	1-97	2-00	1-37	1-00
Kama	1-14	1-90	2-66	2-66	1-91	1-56	1-87	2-00	1-25	0-94
Deeg	1-08	1-90	2-32	2-32	1-82	1-42	1-90	2-00	1-19	0-90
Kumher	1-16	1-26					2-54		1-80	1-53
Akheygarh	1-36	1-31					2-54		1-80	1-53
Bharatpur	1-29	1-23					2-58	1-80		1-48
Nagar	1-10	0-81					2-54		1-80	0-78
Rupbas	1-70	1-48	3-62	2-14	2-10	1-16	3-87	2-14	2-10	1-16
Oochain	1-57	1-45	3-14	2-30	1-56	1-23	3-02	2-30	1-56	1-23
Biyana	1-66	1-51	3-51	1-91	2-56	0-90	3-91	1-91	2-56	0-90
Bhusawar	1-14	1-37								

Recorded and Assumed rents at Alwar

Alwar Tehsils	Recorded rent		Khatauni recorded rents per Bigha				Ascertained and assumed rents			
	at owner's rate	at other rates	Chahi average	Dahri Hal	Dahri Sabiqa	Barani	Chahi	Dahri Hal	Dahri Sabiqa	Barani
Kishangarh	1-25	1-38	2-75	2-06		1-19	5-20	3-75	3-25	1-62
Ramgarh	1-94	2-33	3-61	3-35		1-80	5-00	3-71		2-10
Govindgarh	2-06	3-00	4-37	4-25		3-53	4-80	4-80		2-56
Lachmangarh	1-60	1-74	3-28	2-14		1-25	4-57	3-50	2-75	1-66
Tijara	1-03	1-05	2-77	1-50		0-75	4-26	3-00	1-69	
Bahrod	1-27	1-90	4-37	-		1-72	4-05	2-76		2-03
Mandawar	1-87	1-40	4-02	2-36		1-10	4-20	2-75		0-19
Rajgarh	2-56	2-25	4-69	1-87		1-12	5-84	5-12	3-25	1-72
Katumbar	1-75	1-56	3-69	1-87		1-19	4-95	3-37	3-00	1-73
Alwar	1-81	2-06	4-10		2-44	1-51	5-47	3-75	2-50	1-97
Bansur	1-12	1-50	3-90	2-09	1-00	0-65	4-69	3-00	1-87	0-97
Thanaghazi	3-22	3-90	8-03	2-59	1-73	1-16	8-95	3-75	2-62	0-75

rent paid by the tenants-at-will was in relation to the poorer soils. The rents for better and more fertile lands, so he argued, would naturally be higher. In his search for justifying enhancement of cash rents, he even argued that the profits from culturable and unculturable land were considerable (in the upkeep of cattle and profits from the sale of milk and *ghee*). The state had a right to tax the profits from such lands and this could be done by enhancing the cash rents from land.[12] He thereafter enhanced the cash rents so as to provide 1/3rd profit rent to the new intermediary class of owners. His final report on Alwar laid bare his motive. He wanted the distinction between the owners and tenants to become more marked; the owners should assert their claims to receive a profit rent. He impressed upon the zamindars that they were quite free to make their own arrangements with the tenants without fear of interference from the state and to claim from the tenants the margin of profit which the state had forgone in the assessment.[13] He was glad that suits for enhancement of rent and for ejection of tenants who refused to pay enhanced rent, had begun to be filed. Under British administration the old policy of prohibiting profit rents was discontinued because it had obliterated, as he put it, one of the main privileges of ownership. His goal was that a margin of profit should be left to the non-cultivating owner; the foundation for peasant exploitation and enhanced revenue demand was being deliberately laid. For the same reason, the occupancy tenants were subjected to the payment of *malikana* or profit rent to the owners over and above the government demand. The *malikana* was 6 to 20% of the rental.[14] This additional burden on these tenants had not existed earlier.

The cash rents were quite often assumed and not ascertained. He wrote that he assumed cash rents in Bansur and Thanaghazi (Alwar). 'The assumed all round *chahi* rate is slightly below the ascertained *chahi* rate in Bansur and above in Thanaghazi'. 'The assumed *dahri* rates are higher than the actual rates in both the tehsils'. 'I have assumed a low rent of Rs. 0.19 per bigha for new fallow in Bansur and a fairly high rate of Rs. 0.94 in Thanaghazi where the land is of superior quality'. It was Dwyer's assumption everywhere.[15] Regarding Katumbar he wrote: 'I am reluctantly compelled to assume rates which cannot be justified by the existing data as to cash rents'. Dwyer had not considered the rates of settlement of 1890 because their object, according to him, was 'to bring out the assessment considered suitable'. His own method of determining the cash rents was more open to the criticism he had levelled against the old settlement. He had taken the help of 'intensive enquiry' to justify the demand he had resolved upon in advance. He confessed that his 'assumed rents were of a rather speculative character'.

Dwyer went against all written and unwritten evidence about the cash rents which had been paid over the last more than 40 years; he disregarded them for the simple reason that he wanted to justify that the profit rent of a non-existent 'zamindar' class was included in the cash rents. He, by way of justification; argued that his personal enquiry had revealed that the rents paid were higher and 2/3rd share of those assets would lead to a 50% enhancement of state demand which would have been oppressive. Hence the rents were moderated in accordance with one fourth produce estimate.

Thus Dwyer provided for the new class of intermediaries without affecting the state revenue demand from the peasantry. By saying that this intermediary class should have 1/3rd profit rents and by allowing them to eject tenants if they refused to pay high rents, the peasantry was subjected to pay more revenue than the state demand. The peasantry suffered a 65% enhancement when Dwyer was putting forward only a 10% enhancement of the revenue demand.[16] The revenue settlement officers in general and Dwyer in particular very shrewdly tried to justify the fairness of their demand on the basis of gross produce. Since the normal gross produce could not have justified this enhancement, the figures of area under cultivation and the assumed yield of various types of land were kept high. The calculation of gross yield was inflated.

The Criterion Of One-Fourth Gross Produce

The criterion of ¼th gross produce as the state demand had an in built inequity in the way it was worked out and determined: It was one thing to have considered the actual gross produce of a few years prior to the assessment year, formed an estimate of the average on that basis and held that as the basis for determining the one-fourth quantity. It was quite another to assume a certain amount of produce per bigha and calculate the total produce on that basis. The assumed produce was higher than the actual produce in some neighbouring districts of North West Provinces and Punjab, and was also considerably higher than the experimented yield conducted on specially chosen plots of lands in the state under the supervision of O' Dwyer himself.[17]

The principle of assuming a certain yield of crop on a particular type of soil was enforced by the British settlement officers both in Ajmer Merwara and in various states where they got the opportunity to introduce their land revenue settlement.

At Ajmer Merwara, the area of different kinds of soils under cultivation was as follows:

District	Year	*Chahi & talabi*	*Barani*	Total cultivated land	% of *Barani* cultivation
Ajmer	1849	50763	104406	155169	67.27%
Merwara	1874	51949	119467	171416	69.7%
	1884	58079	132242	190321	69.5%
	1908	56074	141442	197516	71.6%

The incidence of land revenue demand has generally been measured only in terms of the rate per acre which, in turn, was based on assumed yield of land. However, the operational incidence of land revenue can be understood in terms of relationship between the assumed and actual yield of different kinds of soil.[18]

Comparative Statement Of Assumed And Actual Yield Of Various Crops in Ajmer Merwara

Crop	Assumed yield per acre	Actual yield per acre
Maize	13.20 mds	9.00 mds
Bajra	3.60 mds	3.5 mds
Wheat	13.20 mds	9.5 mds
Barley	16.70 mds	12.00 mds
Gujai	16.60 mds	13.23 mds
Cotton	8.80 mds	6.69 mds

These 'assumed' yields meant that the average fields were producing a fully-matured crop over the whole area and were giving the assumed crop outturn that they were capable of. These represented the figures of fairly good years. Good years better than these had been very few in Ajmer Merwara. This operated oppressively because Ajmer had no record of '*Kharaba*' percentages as existed in the Punjab. There was nothing on record to estimate the 'true matured' areas on any soil.

It was in 1908 that Lupton for the first time focussed attention on the unjust and iniquitous method of land taxation enforced by the British settlement officers. He compiled cultivation data for 15 years (1893-1907) for *barani* and irrigated lands.[19] The resultant average of *barani* crops is being given on next page (the full data is in Appendix No. D of Chapter 3).

The first thing which strikes significant is that the area assessed (i.e. the area supposed to have been cultivated was 12.4% more than the area sown and 58% more than the

Area sown	Matured area	Failed area	% of failed area	Produce average	Average produce in maunds per sown acre	Average produce in maunds per matured acre
76483	54395	22088	29	147926	1.93	2.72

The area assessed was 85956 acres.

matured area. Even in the area which produced a crop, the average produce variation from year to year was quite heavy. The average produce was 147926 maunds; the variations ranged from 80% above to 40% below the average produce. Thus the mere cultivated or sown *barani* area meant nothing; it was the produce which was relevant. Out of 15 years, only in 6, the produce was more the average while in 9 it was less than the average.

Irrigated Areas

The *chahi* cultivation was the safest since the source of irrigation was assured; the *talabi* was the next best. Here the failed area (*nabud*=less than 25% crop) was only marginal—about 2.5% in *chahi* and 5% in *talabi* areas—but the crop outturn varied quite considerably. Statistics were collected for 55 different villages of Ajmer district[20] (Appendix No. E). The total sown area varied from 37% above to 39% below the average which itself was only 72% of the assessed area. The assessed area was 10683 acres but average sown area was 7692 acres though it varied from 3771 to 10317 acres. The produce also naturally varied from 43% above to 38% below the average. The assumed produce was 93135 maunds; in the best year the actual produce was 72% of the assumed; in the worst it was 31% only. In the *talabi* areas, the annual produce varied from 53% to 151% of the average, after excluding the famine year. Out of 15 years, 7 had below average production; 3 had 5% above the average, 2 had 25%, 1 had 50% and 1 had 151% above the average yield. It was only in 1 out of 15 years that the produce nearly approximated to the assumed yield. A fixed rate of assessment was bound to operate oppressively in such a situation. Lupton observed that a well performed to 1/3rd of its capacity in a dry year. The outturn of produce depended on a favourable rainfall. Even the most assured source of irrigation failed considerably in years of famine and scarcity.

The incidence of land revenue naturally fell heavily on account of the vagaries of nature; it was made calamitous on account of an oppressive administration which assumed an excessive yield per acre. The average assumed yield was 15 maunds per acre. The actual yield was 10.41 maunds per acre on sown area and 10.66 maunds per acre on matured area in the chahi lands; in talabi lands the figures were 8.87 and 9.35 maunds per acre respectively. Thus 100 acres of chahi and talabi lands actually produced 1041 and 887 maunds while they were assumed to yield 1500 and 1500 maunds. The land revenue was assessed on the basis of the assumed yield; the actual yield was 69.4% in chahi and 59.13% in talabi lands. Over a period of 15 years, the average annual incidence of revenue demand came to be 231% higher, as shown in the Table 4.4.

When Lupton argued that the land revenue demand in the district of Ajmer was only about 38% of the net assets, it was in fact 38 x 231% = 87% of the net assets.[21] The British land revenue policy in the closing years of the 19th century in Ajmer district witnessed the phenomenon of the growth of subsistence *chahi* cultivation and of below subsistence *barani* cultivation. This was accompanied by an increase in the number of ploughs and cattle wealth which has been discussed separately later in this book.

The estimate of revenue demand, on the basis of one-fourth gross produce, was projected as an 'independent' estimate of the peasants' capacity to pay. In Bharatpur and Alwar, this provided corroborative support to the demand worked out on the basis of assumed cash rents.[22] Dwyer had rejected

TABLE: 4.4

Incidence of Assumed Yield in *Chahi* and *Talabi* Lands in Ajmer-Merwara (55 villages)

Year *Fasli*	Assessed Area (acres)			Annual Produce (maunds)		Land Revenue increased by percentage	Year A.D.
	Chahi	*Talabi*	Total	Assumed	Actual		
1300	6209	2625	8834	132510	52053	254	1892-93
1301	"	"	"	"	64576	205	1893-94
1302					76970	172	1894-95
1303	"	"	"	"	75177	175	1895-96
1304	"				81767	162	1896-97
1305					91169	145	1897-98
1306					66220	200	1898-99
1307					38620	343	1899-1900
1308					69037	191	1900-01
1309					50746	261	1901-02
1310					55085	240	1902-03
1311					60521	218	1903-04
1312					40136	330	1904-05
1313					31435	421	1905-06
1314					88187	150	1906-07
				Average for 15 year		**231.2%**	

Based on Appendix E of Chapter 3.

the *Khatauni* cash rents (discussed earlier) and determined different, much higher than the recorded, rents. He therefore considered it very important that the one-fourth share of gross produce should be nearer to his estimate of cash rents. However the method of working out the gross produce reduced the whole exercise to window dressing. Although he undertook a large number of experiments in the various tehsils of the two states, but he himself, by calling the 'crop experiments' as giving a very rough indication of the average yield, reduced their importance. These experiments had been carried out on well chosen plots of land under his own supervision; at some places he even conceded that the plots of land 'were often above the average'.[23] He himself was skeptical of their utility and himself moderated the results of crop experiments, thus rendering the whole exercise as full of inequity and unfairness. It was one thing to have considered the average gross produce of previous years as the basis and to have modified the result of experimental crops in the light of actual gross produce. It was quite another to compare the experimental results with those of other tehsils of Alwar and of neighbouring British districts of Mathura, Agra and Punjab. It was still another to moderate the results with 'continual enquiries' from the agriculturists and tehsil officials and to determine the final rates of yield in consultation with the deputy collectors. The rates so decided were held to be representative of the average outturn in different classes of soil. He further undervalued the result of his experiments, by arguing that the outturn depended chiefly not on the classification of soil but on the conditions under which the crop was grown.

His report of northern tehsils of Bharatpur gave the result of his crop experiments but the later reports of central and southern tehsils of Bharatpur did not even give this data in the assessment reports but relegated it to an appendix. He later contented himself by saying that 660 experiments in 6 harvests in the southern tehsils and 839 experiments in the central tehsils were conducted and then finally assumed a certain produce per bigha.[24]

In the northern tehsils of Bharatpur the crop experiments made during 1896-98 were considered imperfect 'as the supervising establishment was very weak and the machinery not in full working order'. This was despite the confession that 'the *rabi* experiments were very carefully and systematically made', and O' Dwyer himself got the experiment carried out under his personal supervision in average plots selected by himself. The experimental yield was low but it was assumed to be much higher for purposes of justifying the revenue demand to be one-fourth of the gross produce. Some data is being given in Table 4.5 in relation to major crops.[25]

The relationship between the experimented and assumed yield did not follow any logical pattern; it was enhanced or reduced at will. The only regulatory relationship appeared to be conected with the growth percentage in the cultivation of a particular crop in a tehsil. The assumed yield of *bajra* was higher in Deeg in comparison to Gopalgarh because the crop cultivation had increased by 234% in the former tehsil; same was the case with the assumed yield of barley in Kama as compared to Deeg or the assumed yield of wheat and *jowar* in Gopalgarh in comparison to Deeg.

In his report on Alwar tehsils he did not prominently put forward his assumptions of crop yield and expressed them in vague terms. He felt that the quality of crops had somewhat deteriorated mainly on account of the drying up of wells. In his report on southern tehsils of the state he expressed that his assumptions of crop yield for barley varied from 10 to 16 maunds in *chahi* and 3½ to 13 maunds in *dahri* lands. When comparing these figures with the neighbouring Gurgaon, he confessed that these were 'on the whole distinctly higher'. The weightage he gave to his experiments may be seen by a few examples.[26]

TABLE: 4.5

Crop yield: Assumed And Experimented Yield
In Maunds per Bigha (Bharatpur state)

	Bajra				Jowar				Wheat				Barley			
Increase in cultivation in relation to 1890	Gopal garh 183%		Deeg 234%		Gopal garh 143%		Deeg 131%		Gopal garh 130%		Deeg 82%		Kama 226%		Deeg 138%	
Type of soil	E	A	E	A	E	A	E	A	E	A	E	A	E	A	E	A
Chahi		5	3.4	5		4	3.4	3.5	6.5	8	6.4	7		8.5	6.6	8
Sairaba Hal		4			5.8	4			4.8	6				7		
Sairaba Sabiq		3		5	4.6	4	2.4	3	1.2	5		4.5		5.5		5
Barani		3	2.8	5	3.3	4	2.8	3		4		4		4.5		4.5

A=Assumed

E=Experimented

Yield per Bigha (in maunds)

Alwar State Tehsils	*Chahi* land								*Dahri* land			
	Wheat		Barley		Bajra		Jowar		Bajra		Jowar	
	E	A	E	A	E	A	E	A	E	A	E	A
Alwar & Bansur	10	12	12½	15	6½	8	7½	8	3.1	4.5	5	6
Difference in %		+20		+20		+23		+7		+45		+20
Govindgarh	6	12							4	6		
Difference in %		+100								+50		

The assumption of yield was generally higher than the experimented yield though in a few cases in some tehsils, he assumed lower yield also. The assumed yield was generally higher by 20 to 30%. For soils in which no experiments were made, the outturn was calculated with reference to similar soils for which experiments were made. The yield of irrigated barley which was par excellence the staple *rabi* crop, was kept at a very high figure, as he himself confessed, because it was sown on the best lands on which labour, manure and irrigation were concentrated. Dwyer claimed that the assumed averages were based on many varying and uncertain factors as soil, rainfall and agricultural conditions, and that these represented as nearly as possible 'the *probable* average rates of yield for a series of years'. He even confessed that 'the rates I assume are on the whole distinctly higher except for cotton and grain'.[27]

In the final calculation of total yield deductions had to be allowed for failure of crops (called *na bud* in Ajmer).

Concession For Failed Crops

The assumption of failed crops in different states was at considerable variance with the actuality. While the settlement officer at Bharatpur and Alwar made a mention of allowing a certain percentage of failure, none was done at Ajmer and at other places. At Bharatpur and Alwar, O'Dwyer was not willing to trust 'the patwari agency to carry out honestly or intelligently' the estimate of failed crops. Till 1897-98, the idea of allowing a percentage of failed crops as a deduction from the total yield had not been entertained. However, the large scale complaints on this account led O' Dwyer to look at the data of failed crops for 5 years (1892-97) preserved in the Ferozepur tehsil of the neighbouring Gurgaon district under British control and administration. He refused to believe the truthfulness of the record because it revealed that 40% of the kharif sowings and 28% of the rabi had failed completely. He even attempted to justify his disbelief of the record; he had to go as far away as Gujranwala in Punjab where 70% of the area was irrigated, to find single digit percentage of failed area (it was 5 to 7.5%). His strange logic was that Alwar should have lesser percentage of failure because the soil was lighter in texture; for Bharatpur his argument was that since there was heavier rainfall than Alwar, the failure percentage should be lower. He knew that there was greater percentage of failure from swamping at Bharatpur as much of the land was low lying and badly drained. Disbelieving the records of the neighbouring Gurgaon or of Ajmer or his own knowledge about the failure of crops, he deliberately cut down the allowance for failed crops.[28] (Table No. 4.6)

Besides allowance for failure of crops, certain allowance was also made for fodder crops and payment to menials. The payment to menials was disallowed by Dwyer; his contention was that this payment was made out of the peasant's share and not out of gross produce. The 1930-31 settlement at Bharatpur made by the ruler allowed 8-11 % deduction for menials and 6 to 10% for harvesting labour, 7 to 15% for failed crops.[29]

TABLE: 4.6

Concession Percentage for failed crops Alwar and Bharatpur

State	Tehsils	Kharif	Rabi	State	Tehsils	Rabi		other crops
						Chahi	Barani	
Alwar	Kishangarh	8	4	Bharatpur	Gopalgarh	5	5	10
	Ramgarh	10	5		Pahari	3	8	8
	Govindgarh	5	3		Kama	4	8	10
	Lachmangarh	12	5		Deeg	4	10	10
	Tijara	12	5		Kumher	4		10
	Bahrod	10	5		Akheygarh	4		10
	Mandawar	10	5		Nagar	4		10
	Katumbar	10	5		Bharatpur	4		8
	Rajgarh	5.5	5.5		Bhusawar	4		3
	Alwar	10	8		Rupbas	4		10
	Bansur	10	10		Oochain	4		10
	Thanaghazi	10	10		Bayana	4		10

The Valuation Of The Crop

Having allowed deductions for fodder and failure of crops, the net produce was evaluated and one-fourth of this valuation was put forth as the government land revenue demand. But the more important question was: At what rates was the crop to be valued? La Touche valued the crop yield at the prevailing market retail rate and showed that the government demand was less than one-fourth.[30] Whiteway had allowed a reduction of 10% on the retail price because the former was paid only at the wholesale price by the traders.[31] It was Lupton who pointed out that the net price paid to the former was 20% less than the prevalent market rate; he further allowed another 10% deduction for payment for cartage and menials.[32] In a fair evaluation this 30% reduction in the retail price, should have been allowed if the real price paid to the cultivator was to be found out. It was not done in any state. Secondly, Dwyer compiled prevalent prices in the various tehsils of the two states for the last three decades. Thereafter he calculated the average price in his own way and arbitrarily fixed prices of major crops which was higher than the prevalent market rate as the following figures show.[33]

TABLE: 4.7

Average Price in Seers per Rupee

Alwar Tehsils	Years	Kharif			Rabi	
		Bajra	Jowar	Moth Masina	Wheat	Barley
Kishangarh	1870-75	28	31	30	23	31
	1876-86*	28	32	31	22	28
	1886-97	22	27	30	19	26
	Average of 26 years	27	30	30	21	27
Alwar	1870-75	28	28	30	23	30
	1876-90*	27	31	29	23	31
	1888-98	23	25	23	20	28
	Average of 27 years	25½	27	27	21	28

Assumed rate for the different tehsils of Alwar		25	30	29	20	28
Bharatpur Teshils						
Gopalgarh	1880-1898	23.44	28.66	24	21.6	31.3
Pahari	"	24	28	22.8	21.1	30.11
Kama	"	27	31	30	24	32
Deeg	"	25	28	28	23	31
Average of 4 tehsils		24.86	28.9	26	22.67	23.5
Average now fixed		26	30	25	21	19

* The famine year 1877-78 was omitted.

The prices now assumed for calculating the value of the crop were definitely higher in Bharatpur for wheat and barley and moth masina; in Alwar and Kishangarh the prices for wheat and bajra were higher in most of the years; for barley in some years. These were cheaper for jowar in both the states. The fixation of a higher price secured a higher notional value for the crops in a particular year. The total crop yield had already been estimated higher by postulating a higher output, the *chahi* and *sairaba* cultivated area had been taken to be much higher than actually cultivated. Thus, a far larger area was supposed to have been cultivated and the crop yield was assumed to be higher. By allowing a lower percentage of failed crops, the quantity of output remained much greater than the actual produce; by evaluating it at a higher price than the prevalent or the past average rate, the money value of the total crop was enhanced automatically. Thus the notional value of the total crop had been enhanced considerably at both the levels—the yield per bigha and the rate per maund. The valuation of the gross produce thus calculated justified a higher revenue demand on the basis of one-fourth produce. An equitable principle had been so mutilated and distorted that 25% produce became a much higher percentage. That this

TABLE: 4.8

Assessed and cropped areas (Bharatpur and Alwar)

State	Year	*Chahi* area (bighas)			*Sairaba*			*Barani*		
		Assessed	Cropped	%	Assessed	Cropped	%	Assessed	Cropped	%
Bharatpur	1897-98	340270	247794	72.8	335224	196388	58.6	923495	1254582	133
Alwar	1897-98	264796	156229	59						
4 Eastern Tehsils		79338	47297	59	68642	62265	90	257508	306816	119

estimate of gross produce at Alwar and Bharatpur was totally imaginary and highly oppressive for the peasantry can be easily verified by some objective data.

In Bharatpur, *chahi* cultivation had gone down by 5.32% but the cropped *chahi* area had gone down by 7.14%. The *sairaba* cultivated area had been enhanced by 50% adding *sairaba sabiqa* to the *sairaba* area; but only 57.6% of the *sairaba* was cropped. The *barani* area was double cropped with what output can only be a wild guess. (Table No. 3.22) Out of a total cultivated area of 1698764 bighas cropped in the year, only 247794 bighas was *chahi* and 8498 was *sairaba hal* = 256292 i.e. 16% was irrigated.

The above cropped statistics in the *chahi* and *sairaba* area of Bharatpur are significant. It shows that 27% *chahi* land remained uncropped and probably uncultivated also and yet paid the land revenue on the basis of *chahi* crop yield. (Table No. 3.13) Thus the incidence of land revenue demand had increased by 38.8% on *chahi* and 70% on *sairaba* lands. This has been worked out by dividing the land area uncropped by the land are cropped (28 ÷ 72 = 38.8% and 41.4 ÷ 58.58 = 70%). The incidence on *barani* can be guessed only because the peasant was compelled to cultivate only on the basis of rain god. The percentage of failure may not have been as high as Ajmer Merwara but would certainly have been higher than *sairaba* which at least had the benefit of flood water for growing rabi crops. The incidence of 25% of gross produce may be seen in the case of one of the tehsils for which figures have been worked out.[35]

Tehsil	*Chahi* area bighas		Produce per Bigha		Price per rupee (seers)	
	assessed	cultivated	actual	assumed	prevalent	assumed
Kama (Bharatpur)	19221	11115	7.2 mds	7.5 mds	24	21

By the above figures the total assumed yield would be 19221 X 7.5 = 144157.5 mds while the yield actually was 11115 X 7.2 = 80028 mds. Its value according to the assumed rate was 144157.5 X 40/21 = Rs. 274585.71; the market value of the crop was 80028 X 40/24 = Rs. 133380. The land revenue on the basis of ¼ gross produce according to the assumed figures would be Rs. 274585.71 ÷ 4 = Rs. 68646.43 when it should have been Rs. 133380 ÷ 4 = Rs. 33345. By assessing a higher than normally irrigated area per well and by small differences in the yield and prices assessed the *chahi* area in Kama had to pay 51.47% of its produce when the settlement officer was saying that he was taking 25% of its gross produce. The incidence of revenue demand was enhanced more than 100%.

In the case of Alwar, the result of ¼ gross produce was even worse because land has been transferred from bhur to mattiyar category. Let us take the detailed calculations for one tehsil.

Tehsil	Year	Land area in Bighas			
		Chiknoot	Mattiyar	Bhur	Total
Kishangarh	1876	19959	69701	52136	141796
	1898	19620	96656	29112	145388
Difference		-339	+26955	-23024	+3592

The impact of ¼th gross produce may be judged by the division of these three soil categories into *chahi, dahri,* and *barani* and the assumed yield of each class of soil.[36]

TABLE: 4.9

Changes in Natural and Artificial Classes of Soil

Tehsil	Natural class of Soil year of Settlement		Artifical class of Soil			Total
			Chahi	Dahri	Barani	
Kishangarh (Alwar)	Chiknoot I + II	1876	5864	4710	9385	19,959
	" "	1898	6284	5497	7839	19,620
	Mattiyar I + II	1876	14439	6210	49052	69,701
	" "	1898	20597	8289	67761	96,656
	Bhur	1876	3265	1711	47160	52,136
	"	1898	1360	2019	25733	29,112

(Contd.)

(Table 4.9 Contd.)

The yield was to be calculated on the following basis:

	Chiknoot				Mattiyar			Av. of MI&II	Bhur				Bhur II
	Chahi	Dahri		Barani	Chahi	Dahri		Barani	Chahi	Dahri		Barani	Barani
		H	S			H	S			H	S		
Wheat													
Yield Experimented													
Yield Assumed	10		6	4	10	6	6	3½	8	5	4	2½	-
Barley													
Yield Expreimented													
Yield Assumed	14	9	8	5½	14	9	8	5	11	7	5	3½	2
Bajra													
Yield Exprimented	8½												
Yield Assumed	9	8	6	5	8	8	6	5	6	6	5	3	2½

H = *Hal*

S = *Sabiqa*

Even if for the sake of argument we accept that the assumed yield was the actual yield in 1876 also. The difference in revenue demand would work out as follows:

Gross produce of wheat in 1876

Chiknoot (5864 X 10) + (4710 X 6)+(9385 X 4)	=	124440
Mattiyar (14439 X 10) + (6210 X 6) + (49052 X 3½)	=	353332
Bhur (3265 X 8) + (1711 X 4½) + (47160 X 2½)	=	151719.5
		629491.5

Gross produce of wheat in 1898

Chiknoot (6284 x 10) + (5497 X 6) + (7839 X 4)	=	127178
Mattiyar (20597 X 10) + (8298 X 6) + (67761 X 3½)	=	492921.5
Bhur (1360 X 8) + (2019 X 4½) + (25733 X 2½)	=	84298
		704397.5

In terms of gross produce, the significance of shifting of soil from bhur I to mattiyar can now be seen. The gross produce had increased by 11.9%. The assumed yields of Bajra and Jowar assumed in relation to different kinds of soils in the eastern tehsils of Alwar, is being given.

By shifting soils from bhur to mattiyar category, Dwyer was able to increase the gross produce of wheat by 74906 maunds which fetched Rs. 159812 or Rs. 37453 revenue as ¼th gross produce. Accepting the assumed produce figure to be real (which they were not) he was able to collect 30% revenue when he was claiming only 25%. The other expenses and losses which the cultivators had to bear are not being taken into account here. By marginal changes in yield and the rate and quality of soil, he raised the revenue by 20% over ¼th demand. The pretensions to equitable settlement were maintained in order to establish an inequitable settlement. The yields assumed for mattiyar and bhur soils explain the mechanism of enhancement of revenue demand. The data for the four eastern tehsils of Alwar is being given to explain it.[37]

TABLE: 4.10

Assumed yields in different kinds of soils (for Bajra)
(Alwar four-eastern Tehsils)

Tehsil	Chiknoot				Mattiyar				Bhur I			
	Chahi	Dahri		Barani	Chahi	Dahri		Barani	Chahi	Dahri		Barani
		H	S			H	S			H	S	
Kishangarh	9	7	5½	5	9	7	5½	4½	8	5½	3	2½
Ramgarh	8	8	6	5	8	8	6	5	6	6	5	3
Govindgarh	-	9	7	6	-	9	7	5½	-		-	3½
Lachmangarh	7	7	5	4½	7	7	5	5	-		-	3
For Jowar the assumed yields in the four tehsils were:												
Kishangarh	10	7½	6½	4½	10	7½	6	4½	9½	6	4	2¼
Ramgarh	10	10	7	5	10	10	7	5			4	3
Govindgarh		13	-	5½		13	11	8			5	
Lachmangarh	8	8	6	5	8	8	6	5			2½	

H = *hal*

S = *Sabiqa*

The above figures explain the difference which would be caused in revenue demand by shifting soil category from *bhur* to *mattiyar*.

In Bharatpur the main difference in the area under cultivation as compared to 1890 was:

	Chahi	Sairaba	Barani	New fallow	Total cultivated
1890	366437	212467	797646	496318	1376550
1897-99	340270	335224	923495	119168	1598989
	-26167	+122757	+125849	-377150	+222439
		248606			

The total cultivated area had increased by 222439 bighas net though *chahi* cultivation had gone down by 26167 bighas. The yield of 248606 bighas of *sairaba* and *barani* was:

Barani bighas 125849 X 3 = 377547 maunds *kharif* yield (Bajra) Rabi yield of 122757 *sairaba* bighas X 5½ = 675163.5 maunds *rabi* yield (wheat and barley).

Evaluated at the assumed prices it would amount to 377547 X 40/25 + 675163.5 X 40/19 = Rs. 604075.2 + 1421396.8 = Rs. 2025472 = Net increase of value of gross produce.

Thus by means of adding to the *sairaba* and *barani* area had led to an increase of Rs. 20.25 lakhs in gross produce.

The apparently equitable revenue demand had become inequitable.

The gross revenue demand would not increase by that amount because the *chahi* cultivation had gone down. But the fact was apparent that the revenue demand though claimed as ¼th gross produce was more than 50%. By assuming a higher yield for crops, by transferring land from fallow to *barani* and *sairaba*, and by fixing a higher price than the average rate of the last 20 years the revenue demand could be enhanced easily when the *chahi* cultivated area had gone down by 26167 bighas.

The actual and assumed yield served another subtle purpose which was not apparent. The assumed yield of certain crops was kept at a low figures specially in the case of crops which were sought to be encouraged; it was used to benefit the cultivation of wheat in certain tehsils or the owners of irrigated lands. For example in the four eastern tehsils of Alwar, the assumed yield for *chahi* crops was lower than for unirrigated crops. The relative assumptions were[38]:

	Produce per bigha in maunds			
	Wheat		Jowar	
	Actual	Assumed	Actual	Assumed
Kishangarh	19	10	7.25	10
Ramgarh	11½	10	3.37	10
Govindgarh	6	12	4	6
Lachmangarh	16	9	4.5	8

This was a general assumption which operated against the cultivators of coarse foodgrains or unirrigated crops; it was in accordance with the general principle behind the land revenue settlements that the cultivators of unirrigated lands were to be subjected to heavier taxation than those of irrigated lands.

Appendix-F

Cropping pattern of Alwar and Bharatpur (in Percentage)

Alwar tehsils	Kharif Foodcrops			Non food		Total Area		Rabi Foodcrops			Nonfood crops			Total Area	
	Maize Bajra	Jowar	Masina	Gawar chari	Cotton	Kharif	Total Area	Wheat	Barley	Gram	Gochni Bejhar	Sarshaf Linseed Taramira	Tobacco & poppy	Rabi	Total area
Alwar															
Kishangarh	76.0	10.0	2.5	7.25	4.25		101085	8.5	30.7	19.3	21.12	17.8	0.3		63665
Ramgarh	58.0	13.0	3.5	9.7	15.8		80946	8.3	25	17.5	19.9	27.0	1.0		47802
Govindgarh	45.0	30.0	5.2	4.25	15.55		29475	6.7	32	41	6.7	10.6	0.8		12941
Lachmangarh	47.0	19.0	17.2	8.4	8.4		61177	7.6	26	52.9	7.1	2.34	0.8		32719
Tijara	72.0	1.4	9.8	14.6	2.2		147040	12.0	40.5	27.4	6.2	10.48	0.5		53796
Bahror	68.0	10.3	23.5	3.6	4.6		139388	4.2	30	52	3.9	7.5	0.2		48787
Mandawar	52.0	7.5	34.0	3.7	2.8		99863	7.87	29.7	31.5	4.6	21.56	0.3		49729
Rajgarh	38.0	39.5	9.5	-	13.0		46351	11.6	39.7	26.3	4.9	-	0.9		23233
Katumbar	46.7	16.0	22.6	5.6	9.1		69272	9.9	37.2	45.56	7.8	2.2	2.9		25667
Alwar	40.0	33.5	10.6	6.0	15.3		108713	7.6	19.5	62	3.2	3.4	0.7		64158
Bansur	62.8	1.9	30	3.2	2.1		125611	13.5	42.7	15	2.9	15.6	2.2		36344
Thanaghazi	57.8	18.7	13	-	10.5		32797	10.3	55.9	19.7	3.4	-	2.5		16864
Total	58.6	13.4	15.6	6.6	5.8		1041638	8.8	31.9	34.8	8.5	11.6	.86	475	705

(Contd.)

(Contd.)

Bharatpur tehsils	Kharif Foodcrops			Non food			Total Area	Rabi Foodcrops				Nonfood-crops		Total Area	
	Bajra	Jowar	Masina	Gawar chari	Cotton	Til	Kharif Total Area	Wheat	Barley	Gram	Gochni Bejhar	Sarshaf Linseed Taramira	Tobacco & poppy	Rabi	Total area
Pahari	31.6	31.3	5.4	10.27	10	9.8	130052	9.6	15.26	37.12	26.3	11			77150
Kama	45.9	24.5	6.25	9.87	8.8	2.8	104028	7.6	14.85	55.5	15.4	5.93			67065
Deeg	29.5	38.2	11.6	6.5	8.2	5.2	66045	9.23	18.8	57.3	6.1	6.47			45241
Kumher	17.7	46.8	18.9	6.1	3.1	6.6	86986	18	23.6	45.2	.4	11.52			56889
Akheygarh	33	26.76	23.4	5.48	4.92	5	149593	18.6	40.95	26	4.35	3.1			51073
Nagar	33.5	30.5	8.9	9.7	5.88	9.87	138208	11.47	17.48	40.73	19.47	8.37			84573
Bharatpur	23	43.4	19	5.6	2.36	4.5	86001	22.7	17.1	31.13	20.6	6.14			73865
Rupbas	52.48	9.4	7.4	6.3	5.6	12.4	145248	15.1	27.6	16.28	23	11.55			67667
Bayana	48	9.85	19.24	5.2	11.53	4.75	129799	19.9	31.8	16.1	13.24	4.14			53909
Weir	43.9	17.65	18.34	4.6	10.2	4.33	155383	13.11	33.4	26.8	8.97	.85			61265
Total	37.34	25.65	14.2	6.9	7.3	6.78	1191343	14.39	23.2	34.93	14.98	7.17			638697

The above data is based on: O'Dwyer: Final Report on Alwar Settlement, Appendix B, pp. vii-xv; Final Report on Bharatpur Settlement, Appendix no.8, pp. vi-viii.

Notes & References

1. La Touche's Report, p. 109
2. Para 3, Government of India Order no. 615-I of March 10, 1883: cited by Whiteway: op.cit., p.1
3. O'Dwyer: Final Report on Alwar, pp. 71-72
4. O'Dwyer: Eastern Tehsils, p. 72; Northern and Southern Tehsils, p. 63; Central and Southern Tehsils, p. 63; Northern Tehsils of Bharatpur, p. 43; Central Tehsils p. 45; Southern Tehsils, p. 54
5. O'Dwyer: Eastern Tehsils, p. 73
6. Ibid., pp. 73, 76-77; Northern and Southern Tehsils, p. 92; Central and Southern Tehsils, p. 94; Northern Tehsils Report, p. 82; Central Tehsils, p. 76; Southern Tehsils, p. 81
7. Northern Tehsils, pp. 82-95; Central Tehsils, pp. 75-79; Southern Tehsils, pp. 81, 85; Eastern Tehsils, pp. 73-80; Northern and Southern Tehsils, pp. 90-99; Central and Southern Tehsils, pp. 92-99
8. Eastern Tehsils, p. 42
9. Final Report on Alwar, p. 69
10. Final Report on Bharatpur, p. 73; Central Tehsils, p. 80; Southern Tehsils, p. 82
11. Eastern Tehsils, pp. 76-83

11a. The data about cash rents is seattered in the assessment reports of the various tehsils. For Alwar it has been compiled from : Easterh Tehsils, pp. 72, 75, 76, 78, 80; Northern & Southern Tehsils, pp. 90, 92, 97, 99; Central & Southern Tehsils, pp. 93, 96, 98 For Bharatpur : Northern Tehsils, pp. 81, 85, 87; Central Tehsils, pp. 75, 77; Southern Tehsils, pp. 81, 82

12. Northern and Southern Tehsils of Alwar; 99-100, 106-107. O'Dwyer was aware that the last assessment had been heavy and cultivation had been reduced by 5% in Rajgarh tehsil; but his argument was that 'this tehsil had great resources in its cattle and enormous area of pasture'. He raised the revenue by 10%.. Eastern Tehsils, p. 81; Central and Southern Tehsils, pp. 92-98 The fallow land was taken into account in the annual *bachh*. Northern Tehsils Report, p. 96; Central Tehsils, p. 91; Southern Tehsils, p. 83
13. Final Report on Alwar, pp. 78, 109; Northern and Southern Tehsils, p. 100; Northern Tehsils, p. 82
14. Final Report on Alwar, p. 110; Eastern Tehsils, p. 81

15. Northern and Southern Teshils Report, p. 97; Central and Southern Tehsils Report p. 98; Northern Tehsils of Bharatpur, p. 86; Final Report on Bharatpur, p. 69
16. Final Report on Bharatpur, pp.63,65-66,70. The data compiled in Table no.3 substantiates the argument. The 10% enhancement of state demand amounted to 65% enhancement for the peasantry because the state demand was 2/3rd of what the peasant paid to the zamindar. The peasant paid 50% more to the zamindar.
17. Northern Tehsils, pp. 76-77; Central Tehsils, p. 71; Southern Tehsils, p. 77; Eastern tehsils, pp. 66-68
18. Lupton: Water Revenue Report, pp. 67
19. Ibid., Statement no. VI, p. 24
20. Ibid., Appendix no. XII
21. Lupton: Land Settlement Report., p.31
22. Northern Tehsils Report, p. 74; Central and Southern Tehsils, p. 86
23. Eastern Tehsils, p. 65; Northern Tehsils, p. 75
24. Central Tehsils, p. 69; Southern Tehsils, p. 75
25. Northern Tehsils, p. 74
26. Northern and Southern Tehsils, p. 86; Central and Southern Tehsils, p. 86
27. Ibid.
28. Northern Tehsils, p. 78; Central Tehsils, p. 72; Southern Tehsils, p. 78; Northern and Southern Tehsils, pp. 86-87; Central and Southern Tehsils, p. 88
29. Bharatpur Settlement Report of 1930, pp. 48-50.
30. La Touche's Report, pp. 94-95, 216.
31. Whiteway raised the revenue demand by 7.4%. op. cit., p. 32
32. Lupton: Land Settlement Report, pp. 21, 30
33. Northern Tehsils, pp. 66-68; Eastern Tehsils, p. 56; Central and Southern Tehsils, Appendix C, p. 1iii
34. Northern Tehsils, Appendix B, pp. 180-181
35. Ibid., pp. 74-76
36. Eastern Tehsils, Area Statement no.1, pp. 116-117
37. Ibid., Appendix D., pp. 106-107
38. Ibid., pp. 107-108

5

Investment of Capital and Increasing Cattle Wealth

I

Almost all land settlement officers spoke of their object of encouraging investment of capital in land which had not been permitted, as they put it, by the traditional structure of land system. The entire focus was on providing enough foodgrains for the common cultivator. The payment of land revenue in kind to the state met the needs of the royal household and the needs of the state. The trader came into picture largely when the production had been affected by scarcity and famine.

The investment of capital in land had various shades in different state situations. One of them may be understood by a comparative projection of the roles of *ijaredars/mustajjirs* on the one hand and *manotidars* on the other. Both these institutions coexisted in Tonk and Jhalawar, the former exclusively in Dholpur, a variety of the latter existed partly in Kota and Udaipur. The *ijaredars* were a group of wealthy and influential men who invested money in encouraging the cultivation of cash crops like opium. The British Government had conveyed very little information to the opium growing Indian states and the traders and financers therein about the changes in its policy towards opium cultivation after 1884 and the fall in opium prices in the Chinese market. Even in 1893-94 it misinformed the states about the purpose of enquiry by the Royal Commission on opium.[1] The *ijaredars* who had accepted responsibility for revenue realisation in opium growing parganas, suddenly found themselves saddled with loosing investments, some found themselves verging on bankruptcy. Pears blamed the Tonk ruler for not reducing the land revenue demand after 1884 in opium growing areas. He allowed the *ijaredars* a 5% discount on the settlement demand and the option of either retaining or abandoning the *ijara*. In Nimbahera, all *ijaredars*, except a small minority, threw up their leases but in other parganas they continued. Pears reduced the demand in the three opium growing parganas but projected the *ijaredari* system as injurious to agricultural prosperity of the state. He further projected some of the *ijaredars* as not being men of wealth and influence now; they were held guilty of discouraging cultivation, and adopting 'unhealthy practices' towards the close of their contractual terms so that the leases might be renewed at a lower amount.[2]

His attitude to the *manotidars* stood out in sharp contrast to the above. A *manotidar* was one who stood surety (*manoti*) for revenue payment to the state. The *manotidars* mostly belonged to the banking and trading classes, though some patels, cultivators and ex-agriculturists were also included in the group. As an intermediary, he contracted both with the cultivator and the state as regards banking transactions with the former. He provided the cultivators with advances of grain for seed, of money for agricultural operations, ordinary and extra-ordinary expenses, the cultivators in return agreeing not to dispose of the produce of their fields elsewhere until the claims of the *manotidars* have been first satisfied. The price at which the produce was to be credited was settled either by mutual agreement or by state arbitration. The *manotidar's* contract with the state was that he was responsible for the revenue payment of the cultivators on condition that the state undertook to consider the advances made by him to the cultivators on all accounts as 'a first charge on the cultivator's crops' and to afford him all assistance in the realization of his dues, whenever this may be necessary. The *manotidar* could not withdraw except after due notice and with the approval of the Durbar; he could be dismissed by the state for breaking the conditions of the agreement or on the request of the cultivators if found reasonable. If he were dismissed at the request of the cultivators, his claims would have to be satisfied first either by the new *manotidar* or the cultivators; if he were dismissed for breach of contract or exactions, he would not be given any assistance by the state to recover his outstanding balances from the cultivators.[3]

The *manotidar* was thus a surety for the revenue payment and a licensed agricultural banker combined in one. He was spoken of very highly by Pears and Abbott. Pears declared that the land revenue settlement would revive the *manotidari* system which had been disturbed by the inefficient administration. Complaints about the oppressions and tyranny of the *manotidars* in Pirawa pargana (Tonk) or at Jhalawar were considered to have been the result of state inefficiency which did not ensure punctual payment of the loans by the cultivators. If any evils had crept into the system at Jhalawar, the state administration was held responsible for it. The institution was considered a 'good agricultural banking arrangement' which enabled the wealthy and respectable firms to supply the ever needed capital to the cultivators on fair terms. The *manotidars,* because of a permanent interest in the cultivators, could highlight cases of over assessment and the need for remission and suspension of revenue demand. Abbott considered that a *manoti assami* was better placed than either a self supporting *assami* (*gurhu dewal*), or a *bania*-cum-court worried *assami* or a khalsa *assami*.[4]

This difference in attitude and approach to the *ijaredars* and *manotidars* became understandable in the light of the general approach of the British towards the problem of investments in land. They were keen to find a class of men having money and willing to invest in land. The policy was not in favour of a class which farmed the revenues of the parganas and claimed discount from the money which belonged, as they thought, to the state. A class which took peasants' money was welcome but a class which shared state's resources was not. Pears changed the agency of revenue collection; paid 3% commission to the *patels* for the job, called it '*amani*' system, and saved 2%. After the settlement, the *ijaredars* were also paid 3% in place of 5% commission. Any increase or decrease in the revenues of the village would be the share of the *ijaredars*. The *amani* system was a variation of the earlier practice since the *patels* were paid a commission by the state.

Pears developed the argument that the indebtedness of the cultivators was on account of the *ijaredars* who were held guilty of deterring all incentives to improvement. Every increase in output was followed by a proportionate increase in the revenue collected by the *ijaredar* which may not be deposited in the state. This was the great disincentive to all improvements. The system was held to be unprofitable to the government because it led to a continuous scrapping of all surplus production. The *manotidar* was preferred because his demands were limited; he encouraged investment in land and improvement of agriculture 'because the proprietor will be satisfied that he was labouring for himself'. The system ensured regular fiscal receipts.

The figures shown in Table 5.1 clearly show the tremendous changes brought about by a change in the agency of collection.[5] The *ijaredars* were left to collect only 3% of their previous contracts and amounts; the *manotidars* increased their responsibility by 357% and the *amani* system was extended by 434% to new areas to collect the revenues.

TABLE: 5.1

Change in the Revenue Collecting Agency (Tonk)

Tonk Pargana	Year	*Manotidar* Rupees	*Ijaredar* Rupees	*Patel* Rupees	*Amani* Rupees	Total Amount
Nimbahera	1886-87	63173	120737		30799	218709
	1891-92	111636	804	93503	28463	241606
Pirawa	1886-87	2980	160647		1141	164768
	1891-92	86666	9396		102608	198670
Chabra	1886-87	11858	97904		8851	118613
	1891-92	80803	1194		46011	128008

Wingate talked of investment in land in a different context. He was aware that the extension of cultivation could take place only in inferior soil because the best lands for either wet (irrigated) or dry (*barani*) cultivation, had already been occupied. He argued that more revenue could not be looked for till there was extension of cultivation. He, for reasons of his own, believed that there was a good deal of accumulated capital seeking investment, even though labour and cultivators were scarce, the latter could very quickly be attracted from other parts.[6] He was convinced that a favourable moment for adopting a policy intended to induce a large investment of capital in land had come; this would succeed in bringing about an increase of revenue in future. The investment would be in constructing new wells to irrigate the poorer and distant lands which were lying waste at that time. The capital could be attracted, he argued, only if the new wells were taxed at lower rates. He talked of encouragement to new wells by Maharana Swarup Singh during 1841-61; but he was keen to propose more concessional terms for the new wells than had been granted earlier. Formerly, a new well was taxed at a lower rate for a few years and then the taxation was enhanced. Wingate wanted to grant concessions to the new wells for the whole duration of the settlement. He therefore divided the wells into ancient, modern and new wells; wells dug during this settlement period were called new wells; at the next settlement, these new wells would become modern and the modern wells of the last settlement would become ancient. He advocated the view that the profits of labour and of capital must be satisfied before the government assessment and therefore put forth many concessions for new wells.[7]

A separate category of rules was framed for the new wells. Any one could make a new well and get an area allotted to it. 15 to 20 bighas of land was ordinarily allotted though a bigger area also could be given. The maximum area which would be charged for irrigation from the new well varied from three to five bighas depending upon the class of village: three, four or five in a third, second or first class village respectively. Irrigation in the first year was free; the rate of Rs.5/- per bigha would be charged only in the fifth year. This rate was much less than the irrigation rate for the ancient and modern wells. He argued that the agency for digging wells was different and needed attractions for investing capital in land. Wingate suggested revenue demand from new wells at very low rates. His stock argument was that without low rates for new cultivation, *mahajans* and cultivators would not invest their savings in wells.[8]

The rules for new irrigation contained further instructions for *hakims* to enter into a contract with the owners of new wells about the extent of land to be irrigated by a well in accordance with the maximum area defined above. The *hakim* was to be pulled up if he did not enter into such a contract and waited for 5 years (also permitted under the rules) so that a more beneficial agreement for the state could be signed. It was specially mentioned that the object was to multiply wells rapidly and encourage them by a very liberal policy.[9] After the settlement, Wingate hoped that land in the pargana would acquire a high value. The pargana was fertile and a railway passed close to it and there was every prospect of much competition for the waste areas.

More important than the above provisions for extension of irrigation, were rules numbering 18 and 19 for ancient irrigation which were made applicable for all types of irrigation—modern and new included. These rules tightened the *mahajan's* noose round the neck of the cultivator. These rules pertained to a well becoming useless (rule 18) and its re-making (rule 19) afterwards. Rule 18 provided : "When a well for any cause becomes useless, the assessment is to be reduced to the rate for dry manured land prevailing in the neighbourhood..." Rule 19 provided for a permission to remake a well which had been certified useless earlier; the normal rate for land under such a well should not be less than 3/4 of the former payment unless it was certified that the well had become useless and the land had been injured in its fertility.

The rules as such may appear to be harmless but the explanation attached to them brought out their significance. These rules were also applicable to cases where an indebted *assami* could not come to terms with his *mahajan,* the latter taking possession of the former's land and the land lying fallow for a few years, the *mahajan* not getting anyone to work it and the *assami* not allowing the owner to do so. The *mahajan* continued to pay the revenue otherwise he shall have to give up all claim to the land and with it the debt upon it. Under these rules, such a *mahajan* might get the well declared useless and so escape paying at irrigation rates for it. When he and the *assami* had come to terms, he might get the benefit of having remade the well by some minor repair. The intention was to provide relief to a man from the injustice of paying for years for a dry hole at irrigation rates.[10]

The far reaching impact of this change can hardly be over emphasized. It altered fundamentally the terms of trade between a *mahajan* and a peasant. Whatever constraints existed on the *mahajan* to come to terms with his debtor, were now removed. Earlier when the *mahajan* had been paying at irrigation rates for a land which he could not get cultivated, he would be willing to come to terms with the cultivator; now that the liability of the *mahajan* had been substantially reduced, he came to be in a dictating situation. It was the cultivator who was now in the losing situation. If the *mahajan* was later on able to find a cultivator, he could get the same land cultivated and pay for at 3/4th of normal rates which could even be less if the *hakim* so recommended.

The significant emphasis laid on the need to extend cultivation to inferior lands at a time when 'labour and cultivators were scarce', was an acceptance of great pressure of unemployed population, which had been displaced from traditional crafts and cottage industries. Any extension of cultivation was possible only if wells could be dug. Wingate therefore laid great emphasis on investment of capital in land and on providing heavy concessions to the people who did so. The new situation was that the new cultivators were people without resources and the digging of wells would have to be undertaken by a different set of people having resources. Wingate went out of his way to create a new class of wells—new wells—by classifying the earlier wells into ancient and modern. This helped him to lay down different irrigation rates for the new wells which were considerably lower than the other two categories. He made his object clearer when he did not provide for the concessional rates for new wells dug in fields which were irrigated by old wells which had now become useless.

Irrigation and cultivation could only extend to poorer lands yielding comparatively smaller profits. The revenue income of the state could increase only from new cultivation at lower rates for the present but which would lead to increasing revenue yields in the years to come. The object of the settlement was "to lay down such rules and principles for the future as shall lead to an immediate and wide increase in the newly cultivated and newly irrigated area, specially in the latter".[11]

It was Wingate's desire to make well central to the land revenue system. He therefore, by laboured arguments, projected the land revenue demand in Sadri Pargana to have been a lump sum demand on 'ancient' wells. He argued that the total demand for all lands—irrigated, dry, manured, and unmanured—within the range of irrigation of a well was the revenue demand on the well. He came across various forms of keeping accounts while going through thousands of individual *assami* accounts in the *hakim's* note books. He cited account keeping methods of about 20 cases out of which one recommended itself to him. It was in relation to well No.491 where 10½ bighas of irrigated land belonged to three accounts, Nos. 70, 71 and 72. He picked this up as supporting evidence for his suggestion of assessments being based on wells as units. He deliberately ignored the over whelming number of cases denying the practice. In all his instances, there was always a mention of rate per bigha for the three types of land and yet he wanted his readers to believe that the past practice of determining the assessment was based on the well. He was not able to cite a single instance where a cultivator's liability for land revenue was determined by a certain share or percentage of assessment on the well. The absence of any system of accounting by the well (he later introduced the well slip for making well central to the assessment structure) was proof, if any were needed, of the fact that the doctrine of assessment by the well had been non-existent earlier. While explaining settlement rules 2 & 3, he confessed that the reason for binding up all the land under a well and assessing it at a fixed contract sum for the term of the settlement in preference to levying a rate per irrigated bigha was the need to avoid annual measurement or inspection of the area irrigated. He neither credited the cultivator with honesty to abide by the rules nor allowed the *hakim* any discretionary role in the implementation of the recommendations of the settlement. He was keen to ensure fixity of payment for a particular land. He confessed introducing it for the first time. He wrote: 'I have discussed it (assessment by the well) and I think it will work easily'.[12] He was insistent on devising a unit (well) which should not be interfered by sub-divisions and transfer of ownership. He wanted to make the 'well' fundamentally important.

The prevalent practice of entering the name of the *mahajan* in the account books of the *hakim* was misconstrued by Wingate. He cited a number of cases where the names of the *mahajan* and the cultivator were jointly entered, and a few cases where the name of the cultivator was not there or where the name of the *mahajan* was missing. A few instances of only the *mahajan's* name were generalised by Wingate to imply that the *mahajan* had taken over the ownership of land with or without the fact of sale or mortgage having been recorded. He argued that land had changed hands in *katcha* and *pucca bapï* tenures, and thus buttressed his claim that the money lender had taken over possession of land in the past also. This was a misconstruction because a change of ownership had not taken place. The termination of ownership of land was not conceivable, except by sale, in the pre-settlement day. He pretended to confer security of tenure on the cultivator by providing that 'no land could be sold without the written consent of the occupier'. His contention that the creditor was already stepping into possession of his debtor's lands was incorrect. He suppressed the real significance of the *mahajan*'s name being entered in the books of the *hakim* in order to convey a totally wrong impression. The *mahajans* were allowed a concessional rate of land revenue. This was the reason that he did not find a mention of the rate of interest in the accounts cited by him in the Sadri pargana. The *mahajan* made the payment of land revenue at his concessional rates; the cultivator paid the *mahajan* at the rate he would have paid to the government; the difference realised by the *mahajan* was his interest on money advanced to the peasant. His real intentions became clear when he legalised the procedure of making land attractive for capital to be invested in it. He aimed at strengthening the process of *mahajans* acquiring land ownership and claimed this to be equivalent of investment of capital in land. He had prophetically said: 'If this settlement is sanctioned on the basis proposed. . . land will very shortly acquire very high value'. He wanted 'credit for this enhancement in the value of land' on account of investment of capital 'to be due to settlement alone'.[13]

This was the process by which the theoretical acceptability of the money lender with the tiller of the soil was transformed into a situation where the money lender was given the right to push out the cultivator. The settlement facilitated and quickened the process of transfer of land to the money lender; the written consent of a helpless cultivator would be as easy as his oral consent because his liability to pay had been enhanced and his ability to resist the *mahajan* was considerably reduced. The acquisition of land ownership by the *mahajan* after he had advanced money for well construction had been made possible by the land settlement. This was Wingate's encouragement to investment of capital in land.

Bharatpur was agriculturally the most fertile state in the region and the Administrative Reports, during the decade 1866-76 talked of a prosperous peasantry.[14] Walter had calculated in 1866 that the cultivated area was 740,000 acres. When Dwyer found in 1897 that the cultivated area was only 533,392 acres, he was very condemnatory of the state government and even questioned the correctness of the earlier figures. He knew the real cause of the decline of agricultural prosperity of the state, but he chose to blame the land revenue assessment policy of the state for its failure to attract investment of capital in land by the non-cultivating banker. It was his diagnosis that over assessment had left land of no value to the financier; it had kept the zamindars in possession of their ancestral areas which offered no temptations to the outsiders. He did not modify the state prohibition on mortgages and sale of land to the non-agriculturists. He was aware of the fact that the richer elements of the local trading community had migrated out of the state after the prohibition of salt manufacture in January 1879 since there were no alternative areas for investment of capital.

Fearing diversion of capital from the neighbouring districts of Agra and Mathura for investment in land in the state, Dwyer did not create conditions conducive for the banking classes to invest money in land. Instead he created a rentier class of zamindars, provides them with 1/3rd cash rents as profit rents and called this policy as conducive to investment of capital in land. He, by introducing a new class of intermediaries, kept the peasantry in the state backward and over burdened with revenue demand. The new class was provided with ostensible surplus funds drawn from the peasantry. It was given concessions to invest this money in land. Dwyer, in accordance with the changed policy perspective of the British Government towards land alienation, had allowed the restrictions on transfer of land to non-agricultural classes to remain as before; only the mutation fee had been reduced from 10 to 5% on sale and mortgage deeds. He had found that indebtedness to any heavy extent was comparatively rare, and attributed this absence to the restriction of credit, the absence of legal practitioners and other opportunities for expensive litigation. Some villages did not even have a money lender; the indebtedness did not exceed one year's revenue demand.[15] The money lenders were prevented, he argued, from making large advances to the peasantry because of restrictions on land transfer to non-agricultural classes. He had raised the state revenue demand by about 10% but the peasantry had been subjected to paying 65% more land revenue to the new intermediary class. He hoped that by keeping the existing restrictions on transfer of land to non-agriculturists and by reducing the credit worthiness of the peasantry, he would be able to escape the blame for subordinating the peasantry to the money lender. But no amount of restrictions could prevent the peasantry from going under debt when the demand had been enhanced heavily.

The 10% enhancement had practically meant 65% for the peasantry as explained earlier. The practical consequences of this policy can best be seen by a comparison of the figures of mortgages and sales of land to the agriculturists and moneylenders. The tehsilwise data (Appendix No. G and H) has been consolidated to give the following picture.

Land Area Mortgaged and Sold in Bharatpur (In bighas)

Year	Land area mortgaged to		Land area sold to	
	Agriculturists	Moneylenders	Agriculturists	Moneylenders
1855-90	105998	25114	76200	31644
1890-98	135711	28352	24638	10281
1898-1930	112822	15701	70183	10289

The sale price of land in Bharatpur remained far below the value of land in the districts of Mathura and Agra. Though it had increased from Rs. 5/- per acre in 1897 to about Rs.10/- per acre in 1930, still it remained far behind the rates of Rs.20 to 30 per acre in the neighbouring districts.

The gradual impoverishment of the Bharatpur peasantry may also be seen in the reports of the Political Agent in the State. In 1870-71 and 1873-74, he talked of the prosperity of the peasantry; Dwyer at the time of his settlement talked of the standard of living not being below that of the neighbouring districts of British India; the settlement of 1930 confessed that 'the general standard of living is very low'; 'the decline in the state as a whole is. . . due to adverse agricultural conditions including decreased resources of the cultivators'.[17] In 1898-99, many examples of heavy indebtedness could not be found even though the state land revenue demand was held to be high. But by 1930, the indebtedness was to the extent of 10 years' land revenue demand. This indebtedness was the direct result of introducing an intermediary class of land proprietors in the state.

Alwar and Bharatpur were the two states where the land revenue settlements introduced by the British Political officers had been in operation since 1858 and 1855 respectively. The land settlements had been frequently revised leading to a gradual enhancement of revenue demand, reflected in the greater incidence of mortgage and sale of land. Bharatpur had imposed restrictions on land alienations; it was allowed only to fellow agriculturists. Such money lenders whose ancestors were agriculturists or whose collaterals were involved in agriculture could be the mortgagees or purchasers of land. The state had imposed a duty of 10% on all land transactions which led to fewer sale and mortgage transactions being recorded. O' Dwyer got this duty reduced to 5% in order to get all deeds of sale and mortgage recorded.

While the British officers in Ajmer Merwara had considered the high incidence of sale and mortgage of land to be the result of heavy revenue demand, Dwyer thought the absence of sale and mortgage to be an indicator of oppressive demand. It was an indication of his general approach of finding fault with all traditional institutions. He argued that land had been assessed heavily by the state; hence it had no value for the money lender who could derive no profit from it as a non-cultivating landowner. Dwyer himself enhanced the revenue demand by 10% and made the possession of land by non-cultivating owners still less attractive. The restrictions on transfer of land to non-agricultural classes remained as before. Still he claimed that by creating a class of zamindars he had created a class which would invest money in land. By way of persuading the new zamindars to accept responsibility for paying the revenue demand, he remitted all arrears of land revenue prior to 1890. If the arrears of revenue, during 1890-97, were only marginal he found fault with the state administration by saying that the credit should go to years of good rainfall and fresh lands having been brought under cultivation. In the absence of these, the arrears would have increased manifold.

Bharatpur's agriculture was very adversely affected by the prohibition of salt manufacture enforced in 1880. Large tracts of lands were rendered unfit for cultivation on account of salinity of soil. The population of the state declined sharply in the post 1881 period; the value of uncultivated land fell more than that of cultivated land; the mortgage and sale of land also increased.

The average land revenue collections in Alwar state during 1854-59 had been 13.59 lakhs; it had been raised to 20.11 lakhs by Powlett in 1876 by his 16 year settlement. Sale of land had not been resorted to by the peasants till 1876 and mortgage of land had not exceeded 1% of cultivated land. The British practice of recovering land revenue for the famine year had disastrous consequences; during 1876-1896, 36% of *chahi* lands at Alwar had either been mortgaged or sold out.[19] (Appendix No. H). Sales to money-lenders were very few but mortgages to money lenders were 37% of the total. While Jennings talked of an enhancement of 4 lakhs in the revenue demand, the peasantry had been forced to mortgage and sell 8.5 times more land during 1876-98 than in pre 1876 period. The statement of mortgage and sale of land in different tehsils gives the following figures:

	Land mortgaged	Land sold	Total area
Before 1876	9896 bighas	83 bighas	9979 bighas
1876-1898	59028 bighas	25891 bighas	84919 bighas
1876-98 multiplication of area	5.96 times	312 times	8.5 times

Land was not mortgaged or sold for recreation; the fact that 8.5 times the total land mortgaged or sold in the pre 1876 period had been mortgaged during 1876-98 revealed the incidence of heavy land revenue demand imposed in 1876.

The mortgage and sale of land increased on account of heavy land revenue demand imposed by the British settlement officers. The contention that there used to be lesser arrears of revenue and very few mortgages in the pre settlement period was equally true even in the case of a small and comparatively poorer state of Dungarpur. A.T. Holme, Assistant Resident, Mewar and Settlement Officer, wrote in 1905 that 'there is not as yet very much mortgaged land in Dungarpur.'[20] By 1924 when the third land revenue settlement was undertaken, the cultivators and *assamis* often mortgaged their lands to other cultivators. Within a short span of 20 years 4% land area had been mortgaged.[21]

TABLE: 5.2

Land Area (Bighas) Mortgaged (Dungarpur) 1905-24

Circle	Class I	Calsss II	Class III	Class IV	Class V	Total
Dungarpur	125.7	417.95	982.8	729.75	297	2553.2
Sagwara	1421.55	601.6	166.6	27.00	-	2216.75
Aspur	1822.9	541.6	502.0	-	-	2866.5
Total	3370.15	1561.15	1651.4	756.75	297	7636.45

The better quality lands were mortgaged to a larger extent than the lower quality lands. In the case of Jhalawar, when land settlement was first introduced in 1884-85, the area of mortgaged land was less than 1%.[22]

Peasant Poverty and the Money Lender

A study of the British perception of the causes of peasant indebtedness becomes very fruitful and instructive in this context. Though in the beginning there was a fairly objective understanding of the causes of peasant impoverishment, this was transformed slowly. The understanding of the administrators of Ajmer district clearly reflected the changing attitudes of the imperial bureaucracy.

Ajmer was a rich district and was evaluated at Rs. 505,484 in July 1818. The limitations of time frame during which

Hastings had to complete his policy of extending imperial protection over the Rajput states, led him to accept the face value of the district. The attempt to realise 50% gross produce at the prices of 1817-18 was easily approved because the goal of the administration was to realise the sum of Rs. 5.05 lakhs. It resulted in large scale impoverishment as explained earlier. Almost every one of the superintendents of the district conceded, during 1818-36, that the excessive land revenue demand had impoverished the peasantry. The attempt to project the British administration in a better light began in the thirties when the district administration was criticised by the N.W.P. authorities for the impoverishment of the peasantry due to heavy state demand of land revenue. The search for alibis, begun thereafter, was able to locate three forces; two of them pertained to the human element and a third pertained to natural forces. Edmonstone was the first person to talk about the recklessness of the peasantry and the role of the money lenders and *bohras*. He neither gave any factual data to substantiate positively the oppression of the money lender nor adduced evidence to support the lighter incidence of the land revenue.

Dixon, by his own confession, had enhanced the land revenue demand to the maximum. For this and for reasons of his superior ability to propagate his achievements through the 'Sketch of Mairwara', he, of all the administrators, was allowed the longest stay in Ajmer Merwara; but he was not promoted to the post of AGG which required diplomatic skill with the Rajput rulers. He had called upon the bankers/*mahajans* to pay up the land revenue demand on behalf of their *assami* peasants; they were asked to realise it later from them, if necessary through a court of law. Dixon's land revenue demand had been pegged so high that it was not exceeded for the next more than half a century despite three revisions of land revenue settlements, some extension in the area under cultivation and the price rise during the period. He had brought in the *mahajan* because the peasant was not able to regularly pay the heavy demand. During the two decades of Dixonian settlement, the peasantry had been impoverished so much that despite the cultivation of cash crop like opium by a hard working and industrious peasantry, the earlier prosperity of the district could not be restored. The AGG's report on the famine of 1868 and La Touche's settlement report of 1874 had highlighted that the peasant in Ajmer district had been forced to fall into the clutches of the money lender because of the need to pay a fixed heavy demand of land revenue irrespective of the field produce.

The settlement officers—Dixon or La Touche—did not dispute the fact of poverty; but they held the vagaries of weather or the revenue demand in the famine years as the basic cause of this poverty. Col. Brooke, in his report on the famine of 1868, confessed that 'much of the indebtedness of the villagers was caused by the necessity of borrowing money to meet the Government demand'.[23] Notwithstanding the total loss of crops in 1868-69, the irrecoverable balances of the year were only Rs. 35261. This was added to the next year's demand, an unusual procedure in case of famine. The Government resorted to attachment of moveable property of the *patels* in 1868; the number of sales and mortgages of land in order to discharge the government demand went up. La Touche cited the instance of village Rassoolpura where the realisation of revenue demand in the famine of 1868 led to the mortgaging of half the *chahi* and *abi* lands by 1874. The same view was expressed by the Report on the Famine Relief in Merwara during 1891-92. It said that 'there is no doubt that the indebtedness of the rural population of the district was very largely increased by the indiscriminate recovery of Government revenue after the famine of 1868-69.[24]

La Touche lowered the demand by 14% and claimed the incidence of land revenue to be as light as ¼ to 1/6th of the gross produce. The claim was not justified as seen earlier in the

TABLE: 5.3

Mortgage and Sale of Land in Ajmer Merwara 1849-1908

Tehsil	Years	Mortgaged Land (Acres)	% of Increase	Land Sold (Acres)	Total land Sold & Mortgaged	Total Irrigated Area Chahi & Talahi	Abi	% of land Mortgaged & Sold to total area
Ajmer	1849-74	12561		2878	15439	26013	7098	46.6
	1874-84	15662	24.7	4160	19822	26918	7446	57.6
	1884-1908	23327	48.9	11629	34956	30150	7303	93.2
Beawar	1849-74	5541		2325	7866	14336	9562	32.9
	1874-84	6581	18.77	2084	8665	14156	7770	39.56
	1884-1908	10856	65.00	4373	15229	15250	8759	63.45
Todgarh	1849-74	8430		459	8889	10414	2303	70
	1874-84	8076	-4.2	506	8582	10875	922	72.7
	1884-1908	12581	+55	2387	14968	12679	881	110.4*
Total District	1849-74	26532		5662	32194	50763	18963	46.2
	1874-84	30319	14.3	6750	37069	51949	16438	54.2
	1884-1908	46764	54.27	18389	65153	58079	16943	86.87
	1874-1908		76.35		+102.35%			

* Even Barani land had been mortgaged.

chapter on equitable demand because the yield and valuation of the crop was inflated by subtle devices. The end result of the land settlements was reflected in land mortgaged and sold by the peasantry.

The data on mortgage and sale of land in Ajmer Merwara during 1849-1908, given in table 5.3, shows that the percentage of land mortgaged and sold went on increasing. In Todgarh, even *barani* land was sold and mortgaged.[25]

The search for external factors for the poverty of the peasantry, begun much earlier, was, in the post 1874 period, pursued with a vigour. The Government had practically abandoned the attempt to provide additional irrigation resources and had even restricted the maintenance of the existing ones. Both Whiteway and Lupton remarked about the decline of the existing tanks under government management. The harshness of land revenue settlements was replaced by a discussion about the harshness of the weather; the inability of the peasantry to pay was attributed to vagaries of the rain god. This view began to be advocated about other states in the region. Dwyer wrote that the agricultural prosperity of the state (Alwar) 'is almost entirely dependent on the rainfall being adequate and well distributed'. New emphasis on the growth of cattle wealth—cows, buffaloes, beasts of burden—and ploughs was laid; and it was held as a sign of agricultural wealth and prosperity. If despite this growth of agricultural prosperity, the peasant poverty was on the increase, they argued, the fault lay either with the extravagant peasant or with the bloodsucking moneylender. The real implications of growing cattle wealth have been dealt later; the new role of the money lender needs to be analyzed objectively.

The traditional system of revenue collection in the pre settlement period did not bring the money lender into so much prominence. The state collected ¼ to ½ of the gross produce as its revenue through the village officials. Thereafter it was the responsibility of the local officials, under the direction of the state government, either to convert the land revenue collected in kind, into cash or to send the grains to the state granaries. In case of famine or scarcity, if the fields did not produce a crop, the cultivator was normally free from the liability of paying the state demand of land revenue; the state suffered from paucity of resources much like the cultivator. The magnitude of the problem of arrears of revenue was much less. The cultivators borrowed money for personal or family reasons or for improvement of seeds and livestock but the incidence of indebtedness was very much lower in comparison to the post revenue settlement scenario. The phenomenon of land continuing mortgaged for a number of generations was not unknown. The fundamental reason which caused the incidence of peasant indebtedness to grow tremendously was the heavy land revenue demand which had to be paid irrespective of the produce of land; the ownership of land had imposed the duty of payment of land revenue. Since it has been pitched high, indebtedness in years of average production was normal; in years of scarcity and famine it became universal. All other causes of peasant indebtedness in Rajasṭhan were derivative of this first cause.

Besides the data on sale and mortgage, the fragmentation of land holdings in Ajmer Merwara, alongwith the increase in number of ploughs and proprietors of land laid bare the increasing impoverishment of the peasantry in the district and the state. The data on the number of proprietors is being given below[27]:

		Number of Proprietors		
		Non-resident	Resident	Total
La Touche's settlement	1874	8347	39209	47556
Whiteway's settlement	1884	12791	39425	52216
Lupton's Report	1908	19029	56583	75612

This increase in the number of proprietor cultivators was not due to any pressure of population. The population of the district had grown from 460722 in 1881 to 476912 in 1901 or 3.5% only; while the proprietor cultivators had grown from 47556 to 75612 or 59%. The average area owned by a proprietor had come down from 3.6 to 2.42 acres. The increasing fragmentation of land holdings accompanied by the heavy indebtedness of the peasantry was an indication of subsistence agriculture. The high increase in the number of cultivators was the result of the closure of other avenues of employment within the district. Agriculture had become a major source of livelihood for the vast numbers who had been otherwise engaged in arts and crafts earlier. The revenue demand had been so heavy that 93% and 80.4% lands in Ajmer and Merwara tehsils respectively were mortgaged. This abject poverty of the agricultural classes on khalsa land in British administered district was not a heritage from the past; it was the creation of land revenue policy pursued here.

The banker or the *mahajan* had a significant role to play in the peasant economy. With minor variations, he worked in close relationship with the state and the peasant. He financed the peasants in times of need for their extraordinary expenses and sometimes advanced money for the repayment of land revenue also. He converted/marketed the state share of the field produce and paid the same to the state. He was thus more of a trader/banker. Wingate found in 1885 in Mewar that every *assami* had a *mahajan* who stood surety for the payment of revenue by the *assami*. If the *assami* could not produce the guarantee of a banker, he would not be allowed to cultivate for the *rabi*; if the banker did not accept the responsibility for the peasant's payment, he would not be allowed to take any of the crops of the season. The interdependence of both was considerable. Every banker had a considerable number of *assamis* and he, in turn, dealt with a larger banker who dealt with the *hakim* directly.[28] All these transactions were done through *hundis* and the problem of handling much cash did not arise. The *assami 's* accounts for the year with the *mahajan* were closed on *aakha teej* (end of April) and settled much later. The crop rates were finalised at the parganah panchayat of *patels* and *mahajans* who drew up a statement of prices based upon the average of the year. The agreed average price was applied alike to advances of grains by the *mahajan* when the grain was dear and to receipts by him when the grain was cheap. This agreed average price had to be approved by the *hakim* before the accounts for the previous year could be finalised. This practice was prevalent till 1885 when Wingate introduced the settlement. Any variations of the practice which the British attributed to the money lenders were either the result of administrative changes which had allowed the traditional control mechanism to collapse or else were based upon ignorance of the actual system. The peasant interests were not left at the mercy of the *mahajan*; the village *patel* and pargana *hakim* who had direct care of the farmers had an equal role to play. Wingate called this practice as revolving `around the banker' which was not only an incorrect description of the system but also a projection of the situation which he wanted to be created. He cited a number of instances where the name of the *mahajan* was entered alongwith the cultivator; he considered this as equivalent to lands having passed into the possession of *mahajans,* sometimes their name was in the accounts with or without a note of the fact of sale, seizure or mortgage, and sometimes the *assami's* name was retained without any notice that he had no longer any interest in the well. He qualified his statement considerabely when he said that the *mahajan* paid the assessment as he always did and he did not choose to give notice that he had supplanted the owner, and the *hakim* did not enquire so long as he got the assessment. He contradicted himself considerably. The *bohra* or the *mahajan* was basically a trader or a banker-cum-trader. Land ownership had been hereditary and mortgages of land did not normally lead to a termination of the ownership rights of the peasant proprietor. The role of the *mahajan*/banker/trader was transformed after the British land revenue settlements; he now came to play a greater role in determining the terms of trade between the peasant and the market.

The transformation of the relations between the peasant and the *mahajan* began after the assertion of state's right to terminate peasant's land ownership right in case of non-payment of land revenue. The arrears of land revenue had not led to the termination of ownership of land earlier. If the peasants produced less, he paid less; famines and scarcities happened as nature's variations which affected both the state and the farmer equally. In the post settlement period, the nature's vagaries were only for the peasant; the state should have its revenues as usual. In Alwar and Bharatpur, there were no outstanding arrears of revenue of a period prior to the introduction of British settlements which postulated fixed revenue payments irrespective of field produce. Mortgages of lands had continued for generations without affecting either the peasant's right to cultivate or his title to ownership. The practice of the *mahajan* lending seed to the peasant for sowing and recovering it with addition at harvest time had been age old. Its operation was different in the past as Wingate had noted in 1885 in Mewar.[29]

La Touche, Wingate, Dwyer and others did succeed in attracting investment of capital in land in the specific sense of making fallow land cultivable so that the unemployed could find a means of livelihood by spending their labour. But they had to create a legal framework whereby the banker/*mahajan* could be attracted to invest money; this framework consisted in enabling him to acquire land ownership if the farmer failed to repay. By a statistical jugglery, the settlement officers claimed that the state demand of land revenue was one fourth (or even lesser) gross produce. If the cultivator was not able to pay even such a low revenue, it was, they argued, either on account of the expensive prodigality of the farmer or the high interest rate of the money lender. In other words, the poverty of the agricultural classes was a result of the social forces and not of government policy.

The basic reason of farmer's impoverishment had been the land settlements which methodically inflated the figures of area under cultivation, the assumed yield of fields, the quality of soil and the prevalent market rates. The net result of their attempt was that the land revenue claimed 1/2 to 2/3rd of the gross produce and in Alwar and Bharatpur even more than 2/3rd produce. The settlement officers ensured that the new intermediaries or the moneylenders who invested money in land earned profits; if the farmer who spent his labour on the fields did not get enough profits it was none of their concern. This was the secret of agricultural poverty after land settlements. Capital could not be attracted to land in the sense of making agricultural operations profitable. The banker knew that the agricultural operations did not pay for the wages of the manpower of the cultivator and his family members; how could he hope that agriculture by hired labour would be profitable. The settlement officers never aimed at the second eventuality; they only wanted that the surplus money, left with the trader, may be diverted to finance the agriculturist to pay the government revenue.

The settlement officers conferred the legal right on the money lender whereby the landowner could be deprived of his land in the event of non payment of money borrowed; the creation of this right amounted to putting a value on land. It was not and could not be an invitation to invest capital in land. Secondly the peasant was not a free agent when he borrowed; he borrowed money to protect his only means of production which was in danger of being lost if the government demand was not paid. In states where the British did not want the land value to go up, like Bharatpur and Alwar, it did not allow the trading classes to dispossess the farmer in the event of nonpayment of money. The creation of an investment climate could be upheld where cultivating land was more profitable than earning interest on money advanced on the security of land.

Mewar, Tonk, Jhalawar, Bharatpur, Alwar, Dungarpur, and Ajmer Merwara illustrate different policies of encouraging investment of capital in land. In none of these areas, the peasant indebtedness in the pre settlement period was a common feature; in all of them, peasant indebtedness multiplied fast in the post settlement period.

The increase in cattle wealth which was put forth as growth of prosperity among the cultivating peasantry was in reality a return to dependence on animal husbandry because agriculture had ceased to provide even subsistence. The phenomenon of increasing cattlewealth was accompanied by declining pasture land area and, in some states, even by an absence of increase in area under cultivation.

II

Increasing Dependence on Animal Husbandry

In Ajmer Merwara and in such states where the British settlement officers had the opportunity to revise land settlements frequently, it was one of their oft repeated observations that their land revenue policy had led to the growth of cattle wealth and increase in the number of ploughs among the peasantry. These developments were quite naturally held as substantial evidence for the growth of peasant prosperity.

La Touche had been sent to Ajmer after the severe famine of 1868-69; there was considerable awareness of the increasing misery and impoverishment of the peasantry of the district. Amidst the overwhelming evidence of hardship of the last settlement, he found a sizeable number of cattle of all descriptions in the district. Even though the Deputy Commissioner, Ajmer had estimated a loss of 1/3rd cattle in the famine of 1868, and even though the cattle population had declined considerably in all the three tehsils of the district, still La

Touche projected that the district was 'full of agricultural wealth'. He gave figures of cattle population in 1849 and showed that in 1874 the cattle wealth was more than at the time of the last settlement.

	Year	Plough cattle	other cattle
Ajmer-Merwara District	1849	30814	163364
	1874	38072	257011

It appears that he was preparing a justification for acquiring culturable pasture land as reserve forest area under government control. After 1874 'a large proportion of grazing grounds' were taken over as 'forest reserves' by the Government thus denying grazing facility to the villagers which had been available earlier. By 1884, 92180 acres of unculturable land had been taken over, so much so that Whiteway felt that no more land could be taken for government reserve forest area. The measure had been very unpopular. It was natural to anticipate that the decrease of grazing lands and facilities would have resulted in a decrease of cattle wealth. Therefore Whiteway's greatest surprise was the large increase in the number of cattle. He was exultant at this increase since it was held to be 'one of the surest and most certain signs of progress amongst an agricultural population.'[1] The data of increasing cattle wealth with decreasing grazing areas was naturally considered 'a matter for congratulations'. In table no. 5.4 statistics are being given for three different classes of reserved areas (i) created in 1875, (ii) in 1876, and (iii) in 1880; the percentage of growth in these areas has also been compared with the growth percentage in the district as a whole.[2]

Despite available overwhelming evidence of prevalent poverty—72.7%, 39.56% and 57.6% land had been mortgaged by 1884 and 91%, 68% and 62% of landowners were in debt in Todgarh, Beawar and Ajmer tehsils respectively—the growth of cattle wealth was presented as evidence of 'increasing

TABLE: 5.4

Growth of Cattlewealth in Ajmer-Merwara

Class	Cows & Bullocks 1874	Cows & Bullocks 1884	% of Increase	Buffaloes 1874	Buffaloes 1884	% of Increase	Beast of Burden 1874	Beast of Burden 1884	% of Increase	Sheep & Goats 1874	Sheep & Goats 1884
I	7574	16472	119	2422	4128	71	790	1193	50	15839	14876
II	5049	12315	145	858	2179	146	242	496	105	10146	12943
III	2546	5220	105	1101	1531	39	101	161	59	5789	4748
Total	15169	34007	123	4381	7838	78	1133	1850	65	31774	32567
District as a whole	75615	186608	147%	17696	37531	112%	3406	7210	111%	151928	183855

Class I = Reserved area created in 1875
Class II = Reserved area created in 1876
Class III = Reserved area created in 1880

prosperity of the cultivating peasantry'. Whiteway did not perceive the real implications of enhanced cattle wealth with decreasing grazing facility. A large majority had fallen back on animal husbandry to supplement their income. The increase in cattle wealth was primarily a subsidiary turned primary source of income. It was also the only source of manure needed for land which had to be cultivated for whatever it yielded. The growth of cattle wealth could be called by the settlement officers as abundance of agricultural wealth but it was a significant change from agriculture to animal husbandry which now provided means of subsistence better than the former. Whiteway and Dwyer both were interested in finding something which could be held forth as an outward sign of prosperity and growth. Wingate had, in a different connection, made an important observation that if cultivation extended considerably, the number of cattle must either decrease or else more land must be devoted to growing fodder or more land must be available for pastures. Whiteway conceded the lack of land for pastures; the growth of cultivated land in the entire district did not increase in proportion to the growth of cattle population, the only alternative left was to devote more land to fodder crops. The restrictions on natural grazing lands meant that agricultural land provided for the maintenance of both—human and cattle population. In years of scarcity of rainfall, man would first have to find food to keep himself alive. With limited cultivation in famine years, cattle perished in a far larger number than had happened earlier.

The result of the policy of acquiring control over grazing areas was visible when Lupton was hard put to justify the sharp decline in cattle population in 1908. Unwilling to confess the impact of Government policy, he took cover by questioning the correctness of the figures of 1884; he said that the figures had been counted twice over in some tehsils in 1884. The remaining responsibility was attributed to the famine of 1899-1900.[3] Table 5.5 reveals the extent of decline in cattle wealth.

TABLE: 5.5

Decline of Cattle Wealth in Ajmer-Merwara

Tehsil	Year	Cows & Bullocks	Buffaloes	Beasts of Burden	Sheep & Goats	Total
Ajmer	1884	93486	18597	3965	88418	204466
	1908	45955	10243	2436	64628	123262
Beawar	1884	48975	8336	1638	55375	114324
	1908	27657	4722	718	64320	97417
Todgarh	1884	44147	10598	1607	40062	96414
	1908	24426	4717	514	73767	103424
District Total	1884	186608	37531	7210	183855	415204
	1908	98038	19682	3668	202715	324103
Decline %		-47.5	-47.6	-49.2	+10.2	-21.9

Similarly at Alwar and Bharatpur where the land revenue settlement was being revised fifth time during 1896-1900 by the British after they had first introduced it during 1855-59, Dwyer focussed attention on the growth of agricultural wealth and held it as an index of the growing prosperity of the peasantry. The enumeration of the cattle during 1897-1900 in the two states had brought out a phenomenal increase as compared to the last enumeration of 1876 at Alwar and of 1890 at Bharatpur. The increase in the cattle population of all kinds—horned cattle, sheep and goats and beasts of burden—was so great that Dwyer was not able to rationally explain it. He, to begin with, expressed serious doubts about the correctness of the earlier enumeration and held the view that the cattle population must have been larger earlier because his enumeration in the closing years of the 19th century had been held after two years of drought in which the losses of cattle should have been heavy on account of the dearth of fodder. His predicament at the phenomenal growth of cattle population was further complicated by the fact that in some eastern tehsils of Alwar—Kishangarh and Govindgarh particularly—the villages did not have even 100 bighas of culturable land which could be used as pasture. On the contrary the abundance of pasture land in Bharatpur tended to partially explain the growth of cattle wealth and helped Dwyer in putting forward this growth as an evidence of agricultural prosperity and of subsidiary income to the peasantry.

He compared the two states with the agriculturally prosperous Punjab where there was 1 horned cattle, excluding sheep and goats, for every two acres of cultivated land. The statistics of cattle population during 1897-1900, in all the tehsils of Alwar and Bharatpur alongwith the availability of culturable and cultivated land, are being given in table 5.6. The tehsils have been grouped together on the pattern used by Dwyer in his land settlement reports. The cattle wealth statistics given in the table exclude sheep and goats, which numbered 293525 in Alwar and 169140 in Bharatpur.

The statistics show that the availability of culturable land was less than one bigha per cattle in 20 out of 24 tehsils of the two states. The cultivated area per horned cattle was 2.4 bighas in Alwar and 3.2 bighas in Bharatpur; in both it was far lower than in the Punjab. (1 acre = 2.5 bighas in Bharatpur; and 1.6 bighas in Alwar). In Thanaghazi tehsil of Alwar, it had come down to ½ acre of cultivated land for every cattle. It is relevant to pose the question: Why did the cattle wealth grow when it was not needed for agricultural purposes and was not sustained by the availability of culturable land or natural pastures?

The comparative data of the two states also highlights the fact that the availability of culturable land in Alwar was less than half of Bharatpur and the percentage of growth of horned cattle in 9 out of 12 tehsils of Alwar was almost double the percentage of growth in 8 tehsils of Bharatpur. The cultivated land area per cattle was much lower at Alwar than at Bharatpur; rainfall, pasture land and forest area were more conducive to the growth of cattle at Bharatpur than Alwar. Under these

TABLE: 5.6

Cattle Population and Land Area

State-Tehsil	Horned Cattle	% of Increase	Beasts of Burden	% of Increase	Total of Cattle	Culturable Land Area (Bighas)	Culturable Land % of total Land	Bighas per Cattle	Cultivated Land Area (Bighas)	Land Per Cattle Bighas
Alwar										
4 Eastern Tehsils										
1898-1900	147407	88.2	2954	NA	150361	48973	8.7	0.32	405488	2.7
5 Northern & Southern Tehsils										
1898-1900	233141	68.3	9733	195	242874	129598	13.23	0.53	621410	2.55
3 Central & Western Tehsils										
1898-1900	176124	51.7	7032	438	183156	107821	13.15	0.58	367640	2.00
Total State										
1898-1900	556672	61.67	19719	252	576391	286392	12.14	0.49	1394538	2.4
In 1876	344342		5577		349919	255539			1372714	

Bharatpur										
4 Northern Tehsils										
1897-1900	149256	45	7608	245	156864	92170	11.82	0.58	585477	3.7
4 Central Tehsils										
1897-1900	144233	33.8	6784	125	151017	365020	31.3	2.41	494432	3.27
4 Southern Tehsils										
1897-1900	183342	51.7	6863	96.8	190205	188486	22.5	0.9	519080	2.7
Total State										
1897-1900	476831	43.8	21255	144	498086	645676	23.2	1.3	1598989	3.2
In 1890	331526		8699		340225					

circumstances, the growth of cattle wealth becomes inexplicable in terms of agricultural prosperity which Dwyer wanted to convey. In fact this data reduces the relevance of the availability of pasture land as a conducive factor for the growth of cattle wealth. The increase in cattle population helps us to understand the events which had happened during the two decades 1876-96. A large number of cattle wealth was raised at Alwar because it was the only way out of the below subsistence agriculture after Powlett's harsh settlement.

Despite the abundance of pasture land, the peasantry at Bharatpur devoted a larger area to the cultivation of gawar and charri, fodder for the cattle. (Appendix no. F) The peasantry was diverting agricultural land to fodder crops because it found that cultivating land for growing other crops was not so remunerative. The land revenue had to be paid since possession of land could not be abandoned in the absence of other avenues of self employment. The cultivation of land for agricultural purposes had ceased to provide subsistence; taking to animal husbandry was the result of unprofitability of agriculture. The peasantry of Alwar was rearing up cattle because the land revenue settlement of 1876 had been more oppressive than the settlement of 1890 at Bharatpur. Powlett did not give an account of the process of working out his revenue demand, based his assessment on the supposition of 'immense increase of cultivated area' and kept even the AGG ignorant of the 'precise incidence of the new assessment'. The settlement had been approved by the AGG 'as practically good and sound' without sufficient material to form that opinion. The revenue demand had been so heavy that a large number of people deserted the state during the famine of 1877-78 and cared to return only in 1897 when a record of land rights was being created for future. Dwyer introduced a new class of intermediaries at Bharatpur which was aware of the unprofitability of agriculture under the new settlement. Hence it told Dwyer that concessions for fodder had to be allowed.

Dwyer's keenness to keep the new intermediaries contented and satisfied was evident when he recommended the acceptance, by the Government of India, of an 'extremely oppressive' assessment. He wrote: 'combined... with a remission of all old arrears, an equitable distribution by estates, a fairly complete and correct record of rights, and a long term of assessment during which the zamindars will be guaranteed against any extra cesses or enhancement... I think it will be accepted willingly and adhered to loyally by the zamindars...'[4a] He had allowed them to charge profit rents from the tenants and had imposed *malikana* on the occupancy tenants. The fodder crops were called 'a tax on the crops which must be allowed for'. The crop pattern in the two states given at the end of fourth chapter (Appendix F) was prevalent around 1900.

The cropwise distribution of *kharif* and *rabi* crops clearly brings out the fact that the percentage of *rabi* had gone up to 31.35 at Alwar and 34.9 at Bharatpur in 1897-98. However the more relevant question is: What crops were grown in *rabi*? Gram and barley, for which some concession in land revenue demand had been allowed on account of fodder were the major *rabi* crops, and occupied 66.7% and 58.1% area at Alwar and Bharatpur respectively. This area went up to 78.3% and 65.3% in the two states when 11.6% and 7.17% oil seed crops (for which again concession had been allowed) were added to fodder crops. Cash crops like tobacco and poppy occupied less than 1% area in Alwar and nil in Bharatpur state. Wheat cultivation was in single digit percentage at Alwar and was less than 15% at Bharatpur. Inferior food grains in *Rabi* were 8.5% at Alwar and 15% at Bharatpur. The *kharif* crop of inferior food grains covered 58.6% area at Alwar and 37.3% at Bharatpur. The rest was for cattle in one or the other form except 5.8% and 7.3% for cotton at the two states respectively to meet their clothing needs. In *rabi* cultivation the peasants did not encourage cash crops because they could not find them rewarding. Animal husbandry provided manure and substitute fire wood.

Once the concession for fodder crops were allowed, the shift from agriculture to animal husbandry became very quick and rapid. Concessions were allowed for fodder in the two states because the cattle was stall fed during the cold weather on *jowar* and *bajra* stalks mixed with *pala,* in the spring months on the same mixed with *sarson* and turnips or green barley, and in the summers on the *bhusa* of wheat or barley together with root crops. At ploughing time, the cattle was given a seer of grain, barley or *jawar* mixed with cotton cake. The fodder needs were met by some concessions which were as follows:[5]

TABLE: 5.7

Fodder Concessions

State Tehsil	Gawar & Chari	Moth masina	Jawar	Barley Gram	Rabi oil Seeds	Carrots & Vegetable	Total Percentage
Bharatpur							
Gopalgarh	All	25%		5%	5%		8 to 12% (Gopalgarh to Deeg)
Pahari	"	"		"	"		
Kama	"	"		"	"		
Deeg	"	"		"	"		
Kumher	"	"		"	"	all	6.3
Akheygarh	"	"		"	"	nil	4.9
Nagar	"	"		"	"	nil	9.4
Bharatpur	"	20%		"	"	nil	3.6
Rupbas	"	25%		"	"	all	6
Oochain	"	"		"	"	all	7
Biyana	"	15%		"	"	all	8
Bhusavar	"	25%		"	"	all	4

Alwar							
Kishangarh	All	25%	10%	5%	25%	½	8 to 12%
Ramgarh	"	"	10%	"	"	½	
Govindgarh	"	"	12%	10%	"	½	
Lachmangarh	"	"	10%	5%	"	½	
Tijara	"	20%	12%	6%	1/6th	½	15
Bahror	"	25%	10%	5%	25%	½	12½
Mandawar	"	"	"	5%	"	½	10
Katumbar	"	"	"	5%	"	½	12½
Rajgarh	"	"	6%	3%	nil	¼	6
Alwar	75%	"	10%	4%	25%	½	11
Bansur	All	"	10%	5%	20%	½	16
Thanaghazi	"	"	6%	4%	20%	½	7

Another variant evidence of increasing agricultural prosperity was seen in the increasing number of ploughs. This could have been conceded as an evidence of prosperity if the increase in the number of ploughs had led to proportionate increased cultivation. As things happened, the increase in the number of ploughs had led to reduction in the area cultivated per plough in Ajmer Merwara during 1849-1884. The area per plough did not increase till the number of plough went down during 1884-1908. (Table 5.8)

In 1908 the number of ploughs came down from 27088 to 20068 (26% decline); the area under cultivation came down from 190321 acres to 183289. The area per plough could increase only thereafter from 7.02 acres to 9.13 acres.

The argument was repeated in the case of Alwar and Bharatpur states also to sustain the theory of agricultural growth. The relevant statistics are being given below tehsilwise in the two states since there were considerable tehsil variations.

TABLE: 5.8

Area per plough in tehsils of Ajmer-Merwara District

	Ajmer			Beawar			Todgarh		
	1849	1874	1884	1849	1874	1884	1849	1874	1884
No. of Ploughs	6004	8420	11387	4420	5113	9053	3941	4720	6648
Acres per "	15.2	12.9	10.2	9.7	8.2	5.45	5.3	4.4	3.7
Cultivated Acres	91206	108920	116440	41766	49408	48336	20898	20730	24473
District average cultivation per plough			10.8	9.47	7.02				

TABLE: 5.9

Growth of Ploughs, Bharatpur 1890-99

Bharatpur	Cultivated Area in Bighas		Difference In		Number of Ploughs in		Difference in Percentage
Tehsils	1890	1897-99	Area Bighas	Percentage	1890	1897-99	
Gopalgarh	147704	172739	+ 25035	+ 16.9	4247	5650	+ 33
Pahari	102709	112470	+ 9761	+ 9.5	2694	3019	+ 12
Kame	124454	139885	+ 15431	+ 12.4	3195	4317	+ 35
Deeg	126438	160383	+ 33945	+ 2.7	4195	6099	+ 45
Kumher	117329	139694	+ 22365	+ 19	4404	5009	+ 14
Akheygarh	118474	125156	+ 6682	+ 5.6	3042	3465	+ 14
Bharatpur	101019	129734	+ 28715	+ 28.4	3643	4397	+ 21
Nagar	82740	99848	+ 17108	+ 20.7	1864	2693	+ 44
Ruplias	51545	83049	+ 31504	+ 61	1991	2915	+ 46
Oochain	102981	123593	+ 20612	+ 20	3744	4451	+ 18.9
Bijane	134561	142060	+ 7499	+ 5.6	5300	5500	+ 4
Bhusavar	166596	170378	+ 3782	+ 2.3	4827	5873	+ 21
	1376550	1598989	+ 222439	+ 16.16	43146	53388	+ 23.7

(Contd.)

(Table 5.9 Contd.)

Growth of Ploughs, Alwar 1876-99

Alwar	Cultivated Area in Bighas		Difference In		Number of Ploughs in		Difference in Percentage
Tehsils	1876	1897-99	Area (Bighas)	Percentage	1876	1897-99	
Kishangarh	141796	145455	+ 3659	+ 2.5	4751	6780	+ 42.7
Ramgarh	101919	106407	+ 4488	+ 2.3	4572	5216	+ 14.1
Govindgarh	39760	39676	- 84	- 0.2	1654	2029	+ 22.7
Lachmangarh	112534	113950	+ 1416	+ 1.25	4184	4759	+ 13.75
Tijara	167062	169739	+ 2677	+ 1.6	4192	6619	+ 58
Behrod	159142	159821	+ 679	+ 0.4	3871	5428	+ 40
Mandawar	124988	129303	+ 4315	+ 3.4	3706	4647	+ 25
Katumbar	102718	97811	- 4907	- 4.8	3244	3938	+ 21.4
Rajgarh	68463	65093	- 3370	- 4.9	4849	4844	- 0.1
Alwar	165159	169314	+ 4155	+ 2.5	8011	7885	- 1.6
Bansur	143969	155389	+ 11420	+ 7.9	4772	5444	+ 14
Thanaghazi	45127	44937	- 190	- 0.42	4402	4783	+ 8.6
State Total	1372636	1396895	+24259	+ 1.7	52208	62372	+ 19.47

Based on O'Dwyer's Assessment Reports: Bharatpur: Northern Tehsils, pp. 57, 59 & 63; Central Tehsils, pp. 57-59; Southern Tehsils, pp. 62-63 & 66; Alwar: Eastern Tehsils, pp. 47-48; Northern and Southern Tehsils, pp. 73, 75; Central and Southern, pp. 73, 75.

These statistics show that the increase in the number of ploughs did not lead to a proportionate increase in the area under cultivation. In Punjab one plough was enough for 12.5 acres in 1898; in *barani* land, a plough could easily cultivate much larger area. Even then, the average per plough came to be only 12 acres in Bharatpur and 14 acres in Alwar. 57% cultivation in Bharatpur was in *barani* area; this percentage went up to 71.8 in the case of Alwar. In less than a decade in Bharatpur state, the number of ploughs had increased by 24%; the area of cultivated land per plough had gone down by 6%. At Alwar the increase during two decades had been 19.5% in the number of ploughs and the area per plough had come down by 14%. Since the land under cultivation did not increase at Alwar and since the population of Bharatpur state had declined during the last decade, the increase in the number of ploughs could only mean that more people, from within the state, were taking to agriculture. This was partly the direct result of division of joint estates and fragmentation of land holdings deliberately encouraged by Dwyer. It also meant that a far larger number of men were taking to agriculture and sharing the same area. The population of Bharatpur state had declined by about 14000 during 1891-1901. The urban population in the state declined by 27004 during this decade, i.e. 13000 people had gone from the towns to villages to fall back upon agriculture and animal husbandry. Thus declining population (Bharatpur) and negligible increase in cultivation (Alwar) were accompanied by 20 and 24 percent increase in the number of ploughs. The people were being forced out of other vocations and professions and had to fall back on agriculture. The increasing incidence of land mortgage and sale in the two states (Appendix G & H) also does not support the hypothesis of increasing prosperity among the cultivating population.

Appendix G

Sale and Mortgage of Land in Bharatpur

Tehsil	To whom	Sale and mortgage of land 1855-90				Sale and mortgage of land 1890-97			
		Sale		Mortgage		Sale		Mortgage	
		Cult.	Uncult.	Cult.	Uncult.	Cult.	Uncult.	Cult.	Uncult.
Gopalgarh	Zamindar	623	64	5696	67	1377	131	3856	6
	Moneylender	58	11	511	1	96	24	549	-
Pahari	Zamindar	2432	49	3442	11	1922	31	2980	11
	Moneylender	105	-	609	-	-	-	825	-
Kama	Zamindar	1830	670	2111	125	270	68	2553	15
	Moneylender	154	8	943	22	-	-	762	19
Deeg	Zamindar	2744	-	6542	1671	434	518	3592	298
	Moneylender	2521	-	1541	233	491	574	492	136
Nagar	Zamindar	1464	519	1097	227	770	287	905	15
	Moneylender	18	2	271	3	75	61	53	1
Kumher	Zamindar	5160	3203	15954	3122	1441	1041	2486	127
	Moneylender	804	1352	3378	942	163	97	989	136

Bharatpur	Zamindar	3724	3334	4860	3833	1341	1384	3936	1064
	Moneylender	1955	1028	3171	1412	-	-	-	-
Akheygarh	Zamindar	11492	4414	2261	431	1564	857	821	160
	Moneylender	11011	4850	220	49	2272	945	463	224
Rupbas	Zamindar	1701	4166	11524	8030	2095	1191	2307	1319
	Moneylender	536	213	2626	375	130	81	906	350
Oochain	Zamindar	1349	4557	10566	6242	1409	753	2003	1159
	Moneylender	91	21	893	259	73	52	217	182
Biyana	Zamindar	2087	1922	8310	4932	251	178	3364	2609
	Moneylender	394	1255	3131	-			1015	307
Bhusawar	Zamindar	8925	9477	3870	1342	3093	3247	2091	421
	Moneylender	3271	1978	2067	1306	1237	620	676	68
State as a Whole	Zamindar	43531	32375	76233	30033	15967	9686	30894	7214
	Money lender	20918	10718	19361	4602	4537	2504	6947	1423

Cult = Cultivated

Uncult = uncultivated

Based on Dwyer's Report on Northern Tehsils, p. 43; Central Tehsils, p. 51; Southern Tehsils, pp. 57-58.

Appendix H

Alwar

Tehsil	Mortgaged In	Mortgaged (Bighas) To Zamindars Total Area	Amount Rs.	To Moneylenders Total Area	Amount Rs.	Sales (Bighas) To Zamindars Total Area	Amount Rs.	Sales To Moneylenders Total Area	Amount Rs.
Kishangarh	1876	112	1792	45	1930	-	-		
	1876-98	5074	81663	1361	20054	168	280		
Ramgarh	1876	1457	15027	660	5405	-	-		
	1876-98	6051	82017	1943	30458	17	445		
Govindgarh	1876	834	2195						
	1876-98	6156	23186	412	3234	2	33		
Lachmangarh	1876	565	631	28	135				
	1876-98	1156	3551	244	1304	5758	8238		
Tijara	1876	125	534	22	25				
	1876-98	4806	36937	1580	22272	4482	10263	306	336
Bahror	1876	427	1536	20	-				
	1876-98	2202	22909	3612	31213	463	4308	110	2106
Mandawar	1876	-	-	16	147				
	1876-98	2290	18587	2743	25475	1769	4416	124	1395

Katumber	In 1876	19	274	580	363				
	1876-98	997	3423	621	1899	1596	3204	351	400
Rajgarh	In 1876	2233	13499	327	3876				
	1876-98	2541	30643	1143	18429	655	4701	313	808
Alwar	In 1876	406	4998	292	3050				
	1876-98	3347	36210	3012	34727	3512	2998	1695	6814
Bansur	In 1876	11	160						
	1876-98	1830	8041	3391	7790	1234	1739	698	1831
Thanaghazi	In 1876	1426	17335	291	12120	69	889	14	313
	1876-98	1221	38514	1295	54303	2183	8516	455	1167
Total	In 1876	7615	57981	2281	27051	69	889	14	313
	1876-98	37671	385681	21357	251158	21839	49141	4052	14857

Based on O'Dwyer's Report on Eastern Tehsils, p. 43; Northern and Southern Tehsils Report, p. 69; Central and Southern Tehsils Report, p. 68 1905-15 Area Mortgaged & Sold = 5235 acres = 8376 Bighas.

Based on Agricultural Statistics of India (for Indian States) Vol.II, for the years 1904-05 to 1908-09, p.113; 1914-15, p.110

Notes & References

1. Report of the Indian Opium Commission, vol.IV, Appendix iv, pp. 384-386 The First Assistant AGG had written to all Political Officers to highlight the amount of compensation which would be needed if the Commission decided to prohibit its cultivation in the Indian States also.
2. Pears: Tonk Settlement Report, Pt.II, pp. 92-93
3. Tonk Settlement Report, Pt.I, p. 33; Pt.II, pp. 93, 128-129, 152; also Abbott: Jhallawar Land Settlement Report, pp. 25-31
4. Jhalawar Land Settlement Report, p. 33
5. Tonk Settlement Report, Pt.I, p. 34
6. Wingate: Sadri Settlement Report, p. 67
7. Ibid., pp. 25-26
8. Ibid., also rule no. 10, p. 64
9. Ibid., rule no. 11, p. 65
10. Ibid., pp. 52, 56, 57
11. Ibid., p. 25
12. Ibid., p. 55
13. Ibid., p. 71
14. R.A.R., 1868-69, pp. 125-126; 1870-71, p. 164; 1873-74, pp. 155-156
15. Northern Tehsils, pp. 61-62
16. Northern Tehsils, p. 47; Central Tehsils, pp. 50-51; Southern Tehsils, p. 57
17. The consequences of the Settlement of 1897-1900 may best be seen in the Settlement Report of 1930, pp. 22 and 39
18. Final Report on Bharatpur, p. 86; Northern Tehsils, p. 50
19. Eastern Tehsils, pp. 34, 43; Northern and Southern Tehsils, p. 69; Central and Southern Tehsils, p. 68
20. A.T. Holme: Report on the Land Revenue Settlement of the Dungarpur State, p. 8 This was the first land revenue settlement and hence it gave a good idea of the pre settlement period; two decades later the situation had changed. The Settlement Report of 1924 gave a different picture. (pp. 9-10)
21. Report on the Revision of the Settlement in the Dungarpur State, 1924, p. 34

22. Abbott: Jhalawar Settlement Report, pp. 33-34
23. La Touche's Report, pp. 88-89
24. Report on the Famine Relief in Ajmer Merwara, 1891-92, pp. 110-111
25. La Touche's Report, p. 90; Whiteway's Settlement Report, p. 30; Lupton's Land Settlement Report, pp. 26, 49 and Appendix IX Lupton had provided statistics, in a time frame, which highlighted that both mortgages and sales of land had increased after the middle of the 19th century.
26. Wingate: Report of 1881, para 38: Foreign, Revenue A, May 1881, no.6
27. Lupton: Land Settlement Report, p. 25
28. Wingate: Sadri Report, p. 7
29. Ibid., pp. 9-10
30. Northern Tehsils Report, pp. 47-50; Central Tehsils Report, pp. 50-51; Southern Tehsils Report, pp. 57-58 (Statement no.IV given as appendix)
31. Eastern Tehsils Report, p. 43; Northern and Southern Tehsils Report, p. 69; Central and Southern Tehsils Report, p. 68

II

1. La Touche's Report, pp. 121-125
2. Whiteway: Summary Settlement Report for Ajmer, pp. 7 and 26
3. Whiteway's Settlement Report of 1887, pp. 48-49; La Touche's Report, p. 121
4. Lupton; Land Settlement Report, Appendix V, p. 45
5. Eastern Tehsils Report, pp. 47, 53; Northern and Southern Tehsils Report, p. 72; Central and Southern Tehsils Report, p. 70; Northern Tehsils Report, p. 63; Central Tehsils Report, p. 59; Southern Tehsils Report, p. 66
6. Northern Tehsils Report, p. 64; Central Tehsils Report, p. 72; Southern Tehsils Report, p. 78; Eastern Tehsils Report, pp. 63-64; Northern and Southern Tehsils Report, pp. 86-87; Central and Southern Tehsils Report, p. 88
7. Lupton: Land Settlement Report, Appendix V, p. 45
8. Eastern Tehsils Report, pp. 47, 53; Northern and Southern Tehsils Report, pp. 73, 75; Central and Southern Tehsils Report, pp. 73, 75

9. Final Report on Alwar, Appendix B, pp.vii-xv

   Final Report on Bharatpur, Appendix VIII

10. Northern Tehsils, p. 63; Eastern Tehsils Report, p. 47, 53; Northern and Southern Tehsils Report, p. 72; Central and Southern Tehsils Report, p. 70; La Touche's Report, pp. 121-125; Whiteway's Settlement Report, p. 31 & Appendix II,III; Lupton's Land Settlement Report, Appendix V

6

A Retrospect

The land revenue settlements in the states of Rajasthan were part of the policy to build a leviathan of state power. The ruler representing state authority had surrendered in 1818; the nobility surrendered by 1868-70 in all major states. The stage was thus cleared for the utilisation of state power to serve imperial interests since both the components of the clan based feudal state had surrendered to effectual British control, and were in no position to object to state economy being subjected to colonial goals. Opium, a major cash crop, and salt, nature's gift to the region, had been taken by the colonial power under its control. The agricultural sector in the Indian states which had escaped actual British control, was brought under it during 1870-1910. The new leviathan state claimed proprietary rights over all peasant holdings in the khalsa lands. The state had earlier confined itself to the performance of the basic function of removal of hindrances; the civil society, at the pargana and tehsil levels, had developed its own regulatory institutions. By depriving the peasant proprietors of their secure and inheritable right of ownership, the independent strength of the peasantry vis-a-vis the state was considerably weakened. Wherever possible, a new intermediary class of landowners was created so that the centrally determined goals could be transmitted for achievement. The creation of a leviathan of state power also sapped the vertical links of the village community with the state. The capacity of the peasantry to make the state bow down to its will, by a policy of not cultivating the fields, was virtually crippled by disconnecting the land revenue demand from the gross produce of the fields. The instance of Mewar peasantry, compelling the state by its passive resistance in 1875, could not be repeated after the land revenue settlement of 1885-93.

Alongwith the curtailment of the peasant's proprietary right, the leviathan of state power brought about a change in the psychological make up of the officials at the local level. In each state, the pargana official was made, after the land revenue settlement, the centre of all operative autocratic power. It has been seen earlier how the various officials *patwari, kanungo, patel* and *lambardar* were subordinated to state control. Under the pretext of improving their performance, they had been dismissed, and subjected to pass a qualifying examination. Even their hereditary character was abolished theoretically, though in practice it was allowed for all those who had been properly indoctrinated. Different grades were introduced with a view to break the unity nurtured by uniformity; the promotion was made dependent on state's good will. Their functions had been transformed; they were now to realise state land revenue demand irrespective of any sympathetic considerations for the peasantry. The link between the peasantry and the local official machinery had been snapped.

Once the leviathan of state power had been built up, the local interests of the rural community were subordinated to state interests for the common good. The adherence to the fiction of state authority under the ruler was maintained, though it did not prevent the paramount power from either dethroning a ruler or selecting a new one, in case of failure of direct heirs. The facade of state autonomy was maintained since its growth was the only way to crush the self governing autonomous village communities. British colonial interests became state interests. When the settlement officers laid emphasis on state's desire to enhance revenue demand, it was only a figurative way of saying that the British interests demanded it. The individual interests of the ruler or the state concerned were not so relevant. The growth of state power enabled the British to adjudicate the distribution of scarce resources: the replacement of the *ijaredars* at Dholpur and Tonk by a new class of zamindars and *manotidars* respectively was the most significant illustration. The policy pertaining to the cultivation of particular crops—cotton, opium or foodgrains—was now determined by imperial and colonial and not by particular interests of the state concerned. Only the British understanding of state interests was relevant and meaningful.

The state was now made to distance itself from its dependence on the goodwill of the cultivating peasantry which gradually realised its helplessness before state authority. The instance of Bijolia peasantry is significant in this connection. It surrendered its ownership of *mal* lands in 1927 on the advice of its popular leaders who had helped the movement earlier. The peasantry later tried to re-acquire its ownership. For the next 10 years it realised its helplessness against state authority which did not restore the lands till the peasantry had assured the Maharana of Mewar of its absolute unconcern with the popular praja mandal movement in the state.

The land revenue settlements, through their concept of ownership of land, proved to be instruments of tremendous social engineering. Some facets of this engineering can be understood only in the context of the states where the traditional fabric had remained comparatively more intact than in British India. During the seventies and eighties, the settlements encouraged and protected the money investing class in land. The settlement at Mewar was carried out when this school held sway in India. By the nineties, the evil consequences of transfer of land to the banking and trading classes which had invested money in land, had become apparent. By 1895, the British policy had been revised. It emphasized that the transfer of proprietary rights in land should be restricted to the circle of near agnates amongst the agriculturists only. This policy change shaped the land revenue settlements at Alwar and Bharatpur brought about during 1896-1900. Dwyer even restored lands to those original owners who had deserted them during and after the famine of 1877-78; they had lost their lands on account of non-payment of land revenue. The restoration of lands to the original landowners was a reversal of an earlier British decision. It was unfair to all those who had come forward to pay land revenue during the difficult years.

The proprietors who had gone out during the famine were unaware of the new legal doctrines enforced by the British. Since the exhaustive record of land rights being prepared during 1897-1900 was conclusive proof of ownership, all former owners rushed back to get their ownerships registered as a danger to their rights had arisen. Dwyer found it impossible to lay down general rules covering all cases of restoration of land. He tried to bring the parties to a compromise because the new owners had equitable claims and had acquired their rights under rules framed by the British themselves. The principles of restoration could not be either defined or laid down. The result was that while in Ramgarh, Govindgarh and Lachmangarh tehsils (where the Meos predominated) and in Rajgarh (where the Meenas and Meos held a majority of the villages), the percentage of restoration to original owners varied from 2% to 7%; in Behrod and Mandawar tehsils, the percentage of restoration to original owners was 26% and 40% respectively; in Bansur and Thanaghazi tehsils, where hereditary ownership, according to shares, was very strong, the earlier owners were, in a majority of cases, given back their lands by the new owners themselves either subject to or without settlement of profit and loss accounts.

This was one aspect of the commotion caused by the 'record of rights'. There was another facet of this record preparation which was even more disturbing. Sales and mortgages of land were not generally recorded since it was enough if it was publicly known. The state had imposed a 10% mutation fee and people avoided getting the sale or mortgage recorded. Dwyer reduced the fee to 5%, and wanted all changes to be recorded. The speed with which he wanted the work to be accomplished brought forth widespread litigation. In Alwar 85859 mutation cases were instituted of which 443 pertained to sales, 12675 to mortgages, 72741 pertained to individuals who had migrated out on account of famine and natural calamities. The old owners put forward claims for 274,102 acres out of which 135387 acres were given back to them. The restoration of 49.39% land area was a major reversal of earlier British policy decisions; the induction of new owners in 50.61% land area was significant. The 'record of rights' could be a conclusive proof of permanent rights in land for future generations, but to the contemporaries, it was an agency of great social upheaval and disturbance. Dwyer did not want to displease the old or the new owners enblock. Hence he tried to satisfy both. But the new owners who had been dispossessed and the old ones who could not be reinstated (both for none of their faults) became the breeding ground for social conflict on various issues in the time to come. The tehsilwise details of land area abandoned have been given in Appendix A; the result for the whole state is being given below:

State	Population in 1872	1881	No. of owners migrated	Area of cultivated land abandoned
Alwar	728784	636710	5222	119,651

At Bharatpur, Dwyer's policy was more like a bolt from the blue since the British concept of land ownership had not been enforced earlier. The problem of desertions was much greater because the prohibition of salt manufacture had compelled the people to migrate in a far greater number than at Alwar. The state figures were:

	Population in 1867	1891	No. of owners migrated	Area of cultivated Land abandoned
Bharatpur	743710	640303	18959	434562 Bighas

The area of land abandoned was 31.42% of the total cultivated land in the state. The restoration of this land to the original owners wherever possible or traceable, was part of his scheme to create a zamindar class in the state. He decided to waive off a considerable part, from 2/3rd to 3/4th, of the arrears and distributed the balance to be paid over a period of 20 years. The original owners were also assisted with *takavi* advances for the purchase of oxen and seeds. In cases where the original owners could not be traced, land was made over to male agnates or other agriculturists of the same or neighbouring villages and in extreme cases to other agriculturists of the same tribe. The number of cases involving payment of mutation fee in case of mortgage or sale of land were much less than at Alwar because the British law of forfeiture of ownership rights for non-payment of land revenue had not been operative here. For future, all litigation pertaining to rights in land was withdrawn from the civil and made over to the revenue courts.

The preparation of a 'record of rights' thus had provided the occasion for installing a zamindar class at Bharatpur and for restoring the displaced landowners at Alwar. This proved to be generative of much social tension because the landed intermediary class which had been brought into existence or restored at Bharatpur and Alwar by administrative decisions, had not been thrown up by the prevalent system. This change may have been conducive to the prosperity of the intermediaries who had been provided 33% profit rents but it ensured poverty of the cultivating masses whose revenue payment liability had been enhanced by 65% over and above the enhanced government revenue demand. This 65% enhanced payment had been built into the system; it was not recorded anywhere and was not visible to an observer from distance.

The reports by British commissioners of Ajmer Merwara (which faced droughts and scarcities during 1860-70) and by Political officers, reporting on the famines in Rajasthan in the post 1875 period, developed the tendency to hold the harsh climate of the region responsible for its agricultural poverty. This does not carry conviction because the climatic changes during a century are not so sudden. The uncertain rainfall and the vagaries of the monsoon were a convenient scapegoat in the post 1870 period for shifting the responsibility for the consequences of British regressive land revenue policy. The Political officers, in the pre 1870 period, did talk of prosperous peasantry and surplus production. The Famine Report of 1868 itself had mentioned that the peasants did not reap their entire crop of foodgrains in years of plenty because of limitations of storage capacity. It has been one of the main features of agricultural development in the region that the area under cultivation continued to increase even though the total population did not increase during 1881-1931; in fact there was a decline of 0.9 millions. This happened at a time when there was no mechanisation of agricultural operations. The following (table no 6.1) of land under cultivation, in some states where comparative data is available, shows this development.

The inter relation between the data of population and cultivation is essential to an understanding of the process of impoverishment of the peasantry in the post 1870 period, and for raising the basic question: Wherefrom did the cultivator come? In Ajmer Merwara, the decline in irrigated area was 3.3% but *barani* cultivation had increased by 19.6%. This had taken place when the rural population had declined by 21218 during 1881 and 1901. How did it become possible? Avenues of employment in Ajmer Merwara were going up in urban area; the urban population had therefore increased by 37408.

TABLE: 6.1

Increasing Cultivation and declining population

State/Province	Year	Cultivated Land Area Irrigated	Unirrigated		Total		Variation in Percentage Irrigated	Unirrigate
Ajmer Merwara	1874	50763	104406	acres	155169	acres		
	1908	49063	134907	acres	183970	acres		
Difference		- 1700	+ 30501	acres	+28801	acres	- 3.3	+ 19.6
Alwar	1876	217914	1151045	Bighas	1368959	Bighas		
	1899	264796	1120586	Bighas	1385382	Bighas		
Difference		+ 46882	- 30459	Bighas	+ 16423	Bighas	+ 21.5	- 2.6
Bharatpur	1890	366437	1010113	Bighas	1376550	Bighas		
	1899	340270	1258719	Bighas	1598989	Bighas		
Difference		- 26167	+ 248606	Bighas	+ 222439	Bighas	- 7.14	+ 18.1
Kota	1885	144414	1853496	Bighas	1997910	Bighas		
	1909	112594	1650650	Bighas	1763244	Bighas		
Difference		- 31820	- 202846	Bighas	- 234666	Bighas	- 22	-10.9
Dungarpur	1905	5113	30202	acres	35315	acres		
	1916	5997	39745	acres	45742	acres		
Difference		+ 884	+ 9543		+ 10427	acres	+ 17.3	+ 31.6

Population Data

State/Province	1881			1891			1901		
	Urban		Rural	Urban		Rural	Urban		Rural
Ajmer Merwara	92003		368719	123915		418443	129411		347501
Total		460722			542358			476912	
Alwar	88032		594894	90815		676971	95301		733186
Total		682926			767786			828487	
Bharatpur	124944		520596	123605		516698	96601		530064
Total		645540			640303			626665	
Kota	68957		638445	56451		662320	51074		493805
Total		707402			718771			544879	
Dungarpur	6449		79980	6431		92017	6094		94009
Total		86429			98448			100103	

The population data shows that the famine of 1901 had taken a toll of 70942 in the rural area. The increase in urban populatio during the decade 1891-1901 was only 5496.

In Alwar state the total area under cultivation had in creased during 1881-1901 by a meagre 1.2%; the rural popula tion had increased substantially, i.e. 138, 292 but the cultivatio had increased only by 16423 bighas. It has been shown earlie that people had to take to animal husbandry since more lan was not available for cultivation. The increase of irrigatio sources did not mean increased cultivation as explained ear lier. In some tehsils of the state, the area under cultivation no only did not increase proportionate to the enhancement o means of irrigation but it had also gone down. The wells ha to be sunk to pay the heavy land revenue demand. Th population had to migrate under the circumstances. By 192 the total population was reduced to 701154 (15.4% or 12733 souls). The means of livelihood were simply not available i the state.

In Bharatpur the population of the state had gone down b 18875 during 1881-1901. If we look at the population figure o 1867, a decline of over a lakh—117045—had taken place. Th interesting phenomenon was that the settlement officer foun an increased area of 222439 bighas under cultivation. Even i the population figure of 1867 is overlooked, the total popula tion had declined by 13638 during the decade 1891-1901 eve when the rural population had increased by 13366. The peopl were migrating from the towns to the villages. The reductio between the urban population of 1891 and 1901 was greate than the increase in the rural population. The urban popula tion declined by 27004; nearly one half of it went to the villages the other half simply migrated out. The increase of more tha 13 thousand rural population meant that only *barani* land could be cultivated.

In Kota the total population had declined rathe sharply during the decade 1891-1901. This was particularl oteworthy because Kota had been one of the few states in the egion which had fairly regular rainfall. The entire decline of opulation had been in the rural sector where it had declined y 168515. The argument that new opportunities were openng up after the laying down of railways only meant more abour jobs for the farmers. It strengthens the contention that griculture was the last resort because other avenues were eing closed. It would bear repetition that La Touche, Lupton, aw and others had observed that cultivators were willing to lee from the fields to work as wage labourers on the railway racks or on roads.

The cultivation data makes it clear that it was increasing nly in *barani* land area. Since a greater number of people were eing led to take to *barani* cultivation, agriculture became more nd more dependent on rainfall.[1] It was not so earlier. Even in ne states like Alwar and Bharatpur where the population in ne sixties of the 19th century, according to a special census ndertaken by the British Political officers themselves, was far reater, the dependence on agriculture was much lower. In lwar only 48% population was dependent on agriculture; in haratpur it was the urban population which migrated out fter 1879 since trade was adversely affected.

This migration of population from the urban centres, closng of employment opportunities and the closure of innumerble small cottage industries and crafts meant that only *barani* ultivation could increase; it implied that agriculture became nore and more a gamble in rains. The chart given below hows that the *barani* lands were not only cultivated but doule cropped to the extent of 128 to 199%. The double cropping f the *barani* area raised the percentage of cropped area in very tehsil and of the state as a whole; it was indicative not of ncreasing but of declining prosperity of the peasantry because ne cultivators were helpless. They had to cultivate knowing ully well that the yield was uncertain. The *rabi* crop, in ne absence of timely rains was almost a write off; at best it

TABLE: 6.2

Percentage of Cultivation of *Barani* areas (Bharatpur state) (1898-99)

Tehsils	Particulars	Cultivated area			(Bighas)	Percentage of crops to		
		Chahi	*Sairaba*	*Barani*	Total	Total	*Chahi*	*Barani* area
Gopalgarh	Area	13143	100264	59332	172739			
	Crops	10399	67900	108094	186393	108	79	182
Pahari	Area	8551	47958	55961	112470			
	Crops	5663	1515	111809	118987	106	66	199
Kama	Area	19221	33326	85338	139885			
	Crops	11115	25178	114983	151276	108	58	134
Deeg	Area	35832	22534	102017	160383			
	Crops	24904	23	142178	167100	104	70	139
Kumher	Area	49801	364	98529	139694			
	Crops	26170	368	116231	142769	102	64	118
Akhegarh	Area	34131	432	90593	125156			
	Crops	26842	443	102913	130198	104	79	114
Bharatpur	Area	40919	19093	69722	129734			
	Crops	25452	15633	91439	132524	102	62	131
Nagar	Area	12154	2225	85469	99848			
	Crops	9895	2219	95738	107852	108	81	112

Rupbas	Area	13035	18346	51668	83049	107	64	141
	Crops	8352	7544	73052	88948			
Oochain	Area	23980	55011	44602	123593	108	73	157
	Crops	17559	45472	70110	133141			
Biyana	Area	43462	21642	76556	142060	113	88	134
	Crops	38691	18804	102838	166343			
Bhusawar	Area	54641	12029	103708	170378	105	78	120
	Crops	42752	11647	125197	179596			
Details of Four eastern tehsils of Alwar (1897-98)								
Kishangarh	Area	28293	20413	101348	150054	105	61	118
	Crops	17381	20682	119452	157515			
Ramgarh	Area	19575	35624	57920	113119	107	49	117
	Crops	9600	40429	67559	117588			
Govindgarh	Area	9549	1649	28522	39720	119	56	138
	Crops	5311	2427	39458	47196			
Lachmangarh	Area	21921	30155	69718	121794	93	68	115
	Crops	15005	17926	80347	113278			

provided some *bhusa* for the cattle. Even this had become valuable by the commencement of the 20th century. La Touche, when evaluating the gross yield of the province of Ajmer, had ignored the value of *bhusa*; Lupton in 1908 valued it at 10% of the value of the foodgrains. This difference spoke volumes of the increasing poverty of the agriculturists.

It is significant to find that the percentage of *chahi* lands being cultivated was much less than the percentage of *barani* lands. The percentage of *barani* lands varied from 112 to 199. This meant that it was double cropped. The double cropping of *barani* lands was indicative of the helplessness of the peasant who had to cultivate because of the need to produce food for his maintenance. In case of good and timely rainfall, he had enough to eat and maintain his family; otherwise hunger was always staring him in the face.

Every famine commission report laid emphasis on the role and significance of cattle wealth in increasing the staying power of the peasantry during famines. And equally significantly, every settlement officer either at Ajmer or Mewar, or Bikaner or Karauli, Dholpur or Tonk pursued a policy of taxing grazing lands and making the availability of pastures difficult. Alwar and Bharatpur were exceptions where Dwyer had to provide for concessions for fodder because the new intermediaries were not willing to accept responsibility for the collections from the peasantry. Raw at Karauli had confessed that the cultivators were not inclined to cultivate land because rearing cattle provided them better sustenance than cultivating land.[2] Dwyer, at one stage, even blamed the cultivator for shirking hard work because he was taking to animal husbandry. This was equivalent to a confession that agriculture had ceased to pay the wages of cultivation.

In Ajmer Merwara, the British had created reserve forests and deprived the peasants of culturable land which could help in the preservation of cattle. The result was that the peasants began to abandon agriculture, if they could find other means of subsistence. The population of the Ajmer tehsil during 1881-

1911 increased by 5.8%; the rural population declined by 7.45%. The area under cultivation as assessed had come down by 7.45%. The relevant data is[3]:

Ajmer Tehsil Data

Year	Land under assessment	Number Ploughs	Plough Cattle	Other Cattle	Land under actual cultivation: 1891 1908 (18 years' average)
1884	121046 acres	11387	26386	86883	
1908	111919 acres	8230	16528	42106	97169 acres

The peasantry had thus paid for 24.56% more land than was cultivated. The rural population had declined by 20.7% during 1891-1901. The residual land area, i.e., (121046-97169) = 23877 acres had been left for grazing or fodder crops.

A similar situation had arisen in Mewar where large areas of land were renounced by the peasants after the land settlement.[4]

TABLE: 6.3

Land renounced by the Mewar peasantry

District	Period	Rental value of land
Girwa	1890-1919	Rs. 11118.50
Sahada	1885-1919	" 52882.75
Rajnagar	1892-1919	" 42285.37
Choti Sadri	1893-1919	" 55699.56
Chittor	1888-1919	" 61623.31
Mandalgarh	1889-1919	" 36329.37
Maholi	1890-1919	" 14629.31
Hurda	1888-1919	" 44850.69
Kapasan	1885-1919	" 36928.06
Jasma	1885-1919	" 25123.75
Akola	1888-1919	" 17291.25
Jahazpur	1892-1919	" 62122.40
Bhilwara	1887-1919	" 31086.87
Total		4,91971.19

The total land revenue of settled portions of the state amounted to about 11½ lakhs; renouncement of land paying 43% of the revenue was a major commentary on the helplessness of the peasantry which had found that agriculture was not able to provide subsistence to them. The population of the state declined by about 40% during the famine because the land settlement had not left them enough to face the extremity.

In Bharatpur state during 1900-1920, 8% of the total cultivated land area was either resigned, deserted or voluntarily abandoned in favour of others or confiscated due to arrears of payment.[5] Such an eventuality would not have arisen if agriculture had been able to provide subsistence.

Face to face with the possibility of renunciation of land by the peasants, Dwyer reduced, nay practically abolished, the peasants' right of renunciation in his Alwar and Bharatpur settlements. Knowing the unprofitability of agriculture for the common cultivator, he did not want the payment of land revenue to be waived. He elaborated some general principles operative for future. He justified his doing so by advancing the familiar argument of corruption and unfair dealings of the local officials in distributing the *jama* among the proprietor cultivators. His object was that the revenue demand should not be affected by either a temporary or semi-permanent change of situation. The liability of the peasant proprietor would not be changed even if a new well was sunk or a well went out of work. The individual owner or the joint zamindari village, as the case might be, will bear both profit and loss according to shares or possession. In case the area belonged to common land for a *thok* or *patti*, the loss would be borne by the same owners who were entitled to profit. If any owner relinquished cultivation, absconded or migrated on account of famine or poverty, the next of kin will have the first option of cultivation and of bearing the loss or profit. In case of their refusal, the owners of the *patti* or *thok* will be entitled to take up the holding. In case they also refused, the loss or profit will be shared by the estate as a whole. Thus the *jama* fixed by the settlement shall have to be paid in all cases.

In case of *sairaba / dahri* lands, no remission was to be given in years when the flooded area fell short of the assessed area at the time of settlement. If 10% more land were to become *dahri* in any one year, no extra charge would be levied for it. Exemption from the payment of *dahri* rate would be available only if the lands remained without flood waters for 4 successive years. If the area now assessed as *sairaba* remained uncultivated in any year owing to submerging, the fixed *jama* will not necessarily be altered; since submerging will, it was argued, prove very beneficial to the crops of the next harvest[6]. If the land, now assessed as cultivated, went out of cultivation or deteriorated in quality owing to wells collapsing or going out of work, the *jama* will not be subject to revision. Similarly, where waste land was brought under cultivation or *barani* became *chahi*, no change will be made in the assessment. The owners were now made responsible for the payment of *jama* by the tenants at will; the occupancy tenants remained responsible for their own share.

Dwyer, by thus taking away the right of distribution of *jama* from the local officials, also considered it logical to take away from them the authority to provide relief to the peasants in case of necessity. The authority to make deductions on account of any of the eventualities, mentioned above, from the village *jama* was made over to a Deputy collector; it was taken away from a tehsildar or a local official. The local autonomy of the villages was virtually crippled by state control and authority.

The most significant novelty of the land revenue settlement in this arid zone was to enforce the payment of land revenue by the peasant cultivator irrespective of the crop yield. This was a radical departure from the earlier philosophy of claiming a certain share of the produce. In this way, the stored up surplus wealth of the peasantry was easily mopped up; the land revenue settlements thus facilitated drain of wealth from the states. It is for this reason that whenever an opportunity offered itself, a land revenue settlement was suggested. The states of Alwar and Bharatpur provide enough evidence to substantiate the argument. The land revenue demand was first raised; the peasant, unable to pay the same from *barani* cultivation, took loans or invested his savings in sinking new wells because the revenue demand was not changed during the continuation of the settlement even if the artificial class of land had changed from *barani* to *chahi*. Ten or fifteen years later, when the opportunity for regency administration came, it was easily argued that since the irrigation sources had increased, there was scope for an enhancement of revenue demand. The peasant was not allowed to reap the benefits of either his labour or investment.

The real meaning of the observation made at the beginning should now become clear. The land settlements were carried out only when the administrative power was in British hands. The real incidence of land revenue demand on cultivated area multiplied 1.7 to 2.8 times the incidence on assessed area.[6a] The settlements provided the British the opportunity to utilise the only wealth producing sector in the Indian states for its own good.

The land revenue settlements thus operated to mop up the savings of the peasantry of the state concerned and to transfer the resources from the villages to state capitals where they were spent and an impression of progress and development was given. It was therefore ensured that all land, in the possession of cultivators, was subjected to revenue payment. The mopping up of the resources was done in a very thorough going manner. Besides taxing the cultivated land, incidental income from culturable land, i.e. grazing of animals, was taxed. Dwyer included the 'assumed' income from grazing, in the shape of sale of *ghee* and cattle, in the annual *bach* of the tehsils where enough grazing grounds were available. He confessed that the tehsil of Thana Ghazi 'cannot stand even the pettiest enhancement' and yet he proposed small enhancement 'by distributing it over the villages which have profits from grazing and the produce of their cattle' He calculated that the peasants' miscellaneous income from waste and pasture land, such as sale of fuel, charcoal, milk ghee, wool, grazing fees etc. was about Rs. 30,000/- in Thana Ghazi and about Rs. 20,000/- each in Alwar and Bansur tehsils.[7]

All land settlement officers claimed to encourage investment of capital in land; they had encouraged the *mahajans* and bankers to invest capital in wells and in financing agricultural operations. Concessional tariff for new wells and legal facilities for the recovery of loans had been provided. They had also confessed that the land revenue demand in the native states was so high that the principles underlying it could not be recommended for British Indian provinces. It is therefore legitimate to pose the question: How could an assessment policy which sought to take away a full 2/3rd or 3/4th of the net assets (it was actually of the gross produce) encourage investment of capital. It had been conceded much earlier by the British administrators themselves that the maximisation of revenue demand 'constituted the greatest threat to all private property'.* A policy of taxation which raised the greatest possible revenue was hostile to every species of private property, not to say of accumulation of capital. When the peasant was not getting even the wages of cultivation, and when he was on the look out for an opportunity to abandon agriculture and take to wage earning, the element of risk in advancing money to a peasant was great. The high rate of interest on

* This refers to the debate among British administrators in the last quarter of the 18th century at the time of deciding the type of land settlement in Bengal. The debate at that time was 'free' from the 'imperial' psychology of late 19th century. Sir Philip Francis's Minutes on the subject of a Permanent Settlement for Bengal, Bihar and Orissa, ed. by Romesh C. Dutt, p. 109: cited by Ranajit Guha: A Rule of Property for Bengal, p. 115

loans to the peasantry was fundamentally connected with the risk perception of the banker. The peasant's capacity to repay loans was continually being eroded by the high revenue demand; the diminishing capacity to repay invited high rate of interest and ran counter to investment of capital in land.

The land revenue settlements brought about a major change in the economic condition of the peasantry. The impoverishment of the peasantry in the region, brought about through land revenue settlements, has been amply demonstrated earlier. The objective impact of this policy was the recurrence of famines in the region which were presented, to cover the failure of British policy, as natural to the region. Rainfall—its excess or shortfall—was and remains even today, largely the result of natural forces beyond the control of human beings. The peasantry of the region had, over the years, evolved ways to meet the vagaries of nature which were cyclical and repetitive in their occurrence. It was only after man made policies broke the defence mechanism evolved over generations that the impact of a natural phenomenon was aggravated. It is correct to say that the region was not prone to frequent famines and scarcities in the pre 1870 period. When the famine of 1868 occurred, considerable efforts were made to find out the recurrence of famines in the past. The British officers were able to locate two during the 19th century—1832 and 1812. Famines, so far as the result of a failure of rainfall, were part of a natural phenomenon; but its impact on the loss of human and animal life could be eliminated or enhanced depending on human policies.

The calamitous impact of the famine of 1899 A.D. known as 'chappaniya akal' (on account of vikram samvat 2056) was a fitting commentary on the results of the land revenue policy of the British in Rajasthan. It was comparable to the 1868 famine (pachisya akal due to 2025 v.s.) in its intensity and extent though much worse in its consequences. The rates of foodgrains were almost the same in the two famines.[8] A comparative study of the reports of the famines of 1868 and 1899 in Rajasthan makes clear the difference which had come over the approach of British administrators during the three decades. Brooke, in 1868, had considered the great wealth of the desert lands to consist in the vast herds of camels, horned cattle and sheep; the lands were rich though they remained barren in appearance. The salt lakes of Rajasthan, he pointed out, played a most important part in the economic supply of food to the country since the amount of salt taken out of the province represented an almost equal amount of grain poured into the country. In 1868-69, 2.5 million tons of foodgrains were brought to the region by camel and pack bullock caravans. These vast convoys were the salvation of Rajasthan.[9]

The Famine Report of 1899-1900 did not have one word for the natural wealth and defence mechanism of the region against the famines. The British had already deprived the states of the benefit of all salt resources; the traditional mode of conveyance was on the point of extinction. The Report talked of the speed and volume of goods which could be transported by the railways but were not. The earlier report had questioned the advisability of fixing a land revenue settlement for Ajmer Merwara and had held it as having injured the district absolutely. During the three decades, the land revenue settlements had been fixed for Mewar, Alwar, Bharatpur, Marwar, Bikaner, Tonk, Dholpur, the capacity of these states to face famine had been equally adversely affected.

The question of depletion of surplus stocks of foodgrains from the region was significant because the earlier Report on the famine of 1868 had observed that nothing can tend to prevent a country from distress so much as its retaining within itself the means of producing its grain. The Indian Famine Commission Report of 1898 had conceded the fact that 'the export trade and the improvement of communications have tended to diminish the custom of storing grain, as a protection against failure of harvest. . .[10]'. Therefore the Report of 1900 devoted some space to the import of foodgrains by the railways to counter the argument that the province had been depleted of its reserve surplus stocks through the railways. It went on to say that, before the construction of railways, a famine always meant the depletion of grain stores. It went to the extent of saying that 'it was impossible to bring into the country sufficient food to keep the population alive.'

The 1868 Report described the failure of rains during 1868 in less than a page; it was mentioned as a factual occurrence preceding the famine. The Report of 1900 not only contained a full chapter of 5½ pages to depict the failure of rainfall as the primary cause for the failure of crops and fodder, but also considered it as a sufficient explanation. There need be no debate or dispute on the role of the failure of rainfall in bringing about the famine. The real question is whether the loss of human life and animal wealth was equally natural. It is legitimate to raise the question: Why did Rajasthan suffer in 1899-1900 in a greater measure than in 1868 when the severity of the two famines was almost similar. By 1899 the railways had come to the region. The Rajputana Malwa railway had been completed; Bikaner Jodhpur railway was in operation besides the Jodhpur Railway. The role of the railways in depleting the stocks of foodgrains from the region should be placed alongwith the imports. The Famine Commission had confessed that at Agra and other places in U.P. the traders had to wait for weeks together before the goods could be transported to Rajasthan.[11]

The famine report of 1868 had talked of the inherent ability of the region in meeting famines which visited once in four decades. The region had surplus production of foodgrains; it had vast natural resources of salt which ensured import of foodgrains in case of necessity; the deserts, though barren, were rich enough to sustain a large number of cattlewealth. The region had lost about 1/3rd of its cattlewealth and a sizeable population in 1868 when the traditional mode of transport and communications had prevailed. During the next three decades land revenue settlements had been revised in more than half a dozen states of Rajasthan. Wingate had taxed lands meant for growing fodder, knowing very well that it was not taxed in the past. Pears had done the same thing. Fagan had subjected the villagers to pay grazing tax which had earlier been paid only by outsiders. He had further increased the incidence of grazing tax in the days of scarcity when people had moved out with their cattle and those who remained paid the entire amount.[12] Dwyer had devised ways to increase the burden of land revenue on poorer lands. Butler had increased the incidence of taxation on land by withdrawing the discount available to the peasantry on account of currency change.

The Report on the Famine of 1899-1900 in Rajasthan estimated a loss of 56.1% of the total livestock in the states. This unprecedented heavy loss brought to the forefront the evil consequences of land revenue changes introduced under the new settlements. A number of Famine Commissions suggested preventive measures of general relevance. One of the important area of recommendations was the change in attitude and policy towards fodder cultivation and its taxation. The Handbook of Famine Administration in Native States (1908) emphasised growing fodder, exempting fodder from taxation and even from attachment in satisfaction of execution of court decrees; it recommended remission of revenue demand in whole or in part on the area under fodder crops.[13] This was equivalent to a fire fighting operation to undo the damage done by the land revenue settlements in Rajasthan states without explicitly confessing it.

The famine of 1899 was quite severe in the three desert dominated states of northern, and north western Rajasthan—Bikaner, Jodhpur and Jaisalmer. These states were prone to be affected by shortage of rainfall. The closing years of the 19th century were years of generally deficient rainfall, scarcities and famines. For Jaisalmer it was 'the worst since 1812-13'. But this famine has been talked about more because it affected the entire region. Even those states which were normally not affected by famine, were seriously afflicted by it. Mewar had generally remained unaffected. Similarly half of Tonk had been growing opium because of favourable rainfall generally. In both these states land revenue settlements had been done. A comparative study of the figures of casualties on account of famine, in states where land settlements had been done with such other neighbouring states where land settlement had not been introduced under British advice, should be self explanatory and would be able to convey the real picture.

State	Population in 1891	Population in 1901	% of reduction
Rajasthan	11,990,504	9,841,765	-18.9
Settled States			
Mewar	1,710,579	1,018,805	-40.94
Tonk	380,069	273,201	-28.11
Unsettled neighbour states			
Banswara	180,268	149,128	-17.28
Dungarpur	98,448	100,103	+1.66
Sirohi	187,976	154,544	-17.79

The decline in human population was heaviest in Mewar; it was next followed by Tonk; in both the states it was greater than the average for the region as a whole.

The British administrators did not confess it openly but the arch priest of imperialism—Curzon—had quietly changed the policy towards the land revenue settlements. He wrote to AGG Rajasthan not to undertake revisions of land revenue settlement in native states where, compared to British provinces, there was comparatively very little information about the land structure and the opportunities for correction of mistakes committed were very few. In 1904 a Settlement

Commissioner was appointed by the Government of India 'to control land revenue settlement work in the states':[14] In the post 1904 period, the work of land revenue settlements was considerably reduced. During the next two decades the revenue settlement of Dholpur was revised during 1909-12 where a major change was brought about by abolishing the class of *ijaredars* and restoration of the old zamindars; the revenue settlement of Dungarpur was revised because the Bhils were brought under control. Land Settlement in any major state of the region was avoided; even at Udaipur where the settlement was due for revision after 1905, the settlement officer was not sent till after the first World War, and no revision was carried out except in the hilly regions. Kota was the only major state where a land settlement was carried out when the state was not under minority administration during 1906-9. The state had made special request in order to solve the difficulties created by the abolition of local and adoption of imperial currency.

The Famine Report of 1900 went on to assert that 'it would be superfluous to look for other causes'. It specifically denied the role of land revenue settlements by saying that these 'are neither so severe in themselves nor so rigidly applied as to precipitate distress which could otherwise be avoided'.[15] It was after circuitous arguments that the report conceded that the region had in ordinary years, 'an appreciable surplus for export'. The export of a large quantity of foodgrains out of the region could not be denied. The statistical account of trade carried by rail and water in India bracketed Rajasthan and Central Indian states together.[16]

Exports and Imports for Rajasthan and Central India
(quantity in maunds)

Commodity	Trade	1898-99	1899-1900	1900-01	1901-02	1902-03
All kinds of grains and	Export	3472,342	1311,887	2243,661	1971,356	2033,880
pulses.	Import	2227,343	14787,119	15388,053	8284,103	7755,313

In the absence of a separate category of analysis at that time, it is difficult to exactly quantify the export and import figures of foodgrains from this region. But some approximate idea of the extent of imports (and by implication of exports) can be formed since the exact quantity of foodgrains imported in the region had been mentioned by the famine reports, though they do not have March 31 as the cut off date. During 10 Months (December 1899-September 1900) a quantity of 11,449,597 maunds was imported in Rajasthan.[17] This would come to about 50% of the import figure given above. This showed that a net export of about 625,000 maunds had been taking place every year from Rajasthan (50% of the excess of export over import) in the pre 1899 period. The heavy loss of life during 1899 affected agricultural production in the post 1900 period.

Appendix-I

Land Area Abandoned in Alwar State after the famine of 1877

Tehsil	Population in 1872	Population in 1881	No. of owners	Area of Cultivated land abandoned	
Kishangarh	60,274	52,448	617	2,196	Bighas
Ramgarh	53,499	42,470	385	3,812	"
Govindgarh	38,268	19,615	94	2,587	"
Lachmangarh	66,189	50,982	438	16,931	"
Tijara	51,702	49,451	1,070	29,302	"
Behrod	52,918	60,698	184	3,556	"
Mandawar	40,750	43,035	187	4,602	"
Katumbar	32,189	31,077	280	8,772	"
Rajgarh	60,470	50,866	328	8,387	"
Alwar	1,51,027	1,21,074	1,066	19,186	"
Bansur	69,379	64,055	239	9,293	"
Thanaghazi	52,119	50,939	334	11,027	"
Alwar State	7,28,784	6,36,710	5,222	1,19,651	"

Land Area Abandoned in Bharatpur State during and after the famine of 1877-78

Tehsil	Population in 1867	Population in 1881	Population in 1891	No. of owners	Area of cultivated land abandoned	
Gopalgarh	50,794	45,535	40,791	1,115	11,777	Bighas
Pahari	31,427	29,801	27,737	95	521	"
Kama	43,116	40,375	44,058	509	17,881	"
Deeg	70,003	63,928	62,725	666	15,061	"
Kumher	69,587	45,382	50,705	2,389	46,692	"
Akheygarh	51,294	46,974	44,349	1,151	41,510	"
Bharatpur	1,41,868	1,07,593	1,10,162	1,672	21,079	"
Nagar	29,567	25,266	23,943	1,605	27,733	"

(Contd.)

(Contd.)

Tehsil	Population in 1867	1881	1891	No. of owners	Area of cultivated land abandoned	
Rupbas	36,322	34,134	30,186	1,057	8,309	"
Oochain	50,504	48,849	47,735	1,425	38,872	"
Biyana	76,347	76,559	75,126	3,932	87,380	"
Bhusawar	72,970	72,341	73,728	3,343	1,14,829	"
Bharatpur State	7,43,710	6,45,540	6,40,303	18,959	4,34,526	Bighas

O' Dwyer: Final Report on Alwar, p. 43 and Final Report on Bharatpur, p. 56.

Notes & References

1. The statistics for the remaining 8 tehsils of Alwar are not available. Dwyer:; Eastern Tehsils, p. 48; Northern Tehsils, p. 59; Central Tehsils, p. 58; Southern Teshils, p. 68
2. Raw: Settlement Report, Karauli, p. 29
3. Lupton: Water Revenue Report, pp. 151-159
4. M.P. Jain: Peasant Landlord Relation in Mewar (Unpublished Ph. D. thesis, University of Rajasthan, Jaipur), p. 153
5. Bharatpur Settlement Report, 1930, p. 13
6. Final Report on Bharatpur, pp. 91-92; Final Report on Alwar Settlement, p. 95

6a. This is derived from the data given in Table V of Agricultural Statistics of India, Vol. II pertaining to Native States. This was an annual publication of The Government of India. pp. 92-93 of the Report for the years 1903-04 to 1908

7. Central and Southern Tehsils Report, pp. 92, 98, 103
8. Famine Report for Udaipur State, 1900, p. 3
9. Brooke's Report on the Famine of 1868, para 211
10. Report of the Indian Famine Commission, 1898, p. 363
11. Report of the Indian Famine Commission, 1901, p. 77
12. P.J. Fagan: Settlement Report of Bikaner, pp. 47-48

13. A Handbook of Famine Administration in Native States, p. 48
14. Jaipur Residency Record, File no. 5/1903, p. 27
15. Report on the Famine (Native States of Rajputana) 1899-1900, p. 17
16. Accounts of the Trade Carried by Rail and River in India in 1902-03, Table no. III (for Imports) and IV (for exports), pp. 14-17 and 56-59 Government Publication, Calcutta, 1903
17. Report on the Famine 1899-1900, Appendix no. III, p. 123

Glossary

Abi	Land cultivated in the bed of tanks.
akshay doob	a kind of grass which cannot be destroyed
amani	land revenue collected through the patels who were offered 3% incentive on revenue collected from the village under their charge (in Tonk) only
assami	cultivator
bachh	method of distributing the revenue
bania	a trader cum money lender
bapota	hereditary patrimony
_____puccka	where the owner enjoys the right of alienation by sale or mortgage
_____katcha	where the owner enjoys only the right of alienation by mortgage
barani	dry, unirrigated land dependent on rain
batai (banta)	a division of the produce
bhayachara	land held by possession without reference to shares, i.e. partition has not taken place
bhej	land revenue demand
bhog	a fixed share of the produce of land, either in kind or cash, paid to the state

bhụr	sandy land. It has less clay and more sand than mattiyar and is lighter in texture
bigha	a unit of measurement whose area varied from state to state. In Alwar 1.6 bighas were equal to 1 acre; in Bharatpur 2.5 bighas were equal to 1 acre.
bil ijmal	held jointly by a body of owners
biswadar	individual holding a right to property or share in an estate
chahi	land irrigated from wells
chiknot	stiffish clay or clayey loam; richest natural soil
dahri	land naturally inundated/flooded area (term used at Alwar only)
dahri hal	land crdinarily flooded, ad actually inundated within the last five years
dahri sabiqa	land which was inundated sometimes but not within the last five years (= barani before Dwyer's settlement)
dahri barishi	land benefitted by hill drainage
digar	irrigable by means other than wells or tanks (Dungarpur only)
gaddi	throne
ghee	clarified butter
gol	held jointly
gol ijmali	held by a joint body of owners
gorma	homelands which can be looked after with greater ease than the rest of the area
gurhu deval	self supporting assami (Jhalawar only), comparatively affluent
hakk-i-mokaddami	a percentage by the state to lambardars on the revenue paid in by thern

hakim	chief administrative officer of a pargana
ijaredar	a person to whom an ijara (lease for the collection of rents) is granted.
Kankut	(koota): where the standing crop was evaluated and the state share was fixed on that basis and collected either in cash or kind
khalsa	crownlands where revenue was realised by the state as opposed to revenue due to the assignees
khalis	pure
khasra	field book wherein the fields are entered in a serial order
khewat	a register of proprietary holdings
khatauni	a register of cultivating holdings
kabil	(gorma) in Mewar
korwan	unirrigated land (kota)
jamabandi	land revenue assessment
lao	a well operated by rope
malba	a certain percentage on the revenue levied for village expenses
malikana	profit rent. A rent charge paid to proprietors over and above the revenue
manotidar	a money lender standing surety (manoti) for the revenue payment
mattiyar	ordinary loam with a mixture of sand
milankhasra	a comparative statement of village area of different kinds
mujrai	lambardari dues
mustajjir	a person who became an ijaredar for an area by paying the arrears of revenue on behalf of a zamindar

nabud	no yield (in Ajmer, less than 25% yield was called nabud)
nazrana	sums paid by revenue assignees to the state in recognition of their grant
patti	a division of a village
pattidari	land held by shares ancestral or cutomary
peeval piwat	irrigated land
rankad	the poorest class of unirrigated soil
roahan	land situated in the bed of a tank (Dungarpur)
roznamcha	diary
sairaba sairaba hal sairaba sabiq sairaba barishi	land which was called dahri at Alwar was called sairaba at Bharatpur; the three categories of dahri and sairaba meant the same
seja	a kind of well dug in the bed of a river (Mewar)
serona	2½% paid by a farmer to the patel
shirma	(sirma) unirrigable land but its position or natural qualities ensure it so much moisture that it is able to produce both crops (Dungarpur)
sukhi	a better kind of dry land at Dungarpur
talabi	tank irrigated

Bibliography

The two volume index to land revenue records at the National Archives of India lists the land records preserved there. The records pertaining to Ajmer Merwara are exhaustively available but the records pertaining to the states of Rajasthan are very few in number. The bibliography has been deliberately kept small because the present work is a micro level work based on an interpretation of statistical data supplied by the land revenue settlement reports.

Government Reports on Land Revenue Policy

1. Selections from Papers on Indebtedness and Land Transfer, (Government Press, Calcutta, 1895)
2. Memorandum on the restriction of the Power to Alienate Interests in Land (Government of India, Calcutta, 1895)
3. Selection of Papers on the subject of Permanent Settlements and Redemption of the land revenue in India (Government of India, Calcutta, 1897)
4. Land Revenue Policy of the Government of India, (Calcutta, 1902)
5. On the Improvement of Indian Agriculture by J.A. Voelcker (Government Press, Calcutta, 1897)

Government Publications

1. Jaipur Land Revenue Code, vols. I & II (1947)
2. Jaipur State Grants Land Tenures Act, 1947
3. Tenancy Act, 1945 (Jaipur)
4. Revenue History of Ajmer (1926)

Rajputana Agency Record

Jaipur Residency File nos. 634,1/1889 Settlement
635,2/1889 Settlement
636,3/1889 Settlement
637,4/1889 Settlement
640,9/1897 Settlement
645,5/1903 Settlement
648,1/1923 Settlement

PUBLISHED ORIGINAL SOURCES:

Land Settlement Reports:

Alwar

M.F.O.'Dwyer Assessment Report of Tehsils Kishangarh, Ramgarh, Govindgarh, Lachmangarh, 1897-98 (Calcutta, 1904)

M.F.O.'Dwyer Assessment Report of Tehsils, Tijara, Bahror, Mandawar, Rajgarh, Katumbar, 1898-99 (Calcutta, 1905)

M.F.O.'Dwyer Assessment Report of Tehsils Alwar, Bansur and Thanaghazi 1899-1900 (Simla, 1900)

M.F.O.'Dwyer Final Report of the Alwar state settlement, 1901

Bharatpur

M.F.O.'Dwyer Assessment Report of four northern tehsils of Gopalgarh, Pahari, Kama, Dig (Bharatpur) (Bharatpur, 1900)

M.F.O.'Dwyer Assessment Report of the four central tehsils of Bharatpur: Kumher, Akheygarh, Bharatpur and Nagar 1898-1899 (Simla, 1899)

M.F.O.'Dwyer Assessment Report of the four southern Tehsils: Rupbas, Oochain, Biyana and Bhusawar of Bharatpur 1899-1900 (Simla, 1900)

M.F.O.'Dwyer Final Report on the settlement of the Bharatpur State, 1901

Tonk

T.C. Pears Report on the Revenue Settlement of Tonk, pts. I, II, III (1892)

Dholpur

Umacharan Mukhopadhyaya Report on the Land Settlement of the Dholpur State (Calcutta, Newman & Co., 1894)

W. Raw Final Report of the Revision of the Settlement of the Dholpur state 1909-1912 (Pioneer Press, Allahabad, 1912)

Dungarpur

A.T. Holme Report on the Land Revenue Settlement of the Dungarpur state 1904-05 (Pioneer Press, 1905)

Ganesh Ram Rawat Report on the revision of the Settlement in the Dungarpur state in 1915-16 (Ajmer 1923)

Kahen Nand Joshi Report on the Revision of the settlement in the Dungarpur state, Vikram sambat 1981 (Dungarpur, 1928)

Jhalawar

H.B. Abbott Settlement Report of Jhalawar, 1885

Ajmer Merwara

J.D. La Touche Report on the Settlement of the Ajmer Mhairwara District, 1875 (Government Press, Calcutta, 1900)

R.S. Whiteway Summary Settlement Report, 1884

R.S. Whiteway Report on the Settlement of the Ajmer Merwara District, 1887 (Ajmer Mission Press, 1901)

W.J.E. Lupton Report on the Question of the Assessment of Land and Water Revenue in Ajmer Merwara (Scottish Mission, Ajmer, 1908)

W.J.E. Lupton Final Settlement Report of Ajmer Merwara, 1910 (Scottish Mission, Ajmer, 1910)

Mewar

W.H. Smith Settlement Report 1878 (Foreign, Revenue A, October 1879, nos. 1-17 (National Archives)

A. Wingate Report of 1881 (Foreign Revenue A, May 1881 no. 6 NAI)

A. Wingate Proposals for the Settlement of the Jat Pergannahs of Meywar (Bombay, 1885)

A. Wingate Settlement Report on the Sadri Zillah of the Meywar State (Bombay, 1889)

Kota

M.S.D. Butler Final Report on the Second Settlement of the Kotah State 1904-9 (Kota, 1909)

Karauli

W. Raw Final Report of the First Settlement of the Karauli State 1909-1912 (Pioneer Press, Allahabad, 1912)

Pratapgarh

A.T. Holme — Report on the Land Revenue Settlement of the Pratapgarh State 1904-5 (Thacker & Co., Bombay, 1906)

Bikaner

P.J. Fagan — Bikaner Settlement Report, 1893

Sohan Lal — Completion Report on the Settlement of the Khalsa villages of the Bikaner State (1895)

Famine Reports

1. Famine Report of 1868 by J.C. Brooke (Foreign, General A, March 1871, nos. 3-4)
2. Report on the Famine Relief Operations in Marwar, Jaisalmer, Bikaner and Kishangarh 1891-92 by G.H. Trevor (Bombay, 1892)
3. Report on Famine Relief in Ajmer Merwara during 1891-92 (Ajmer, 1892)
4. Report on Famine Relief in Ajmer Merwara during 1891-1892 by Pritchard and Devenish (Calcutta, 1893)
5. Report of the Indian Famine Commission, 1898 (Simla, 1898)
6. Report of the Indian Famine Commission, 1901 (Calcutta, 1901)
7. Report on the Famine: The Native States of Rajputana in 1899-1900 (Ajmer, 1901)
8. Famine Report of Udaipur State, 1900 (Pionner Press, 1901)
9. Famine Report of Kotah and Jhalawar in 1899-1900 (Ajmer, 1901)
10. The Final Report of the Famine Relief operations in Marwar 1899-1900 by Sukhdeo Prasad (Jodhpur, 1900)

11. Final Report on the Kishangarh Famine 1899-1900 (Ajmer, 1901)
12. Final Report of Famine Relief operations in Sirohi 1899-1900
13. Final Report of the Famine Relife operations in Dungarpur state 1901-1902
14. Famine Relief operations of the Jaipur state for 1905-1906
15. Review of the Famine Relief operations in the Native States of Rajputana and the Districts of Ajmer Merwara during 1905-1906 (Abu, 1907)
16. Final Report of Famine Relief operations in the Tonk state 1905-1906 (Abu, 1907)
17. Report on the Famine in the Mewar state 1905-1906 (Abu, 1906)
18. Final Report on the Alwar Famine of 1905-1906 (Delhi, 1906)
19. Final Report on the Dholpur Famine of 1905-1906 (Abu, 1906)
20. Final Report on the Famine in the Karauli state 1905-1906 (Ajmer 1906)
21. Final Report on the famine in Bharatpur 1905-1906 (Bharatpur, 1906)
22. Note on Famine Relief operations in Marwar in 1905 (Marwar State Press, 1905)
23. A Handbook of Famine Administration in Native States (Government Press, Calcutta, 1908)

INDEX